JAN BELL • ROGER GOWER • with Drew Hyde

# advanced
# expert
## CAE
OURSEBOOK

PEARSON
Longman

# Contents

# Exam overview

▶ See the Exam reference on page 168 for more detailed information and task strategies.

The Cambridge Certificate in Advanced English has five papers, each of which has equal value, receiving 20 per cent of the total 200 marks. It is not necessary to pass every paper, as the pass mark (grade C) is based on an overall score of about 60 per cent. There are three pass grades (A, B and C) and two fail grades (D and E).

| Paper | Task type | Task description |
|---|---|---|
| **Paper 1: Reading**<br>• 1 hour 15 minutes<br>• Four parts<br>• 45–50 reading comprehension questions in total | **Part 1:** multiple matching (12–18 questions)<br>**Part 2:** gapped text (6–7 questions)<br>**Part 3:** four-option multiple choice (5–7 questions)<br>**Part 4:** multiple matching (12–22 questions) | **Part 1:** deciding which text or part of a text contains information given in a set of questions or statements<br>**Part 2:** deciding where jumbled paragraphs fit into gaps in a text<br>**Part 3:** answering four-option multiple-choice questions on a text<br>**Part 4:** as Part 1 |
| **Paper 2: Writing**<br>• 2 hours<br>• Two tasks<br>• Approximately 250 words for each task | **Part 1:** a compulsory task<br>**Part 2:** a choice from four options | **Part 1:** processing the input material provided and using it to produce a text or texts as required<br>**Part 2:** writing for a specific reader, using the appropriate format and style as required in the instructions |
| **Paper 3: English in Use**<br>• 1 hour 30 minutes<br>• Six parts<br>• 80 questions | **Part 1:** four-option multiple-choice lexical cloze (15 questions)<br>**Part 2:** open cloze (15 questions)<br>**Part 3:** error correction (16 questions)<br>**Part 4:** word formation (15 questions)<br>**Part 5:** register transfer (13 questions)<br>**Part 6:** gapped text (6 questions) | **Part 1:** choosing the correct word or phrase to fill gaps in a text; focus on vocabulary<br>**Part 2:** filling in gaps in a text with the appropriate word; focus on grammar<br>**Part 3:** identifying grammar, spelling or punctuation errors in a text<br>**Part 4:** changing the form of a given word to make it fit the context<br>**Part 5:** rewording information from one text in an appropriate style in order to fit gaps in the second text; focus on register<br>**Part 6:** selecting the appropriate phrase or short sentence for each gap in a text; focus on coherence and cohesion |
| **Paper 4: Listening**<br>• Approximately 45 minutes<br>• Four parts<br>• 30–40 questions | **Part 1:** note or sentence completion (8–10 questions)<br>**Part 2:** as Part 1<br>**Part 3:** four-option multiple-choice questions or sentence completion (6–10 questions)<br>**Part 4:** multiple-matching (two tasks) or three-option multiple-choice questions (10 questions) | **Part 1:** a two-minute monologue, played twice; focus on extracting specific information from the text<br>**Part 2:** as Part 1, but heard only once<br>**Part 3:** a four-minute conversation, played twice; focus on understanding specific information, attitudes and opinions<br>**Part 4:** five 30-second monologues heard twice; multiple-matching: selecting the five correct options from a list of eight possibilities; focus on identifying speaker, topic, function, opinion, etc. |
| **Paper 5: Speaking**<br>• Approximately 15 minutes<br>• Four parts | **Part 1:** interview<br>**Part 2:** individual long turn<br>**Part 3:** collaborative task<br>**Part 4:** three-way conversation | **Part 1:** a three-way conversation giving personal information; focus on general social and interactional language<br>**Part 2:** each student speaks for one minute, commenting on a visual prompt<br>**Part 3:** students interact and negotiate to solve a problem or make a decision<br>**Part 4:** examiner-led discussion developing the topic of Part 3; focus on expressing and justifying opinions and ideas |

# MODULE 1
# New directions

## Overview

- **Reading:** multiple matching (Paper 1 Part 1)
- **Vocabulary:** expressions with *on*; phrasal verbs; collocations
- **Listening 1:** main points vs. details; attitudes and opinions (Paper 4 Parts 1 and 4)
- **English in Use 1:** error correction (extra word) (Paper 3 Part 3)
- **Language development 1:** tense review
- **Writing 1:** using an appropriate register
- **Listening 2:** multiple matching (Paper 4 Part 4)
- **Speaking:** personal qualities; long turn (Paper 5 Part 2)
- **English in Use 2:** register transfer (Paper 3 Part 5)
- **Language development 2:** review of passive forms; register
- **Writing 2:** character reference (Paper 2 Part 2)

## Lead-in

- What important aspects of people's lives do the photos show?
- Are any of these aspects important for you? Why?/Why not?
- What other things are important for you at the moment?
- Have your priorities changed over the last five years? In what ways?

# 1A Learning experiences

## Reading (Paper 1 Part 1)

**Before you read**

1 Look at the title and subheading of the magazine article opposite. What do you understand by the expression 'travel broadens the mind'?

**Skimming**

2 a Read through each text quickly. Mark the names of the countries where each person has travelled.

b Can you find one sentence that summarises the importance of travel and exploration for each person?

**Multiple matching**

▶ Task strategies page 168

3 Answer questions 1–13 by choosing from the four people (A–D). Some of the choices may be required more than once. The first one has been done for you. Read the task strategies on page 168 before you begin.

| Which person | |
|---|---|
| feels that he/she turned a setback into an advantage? | **1** __D__ |
| says that travelling abroad can be as valuable as formal study? | **2** ............ |
| wanted to put an aspect of a population's culture on record? | **3** ............ |
| is still trying to compensate for something he/she missed out on as a child? | **4** ............ |
| was awarded money which enabled him/her to achieve a personal goal? | **5** ............ |
| has found a job which finances a passion? | **6** ............ |
| thinks that experiencing hardship has made him/her more resilient? | **7** ............ |
| changed the direction of his/her life after a chance encounter? | **8** ............ |
| believes that potentially dangerous travel is best left to young people? | **9** ............ |
| felt great respect for the positive outlook of a local population? | **10** ............ |
| thinks that his/her university studies have come in useful in later life? | **11** ............ |
| had his/her instincts about people confirmed by experience? | **12** ............ |
| had to make sacrifices before deciding to go off and pursue his/her dream? | **13** ............ |

**Task analysis**

4 Discuss the task.
1 How long did it take you to complete the task?
2 Compare and justify your answers. Which parallel phrases or ideas did you find in the text and questions?

**Discussion**

5 a Do you agree that 'all school-leavers should be able to have a gap year … before going on to further education'? What might be the benefits and drawbacks?

b Prepare a case for funding a research trip abroad related to your studies or work, to be presented to the relevant authority (your parents, head of department, line manager, etc.).

# A passion for exploration

*Four people talk about how travelling helped to broaden their minds.*

## A WILLIAM DALRYMPLE

Before I went to college, I spent nine months backpacking around India. It was a trip that quite literally changed my life. In fact, in an ideal world, all school-leavers should be able to have a gap year like
5 that before going on to further education. I certainly learned as much from living on a low budget in India as I did in three years at university. I'd had a very sheltered upbringing, so sadly I knew very little of the real world outside my home town. I've been trying to
10 make up for it ever since!

It was at university that I got going with my writing, because the history department offered grants if you went on a journey in some way related to your studies. I successfully put forward a scheme to retrace the
15 famous explorer Marco Polo's journey to the palace of Xanadu in China. It had always been my dream to write a travel book, and
20 this provided exactly the material I was looking for.
The trip itself turned out to be one of the most exciting experiences of my life, although I wouldn't dare take risks like that now, 20 years on. The time to do it is
25 when you are 19; you are more adaptable, your body is stronger, your mind more open.

## B JODY SOLOW

It was my geography supervisor at university who encouraged me to undertake some research in the Solomon Islands as part of my degree course. There is
30 no written language on the islands, but I was privileged to meet with village chiefs and tribal historians in my leaf house every day, as I gathered information about their complex land-owning practices. I wanted to write an article about these
35 traditions before the information was lost to future generations. Unfortunately, my visit had to be cut short because I contracted malaria, but it had whetted my appetite for travel.

It was when I was collecting information for my
40 book on Kenya that my survival skills were really put to the test. I travelled on foot with Bante, my guide, through the northern desert, where we built fires at night to keep the lions away and lived almost entirely on camel's milk and goat's blood in the traditional
45 way. Bante taught me 64 different ways of saying 'hello' (there is not a single way to say 'goodbye') in the local languages. Living among people who were on the edge of starvation, but who still found enough energy for song, dance and endless teasing, taught me
50 that it is possible to feel optimistic about life, even in the midst of severe economic deprivation. I have no doubt that my tendency to bounce back from anything life throws at me stems from my time spent with them.

## C ANNE MUSTOE

55 When I made the decision to cycle round the world, I was 54 and unfit. I hated camping and discomfort, and I didn't even own a bicycle. What started it off was coming across a western man cycling through the Thar Desert while I was on holiday in India. Onlookers
60 surrounded him, which made me realise that cycling was an ideal way of getting to know other cultures.

When I was a student, no one took a gap year, so I suppose one of my motives was to catch up with what young people now take as a matter of course. I felt it was
65 now or never, but making the decision to do it was not something I could take lightly. It meant I had to give up my secure job and live off my savings, sell my sports car and exchange my designer shoes for trainers. It took me ages to pluck up the courage
70 to take the plunge.

I've been amazed at the effect this mode of transport has had on people. It brings out protective instincts in
75 strangers, and I've met with nothing but kindness and trust. But I would never actually have embarked on these trips if I hadn't already believed that 99% of human beings are kind and honest. It's just the media that focuses on the 1%
80 who do all the mischief and make us think otherwise.

*'I believe that exploration is not just about finding things, but about understanding what you have found.'*

## D HUGH THOMSON

All my life I have been fascinated by the tale of an Inca city whose ruins were found once and then lost again. So when I was turned down flat by the film school that I had set my heart on attending, I decided on a whim to
85 go to Peru to look for it. Some years later, when I was eventually accepted by that same film school, the reason given was that the rigours of South American exploration were seen as analogous to the process of film-making. In other words, I'd somehow managed to
90 prove something about myself to them.

I believe that exploration is not just about finding things, but about understanding what you have found. I also think that you only ever find what you are looking for. So before (and after) my trips I spend a lot
95 of time in the library doing research. I've always been interested in the intellectual side of exploration. Doing English as my degree subject has proved an invaluable means to an end in that it taught me the importance of gathering information from other disciplines, such as
100 archaeology and history.

My work now takes me all over the world. I've taken filming expeditions to the Himalayas, India and Mexico. So if you want to be an explorer and need funds, my advice is to get a day job! For me, film-making is just
105 that – a second career that converges with and subsidises what I really love doing!

The majority of this material first appeared in CAM, the University of Cambridge Alumni Magazine.

# Vocabulary

## Expressions with *on*

**1** Look at the questions and text on pages 8 and 9 and find expressions containing *on* that mean:

1 wrote down formally (questions)
2 (a period of time) later (section A)
3 walked (section B)
4 very close to (something happening) (section B)
5 decided he wanted very much (section D)
6 suddenly and with no good reason (section D)

## Phrasal verbs

**2** **a** Replace the words in italics below with verb phrases that have the same meaning. Use words from columns A and B in the correct tense.

| A | B |
|---|---|
| turn | back |
| go | out on |
| pluck | off |
| start | down |
| miss | up for |
| bounce | up |
| make | on to |

1 How did the teacher *make* this course *begin*?
2 Would you like to *continue with* another course after this one?
3 Have you ever been *rejected* for a course or job?
4 If you have a problem, do you find it easy to *recover quickly*?
5 How would you *compensate for* forgetting a friend's birthday?
6 Have you ever had to *force yourself to have* the courage to do something?
7 Have you ever *not had the chance to do* something you really wanted?

**b** Ask each other the questions above.

## Collocation: verbs + nouns

**3** Mark one word in each set that does not collocate with the word in bold.

1 **achieve** a goal / a target / a prize / an ambition
2 **take** a risk / the plunge / a chance / a danger
3 realise / gather / collect / come across **information**
4 spend / finish / kill / take **time**
5 **contract** malaria / hepatitis / backache / pneumonia
6 **make** decisions / notice / sacrifices / mistakes

## Collocation: adjectives + nouns

**4** Complete each sentence with an adjective from A and a noun from B.

| A | B |
|---|---|
| open | outlook |
| sheltered | world |
| ideal | goal |
| positive | upbringing |
| personal | generations |
| real | mind |
| future | skills |
| survival | way |

1 Working abroad is an .................... to learn about a country.
2 The world is changing fast, and traditions may be lost to .................... .
3 People with a .................... on life tend to be healthier.
4 Now I've finished university, I've got to go out into the .................... !
5 I've finally achieved my .................... of visiting every European capital city.
6 Before travelling in a remote area, it is important to learn basic .................... .
7 People who have had a .................... are often shocked at how hard life is for some people.
8 When travelling, it is important to keep an .................... and not prejudge people.

**5** Complete the text with words and phrases from Exercises 1–4.

A few years ago, I was stuck in a dead-end job and started thinking about going to college. I'd left school at 18 and hadn't **(1)**.................... higher education, so I felt as though I had **(2)**.................... student life. I'm not the sort of person who does something **(3)**...................., so I spent months **(4)**.................... information about different courses. First, I applied to do a fashion course, but I was **(5)**.................... flat. Eventually I **(6)**.................... becoming a potter and finally **(7)**.................... the courage to apply. Going to college was tough financially, and I had to **(8)**.................... such as selling my car. However, four years **(9)**...................., I have my own business and I'm glad I finally **(10)**.................... .

**6** Discuss these questions.

1 What are your personal goals? Have you achieved any of them yet?
2 Are you the sort of person who likes to take risks?
3 When did you last do something on a whim?

## Listening 1 Developing skills (Parts 1 and 4)

**Before you listen**

1 You are going to hear a university student called Rita, who has been asked to give a talk to students in their last year at her old school. What do you think she might talk about?

**Distinguishing main points from details**

2 a 🎧 Listen to Rita's introduction. What is the main topic of her talk? Choose A, B, C or D.

A How to approach your university studies
B How to manage your time as a university student
C How to set your own learning objectives at university
D How to get the best results from your course of study

b What is Rita going to discuss in the rest of her talk?

3 a 🎧 Rita goes on to make three main points. Listen and number her main points in order. What expressions help you decide?

| Main points | Examples and tips |
|---|---|
| ☐ Set your own learning objectives and deadlines. | e.g. ............................................<br>Tip: ............................................ |
| ☐ Make sure you know what you have to do. | e.g. number of assignments ....<br>Tip: ............................................ |
| ☐ Check what standard of work is expected. | e.g. ............................................<br>Tip: ............................................ |

b For each main point, Rita gives examples and tips. Put the following notes in the correct place above.

- *use a wall planner or diary*
- *get hold of some examples of good work*
- *build in a safety margin*
- *how your work should be presented*
- *decide how many hours a week to spend studying*
- *number of assignments and deadlines for them*

c Listen again and check your answers. What expressions does Rita use to introduce her examples? her tips? Tick the expressions in the box.

> *You know,        … and all that.        One way of doing this is to …*
> *Why not …        For instance, …        The best approach to …*
> *It's a good idea to …        Don't be shy.        … things like: …*
> *… and that sort of thing        I always find it useful to …*

**Identifying attitudes and opinions**

4 a 🎧 Two of Rita's friends, Nick and Ann, heard her talk. Listen to their conversation. What did each of them think of it? Choose from A–D.

A She should have talked more about the social side.
B She was right to emphasise the importance of time management.
C She should have talked about the need to come up with new ideas.
D She was right to stress the importance of knowing what standard of work is expected.

b What expression(s)
- did Ann use to show she agreed with Rita?
- did Nick use to show what he liked best about Rita's talk?

**Discussion**

5 Which of Rita's points do you think are most useful? What other advice could you add from your experience of studying?

# English in Use 1 (Paper 3 Part 3)

**Lead-in**

**1 Discuss these questions.**
1 Can you cook? Were you taught or did you just pick it up? Do you cook just for yourself? for family and friends?
2 If you can't cook, would you like to be able to?

**Error correction**

▶ Task strategy page 169

**2 a** Look at the photo below, read the text through quickly and answer the questions. (Ignore the mistakes at this stage.)
   1 Who is the man in the photo?    3 What kind of teacher is he?
   2 When did he begin to enjoy cooking?

   **b** Read the instructions. What do you have to do?

   **c** Look at the example (**0**). What word class is the extra word? Look at question 1. Which word should not be there? What kind of word is it? How many lines did you need to read to check your answer?

   **d** Do the task. Read the task strategies for Paper 3 and Part 3 on page 169 before you begin. Use the Help clues below if necessary.

   In **most** lines of the following text, there is **one** unnecessary word. It is either grammatically incorrect or does not fit in with the sense of the text. For each numbered line (**1–16**), find this word and write it in the box. **Some lines are correct**. Indicate these lines with a tick (✓) in the box. The exercise begins with two examples (**0**) and (**00**).

**HELP**
➤ **Question 5**
   One of the auxiliaries is incorrect.
➤ **Question 6**
   Is it a verb or a conjunction that shouldn't be there?
➤ **Question 11**
   What is the phrasal verb here?

## LEARNING TO COOK

| | | |
|---|---|---|
| Thanks to Jamie Oliver, is the highly successful TV chef | 0 | is |
| with a casual student image, many young people have learnt | 00 | ✓ |
| that cooking can be fun, creative and satisfying. Oliver who | 1 | |
| himself learnt his trade not only from his formal training at college, | 2 | |
| but by working alongside there some of the very best chefs | 3 | |
| in London restaurants. Before that, though, from the age of eight, | 4 | |
| he had worked with his parents, who having ran a pub-restaurant, | 5 | |
| and when it was there that he realised that being in a kitchen was | 6 | |
| exciting. Oliver believes that children will learn to cook properly | 7 | |
| when they work with enthusiastic adults who to love food and when | 8 | |
| they are given the much responsibility to prepare simple but tasty | 9 | |
| dishes. In recent years, his quite biggest challenge was his | 10 | |
| attempt to turn off 15 unemployed young people into chefs for | 11 | |
| really a new top-class restaurant run by his charity, 'Cheeky Chops'. | 12 | |
| His over-enthusiastic and authoritarian style of teaching didn't suit | 13 | |
| everyone, though, and the five recruits dropped out. However, the | 14 | |
| restaurant is become open, its new chefs are cooking wonderful food, | 15 | |
| and Jamie's success story has been now made into a Hollywood movie. | 16 | |

**3 Answer the questions about the task.**
   1 Which questions test verb forms?
   2 Find an example in the text of
      • a perfect verb form          • a simple verb form
      • a continuous verb form       • a passive verb form

**4 How far do you agree with Jamie Oliver's views about children learning to cook (questions 7–10)?**

# Language development 1

▶ Grammar reference page 173

## Perfect tense forms

**1** Choose the most appropriate form of the verbs in italics: present/past simple, present/past/future perfect simple.

1 Petrus *is / has been* the most expensive restaurant I *ever went / have ever been* to.
2 My grandmother *lives / has lived* with us for years. She *moved / has moved* in after my grandfather died.
3 Claire *was / has been* much happier since she *changed / has changed* her job recently.
4 By the time we *got / had got* to the party, most people *left / had left*.
5 I *practise / have practised* yoga for two years, and before that I *did / had done* judo.
6 At this rate, Michael Owen *has broken / will have broken* the record before the season *will end / has ended*.

## Continuous tense forms

**2 a** Tick (✓) the sentences that use simple and continuous forms correctly. Correct those that don't. There may be one or two mistakes in each sentence.

1 My friend Vanessa has just started a new cookery course and she's loving it.
2 At the moment, she stays at her sister's flat until she is finding a place of her own.
3 Vanessa is enjoying entertaining, so she's always inviting people round.
4 Last week I was visiting her for dinner.
5 I hadn't been seeing Vanessa for over a month and I was looking forward to it.
6 Vanessa cooked when I was arriving at the flat, so I offered to help.
7 It was a great evening; I always enjoy good food and good company.
8 Tonight I cook for her. I will be making my speciality.

**b** Describe the last time you cooked for other people or went to a friend's for a meal.

**3** Match the beginnings of the sentences (1–8) to the endings (a–h).

1 Nowadays, on a normal night,
2 Don't wake John,
3 This time last week
4 I feel terrible today because
5 I felt awful when I arrived as
6 I was so tired that when I got home
7 When I finally woke up,
8 This will be the first time that

a I had been sleeping for 12 hours.
b I hadn't slept the night before.
c he's sleeping on the sofa.
d I slept for ten hours.
e I was sleeping on the beach in Bali.
f I sleep for six to seven hours.
g the baby has slept all night without waking.
h I haven't been sleeping well recently.

## Expressions with future meaning

**4 a** Match the expressions in the box to their functions (1–4).

> *be to (not)* + infinitive    *be due to* + infinitive
> *be bound/sure to* + infinitive
> *be about to* + infinitive    *expect (sb.) to* + infinitive
> *be on the point/verge of -ing*
> *be (un)likely to* + infinitive

1 immediate future
2 expected to happen at a particular time
3 official arrangements, formal announcements
4 probability/certainty

**b** Rewrite these sentences, replacing the words in italics with a suitable expression from the box above.

1 The government *will* introduce higher tuition fees at universities.
2 The new fees *should* come into effect next year.
3 Most students *will certainly* oppose the plans.
4 They *believe* fewer people *will* apply to universities.
5 The government *probably won't* listen to them.
6 The government *will* announce the new fees *within the next few days*.

**c** Do you agree that students should pay for their tuition? Why?/Why not?

## Future in the past

**5 a** Complete the sentences using *would be, was/were going to, was/were to have, would have, was/were about to, was/were due to.*

1 You're lucky you caught me – I ............................... just ............................... go out.
2 We ............................... meet at the cinema, but we've changed our plans.
3 I thought I ............................... finished my degree by now, but I haven't.
4 The match ............................... kick off at 3 p.m., but it didn't start until nearly 4 p.m.
5 I thought this course ............................... really dull, but it isn't – it's very interesting.
6 The exam results ............................... been announced today, but there has been a delay.

**b** Have you had any change of plans recently?

 ▶SRB pp7–8

13

# Writing 1 Using an appropriate register

1 a Look at these extracts from an informal interview with one of chef Jamie Oliver's trainees. Which of the expressions in italics do you think she used? Mark them.
   1 The training was really hard, wasn't it? *There was no messing about. / It was very serious.*
   2 We had to *attend / go through* a *demanding / rigorous* course at college.
   3 *He got us into / We were given* work placements in some *top-class / reputable* restaurant kitchens.
   4 To *round off / complete* our training, we all *worked as chefs / cooked* in Jamie's restaurant.
   5 *It was exhausting. / We were shattered half the time.*

   b 🎧 Listen and check your answers. What were the three stages of training?

   c Which of these features can you find in the trainee's comments in Exercise 1a? Which are you more likely to find in formal writing?
   • phrasal verbs
   • passive structures
   • clear sentence structure
   • linking words
   • colloquial expressions
   • question tags
   • contractions

   d Complete the following extract from a written description of Jamie Oliver's training course. Use information from the trainee's comments in Exercise 1a, and add the information in the notes below. Remember, the written description will be more formal than the trainee's comments!

   – training programme lasted one year
   – course at a London college lasted 14 weeks
   – work placements lasted two months
   – Jamie's restaurant = in London, called 'Fifteen'
   – trainees found course very tiring but rewarding

   (0) The <u>one-year training programme was very</u> serious.
   (1) First, the trainees ............................................. .
   (2) Then they ............................................. . (3) Finally,
   ............................................. . (4) According to the
   trainees, it ............................................. .

2 Rewrite the parts in italics to make the sentences below less colloquial. Use the words in the box and any other language necessary.

| advantage | attended | beginners | completion | congratulate |
| involved | irritated | disorganised | outstanding | prepared |
| presented | publicised | suitable | tuition | |

   1 Everyone thought *the teaching was brilliant.*
   2 It wasn't *the right course for people who didn't know anything.*
   3 *When the course was all over,* everyone *got* a certificate.
   4 The practical parts of the course were *a bit of a mess – no planning.*
   5 *They didn't let people know about the course,* so *not many turned up.*
   6 It was *a real plus* having such an experienced teacher.
   7 Unfortunately, he sometimes *got a bit ratty.*
   8 I'd like to *give a pat on the back to everyone who took part.*

3 a Think of a course you have attended (e.g. a computer course at college, driving lessons). What made it a good or bad course?

   b You have been asked to fill in an evaluation form about your course. Write a paragraph giving your opinions. Use a formal style.

# 1B A job for life?

## Listening 2 (Paper 4 Part 4)

**Before you listen**

1  Discuss these questions.

   1  What do you think are the important factors to consider when choosing a job or career (e.g. salary, training)?
   2  Do you expect to stay in the same job all your life? Why do you think someone might retrain for a different job later in life?

**Multiple matching**

▶ Task strategies pages 170 and 171

2  🎧 Listen and do the task below. Read the task strategies on pages 170 and 171 before you start and use the Help clues below if necessary. Listen to the recording twice.

You will hear **five** different people talking about career changes they have made.

---

### TASK ONE

For questions **1–5**, choose from the list **A–H** the reason each person gives for changing career.

A  I needed a challenge.

B  I did it for financial reasons.          | 1 |

C  I was made redundant.                     | 2 |

D  I wanted to do something more exciting.   | 3 |

E  I witnessed a dramatic event.            | 4 |

F  I did it for family reasons.             | 5 |

G  I got the opportunity of a lifetime.

H  I wanted to do something more worthwhile.

### TASK TWO

For questions **6–10**, choose from the list **A–H** what each person dislikes about their new career.

A  the attitude of colleagues

B  the drop in income                       | 6 |

C  the insecure nature of the work          | 7 |

D  the strain it puts on the family         | 8 |

E  the lack of support from superiors       | 9 |

F  the demanding workload                   | 10 |

G  the stress involved in retraining

H  the amount of travelling involved

---

**HELP**

➤ Question 1
The speaker found her previous job superficial and wanted to make a useful contribution to society. Which reason (A–H) matches these ideas?

➤ Question 2
The speaker didn't feel stretched in the navy, but is happy that his present job is demanding. So why did he change?

**HELP**

➤ Question 6
Listen for what the speaker didn't realise about the work of a lawyer.

➤ Question 9
The speaker talks about his retraining, travelling and his income. But what does he dislike about his new career?

**Task analysis**

3  What key phrases in the recording helped you choose your answers?

**Discussion**

4  Discuss these questions.

   1  Which person do you think made the most difficult career change? Which do you think was the most rewarding?
   2  Which of the jobs would you most and least like to do?

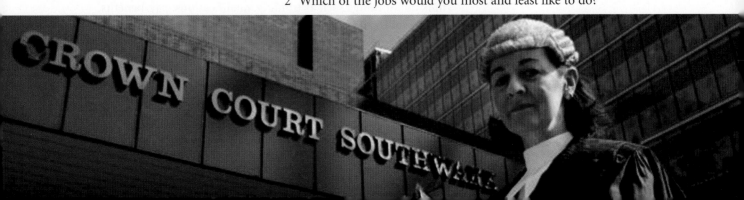

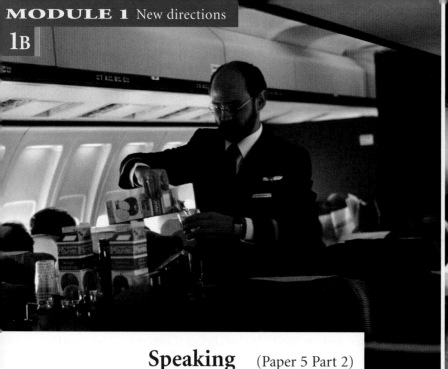

# Speaking (Paper 5 Part 2)

**Vocabulary:**
**personal qualities**

1 a Which adjective in the box below means a person who:
   1 is careful not to say anything that will upset or embarrass others?
   2 is able to understand other people's feelings and problems?
   3 treats everyone in a reasonable and equal way?
   4 is able to get over problems and difficulties quickly?
   5 prefers to be with other people rather than alone?
   6 allows people to do, say or believe what they want, without punishing or criticising them?
   7 is reasonable, practical and is able to judge things well?
   8 continues to do something, even if it's difficult?

| | | | | |
|---|---|---|---|---|
| *assertive* | *creative* | *decisive* | *efficient* | *energetic* |
| *fair-minded* | *flexible* | *friendly* | *gregarious* | *patient* |
| *persistent* | *resilient* | *sensible* | *sensitive* | *tactful* | *tolerant* |

   b Write definitions for two more adjectives from the box. Use a dictionary if necessary.

   c Read your definitions to a partner. He/She should try to guess the words.

   d 🎧 Divide the adjectives into three groups: words with two, three or four syllables. Say each word and mark the syllable with the main stress. Then listen to check. Can you identify any patterns?

2 a Discuss what kind of person you would need to be to do the jobs in the photos. Use different forms of the words in Exercise 1, and any other words you know.
      EXAMPLES: *You'd have to be really practical to be a ... , because ...*
      *A tactless person would be no good in this job, because ...*
      *You'd need to have a sense of humour and good communication skills ...*

   b Complete these sentences with your opinions about the jobs above. Think about things such as training, qualifications, pay, benefits, working hours, job satisfaction.
      1 The great thing about doing/being ... would be ...
      2 What must be really difficult is ...
      3 I don't really think I'd enjoy ...
      4 I can't see myself ...
      5 I don't think I'm ... enough to ...

   c Discuss your opinions with a partner.

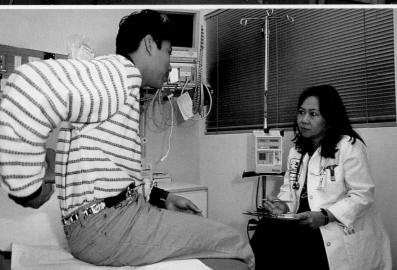

**Sample answer**

▶ Task strategies pages 171 and 172

**3** **a** Read the task strategies for Paper 5 on page 171 and for Part 2 on page 172.

**b** 🎧 Look at the photos again. Listen to the examiner's instructions and answer the questions.

1 What TWO things does the task involve?

2 How long does the candidate have to do it?

**c** 🎧 Listen to someone doing the task. Which jobs did he talk about? Do you agree with the points he made about each one?

**d** How successfully did he complete the task? Did he follow the task strategies?

**Useful language:**
**comparing, contrasting**
**and speculating**

**4** **a** Listen again to the sample answer (Exercise 3c) and complete these sentences.

1 These jobs are similar because they ............................. .

2 To do either of these jobs ........................... .

3 Neither of these people ........................... .

4 The most obvious difference between the jobs is that ........................... , whereas ........................... , I imagine the most important thing would be ........................... .

5 Being ........................... might not be quite as essential for ........................... as for ........................... .

**b** What four expressions did the student use in place of *I think …* ?

**Long turn**

**5** Work in pairs. Take turns to do the task in Exercise 3. Each of you should use a different combination of photos. The person who is not doing the task should time the other one (one minute).

**Task analysis**

**6** Did you

• complete both parts of the task?

• speak for a full minute?

# English in Use 2 (Paper 3 Part 5)

**Lead-in**

1 What advice would you give someone about to go for a job interview?

**Register transfer**

► Task strategies pages 169 and 170

2 a Read both texts below quickly.
   1 Do you agree with the advice?
   2 How is the style of the second text different from the first?

b Do the task. Read the task strategies on pages 169 and 170 before you start and use the Help clues below if necessary.

Read the following leaflet about job interviews. Use the information in it to complete the numbered gaps in the letter from Sarah to her friend Tom, who is applying for his first job. The words you need **do not occur** in the leaflet. **Use no more than two words for each gap**. The exercise begins with an example (**0**).

**LEAFLET**

### The basics

- It will be assumed by your interviewers that you have read all information sent to you in advance about the company. A good piece of advice is that you do some extra research on the company, so that during the interview you appear to be very well informed.
- Be punctual for your interview – even arrive a few minutes early – and try to show respect and consideration to every member of staff you meet. At some time they might be required to give their opinion of you.

### Presentation

- First impressions are lasting ones, and decisions are often made about a candidate within minutes.
- Wear formal clothes for your interview – don't give the impression that you don't care. The clothes you wear could decide your future.
- Your body language is crucial. It is very important that you shake an interviewer's hand firmly and make eye contact.

### Answering questions

- Try to respond appropriately to all questions. If you don't understand a question, make a request – politely – for it to be repeated.

**LETTER**

Dear Tom,

I saw a leaflet in the library about job interviews, which I thought offers some pretty good advice.
First, it covered the basics. The company will take it (0) for granted that you've read all the stuff they sent you (1)............ interview, and the leaflet recommends that you find (2)............ about the company so that you seem to know a lot about it. Of course, you shouldn't (3)............ for your interview – they suggest you (4)............ up a bit early – and when you arrive, make (5)............ to be polite to everyone you meet who (6)............ .
Then the leaflet talked about how you present yourself. How you come (7)............ at the beginning of an interview is critical. Many interviewers make up (8)............ about candidates very early on. For a start, many interviewers won't take you seriously if you dress too (9)............ ! And you should give your interviewers a firm handshake and (10)............ in the eye.
The leaflet also says that during the interview, you should try and answer all the interviewer's questions, but if a question isn't (11)............ , you can always (12)............ the interviewer (politely!) to say it again. Hope this helps!

Best wishes,

Sarah

**HELP**
► Question 1
This paraphrases *in advance*.
► Question 2
Two words: part of a phrasal verb meaning *discover* and a word expressing the idea of *extra*.
► Question 6
Expresses the idea of *staff*.

## Task analysis

3 Answer these questions about the task.
   1 What clues did you find in the words around the gaps to help you think of the words you needed?
   2 Which gaps required a synonym in a different register?
   3 Find examples of passive constructions which make the first text more formal.

## Discussion

4 Have you had an interview for a job? How did it go? Did you follow the advice in the text?

# Language development 2

▶ Grammar reference page 174

## Passive forms

**1** Why is the passive used in the following examples?
1 I was told that if I didn't slow down in future, I would be stopped and charged with dangerous driving.
2 The fire was started deliberately and spread very quickly.
3 I realise that you were overcharged, but nothing can be done about it without a receipt.
4 All visitors must be given an identity badge.
5 The publicity was excellent. The posters were made by Mr Williams.
6 The results will be sent out to candidates in six to eight weeks.
7 He is said to be the greatest drummer alive.

**2** Which sentence is more appropriate in each pair?
1 In a letter from a credit-card company:
   a We must receive your payment within 14 days.
   b Your payment must be received within 14 days.
2 In a note to a friend:
   a Don't forget to bring the book back when you've finished it.
   b Please ensure that the book is brought back when it has been finished.
3 In a company report:
   a We interviewed 1,000 clients and analysed the replies.
   b One thousand clients were interviewed and the replies were analysed.
4 In an advert:
   a You should buy one of these now before it's too late.
   b One of these should be bought by you now before it's too late.

## Register

**3** Look again at the *English in Use* texts opposite and decide if the following statements are *True* or *False*. More formal texts tend to
1 use more passive forms.
2 be more emotional.
3 have more phrasal verbs.
4 use longer, more complex words.
5 use more paraphrases.

**4 a** Look at these examples from the *English in Use* texts. Which one is more formal?
1 Be punctual.
2 You shouldn't be late.

**b** Match the words in column A with the more formal words with the same meaning in column B.

| A | | B | |
|---|---|---|---|
| 1 | places | a | guarantee |
| 2 | expect | b | organise |
| 3 | let down | c | satisfactory |
| 4 | book | d | anticipate |
| 5 | promise | e | reserve |
| 6 | reply (*n.*) | f | sufficient |
| 7 | run | g | enclose |
| 8 | enough | h | destinations |
| 9 | OK | i | disappoint |
| 10 | put in | j | response |

**c** Complete the second sentence in each pair with words from Exercise 4b, so that it means the same as the first sentence but is more formal.

Dear Sir/Madam,
Thank you for your enquiry about our organised tours.
1 a We run trips to the following places.
  b We ..................... excursions to the following ..................... .
2 a In this company, we promise that we will not let you down.
  b We ..................... that you will not be ..................... .
3 a I have put in prices until the end of the year and I hope that is OK.
  b I have ..................... prices until the end of the year and trust that is ..................... .
4 a We expect to get a lot of replies to the advertisement.
  b We ..................... a huge ..................... to the advertisement.
5 a Therefore we suggest you book now while there are still enough places.
  b Customers are therefore advised to ..................... a place now while there are ..................... places available.

Yours faithfully

**5 a** Find these phrases in the *English in Use* texts opposite. Which one is a paraphrase of the other?
1 First impressions …
2 How you come across at the beginning …

**b** Rewrite these sentences with a paraphrase to make them less formal.
1 The tours are extremely popular.
2 Notice of seat numbers will be given one week in advance.
3 Reductions are available for children under the age of five.
4 In the event of cancellation, all fares will be reimbursed in full.

**6** Rewrite these sentences to make them more formal.
1 On some trips, we will ask you to show how old you are.
2 We are sorry to say that we can't get a guide today.
3 The cheap hotel room was fine and what we expected.
4 Not enough people wanted to go on the trip, so we cancelled it.

# Writing 2    Character reference (Paper 2 Part 2)

**Lead-in**    1  Discuss these questions.
  1  What is a character reference?
  2  When do people write them?
  3  Has anyone ever written one about you?
  4  What would you expect to include in a character reference?

**Understand the task**    2  Read the task below and answer these questions.

▶ Writing reference page 189

  1  What is the READER looking for in your reference? Mark the key points you have to cover.
  2  What kind of information will be RELEVANT? Will you only include positive points?
  3  What STYLE will you use: formal? neutral? informal and friendly?
  4  What will make the reader think it is a WELL-WRITTEN reference?

> A family in Britain is looking for a young person to take care of two young children and to do some light domestic work during the summer. A friend of yours has applied for the job, and the family has asked you to write a reference. Your reference should indicate your relationship with the applicant and how long you have known him/her, and include relevant information about your friend's
>
> • character and personal qualities
> • attitude to children
> • any relevant skills and experience.
>
> Write your **reference** in approximately 250 words.

**Plan your reference**    3  a  Look at these notes and match them to the topic areas given in the task.

* went to school together
* did work experience together in local kindergarten
* comes from a large family
* able to handle unexpected situations well
* both of us now training to become primary teachers
* her room at college not always very tidy

* honest and hardworking
* acts in best interest of others
* in school, liked and respected by the children
* children find her fun
* speaks English well

  b  Decide in which order you will deal with each topic area. Add the topic areas to this paragraph plan.

  **Paragraph 1:** Explanation of relationship to applicant

  **Paragraph 2:** ........................................................................................

  **Paragraph 3:** ........................................................................................

  **Paragraph 4:** ........................................................................................

  **Paragraph 5:** Recommendation

  c  Decide which points in the notes you will definitely use and add them to the plan. (For example, you may decide not to include any negative points.) Add any further points you would like to include. Remember, you only have 250 words.

**Language and content**

**4 a** Read this introduction. Mark the verbs and say what tenses are used and why.

> I have known Anna Kurtz for six years, both as a colleague and a friend. We first met at secondary school when we did two weeks' work experience together in a local kindergarten. Since then, I have got to know her very well and have come to appreciate her many talents. At present, we are both at the same teacher training college, learning to become primary-level teachers.

**b** Choose and complete useful expressions from this list for each of your paragraphs.

| | |
|---|---|
| **Talking about your experience of the candidate** | *I have (known) … for … years, both as (a friend) and as (a work colleague).*<br>*In that time …*<br>*Over the years …*<br>*My most recent (contact) with him/her was …*<br>*As part of his/her (duties), he/she …* |
| **Talking about qualities** | *I have always known him/her to be …*<br>*I remember him/her being …*<br>*He/She would bring many (qualities) to …*<br>*He/She always gives the (impression that) …*<br>*He/She has always proved himself/herself to be extremely …*<br>*I can confirm that he/she has always …*<br>*As a (colleague), he/she …*<br>*With (children), he/she …*<br>*On a (social) level, he/she …*<br>*In fact, I would go as far as to say that he/she …* |
| **Talking about negatives** | *I regret having to say anything negative about … but …*<br>*Sometimes his/her … can (lead to) …*<br>*The one (drawback) …*<br>*The only (weakness) …* |
| **Recommending** | *I believe that … would make a (good) …*<br>*For the reasons I have given I have no hesitation/ reservations in (supporting) … application for …*<br>*I am pleased to (recommend) … for the (position) of …* |

Note: it is acceptable to use first names in most character references, particularly after the first time you mention the name.

**Write your character reference**

**5** Now write your character reference, using some of the ideas and language above. Write your answer in approximately 250 words.

**Check your answer**

**6** Edit your work using the checklist on page 188.

▶ Writing reference page 188

# Module 1: Review

**1** Decide which word or phrase best fits each space.

1 Being quite ........., I quickly got over the shock.
   **A** successful   **B** flexible   **C** pliant   **D** resilient

2 Having ........ her heart on university, she'd be upset if she didn't get in.
   **A** laid   **B** set   **C** fixed   **D** positioned

3 He's a very optimistic person with a very positive ........ on life.
   **A** outlook   **B** position   **C** point of view
   **D** stance

4 Do you know anywhere where I can ........ a decent guidebook?
   **A** make up for   **B** take time over   **C** get hold of
   **D** catch up with

5 After working for ten years, I ........ and went back to college.
   **A** missed the boat   **B** took the plunge
   **C** bent the rules   **D** hit the roof

6 He's a bit timid and hasn't yet ........ the courage to apply for the job.
   **A** put on   **B** caught up with   **C** plucked up
   **D** carried through

7 He spends most of his spare time with his ........ stuck in a book.
   **A** eye   **B** face   **C** mind   **D** nose

8 Losing the election was a serious ........ in his career.
   **A** setback   **B** sacrifice   **C** hardship   **D** risk

9 We decided ........ to fly to New York, but we couldn't get a flight.
   **A** far and wide   **B** on a whim   **C** off and on
   **D** once in a while

10 I bought a new dress to ........ not getting the job!
   **A** miss out on   **B** start off with   **C** make up for
   **D** let down

**2** Find and correct the five mistakes with verb forms in each text.

**1**

Sorry I haven't made the plane on Friday. I hope it didn't mess you around too much. I know you have already booked me a hotel room, but presumably you were able to cancel it. Unfortunately, my father isn't very well recently, and on Friday morning, while he cleaned the car, he fainted and was rushed into hospital. Luckily, the doctors say he's likely being home in a few days.

**2**

I got a job in Scotland about ten years ago, and I will have been there ever since. Recently, I met this really nice guy and we'll get married on the 27th of next month. Of course, mother's scandalised because by the time we tie the knot, we'll only be knowing each other for two months! When you'll get some time off, why not come and see us? If you do, I'm going to organise a get-together with some old friends.

**3** Rewrite the sentences in the active or passive.

1 They encouraged me to undertake further research.
   I ............................................................................. .

2 They've transferred my money into my account.
   My money ........................................................... .

3 They'll probably give you a grant.
   You ...................................................................... .

4 They're interviewing the candidates right now.
   The candidates .................................................... .

5 My visit had to be cut short.
   I ............................................................................. .

6 The locals greeted us with nothing but kindness.
   We ....................................................................... .

7 They must receive your proposal by next week.
   Your ..................................................................... .

8 He was bitten by a dog. It must have hurt him badly.
   He was bitten by a dog. He .................................. .

**4** Complete the second sentence so that it has a similar meaning to the first, but a different register. The first letters of the words you need are given.

1 I haven't had a job for three months.
   I've b................. u................. for three months. (*neutral*)

2 Visitors must let the receptionist know when they arrive.
   Visitors are r................. to i................. the receptionist of their a................. . (*formal*)

3 We won't take any applications that arrive late.
   Applications r................. after the deadline will not be a................. . (*formal*)

4 It's important to know what's expected of you.
   You n................. to know what you h................. to do. (*informal*)

5 Take him on, I think he'd be good at the job.
   I'm p................. to r................. him for the p................. . (*formal*)

6 You'd better turn up on time.
   You are a................. to be p................. . (*formal*)

22

# MODULE 2
# Seeing is believing

## Overview

- **Reading:** gapped text (Paper 1 Part 2)
- **Vocabulary:** using the correct word; ways of touching
- **Listening 1:** understanding text structure (Paper 4 Part 1)
- **English in Use 1:** gapped text (Paper 3 Part 6)
- **Language development 1:** relative and reduced relative clauses
- **Writing 1:** planning your writing
- **Listening 2:** sentence completion (Paper 4 Part 1)
- **Speaking:** social interaction (Paper 5 Part 1)
- **English in Use 2:** open cloze (Paper 3 Part 2)
- **Language development 2:** articles, determiners and quantifiers
- **Writing 2:** information leaflet (Paper 2 Part 2)

*Photo of the Loch Ness Monster taken by Marmaduke Wetherell in 1934*

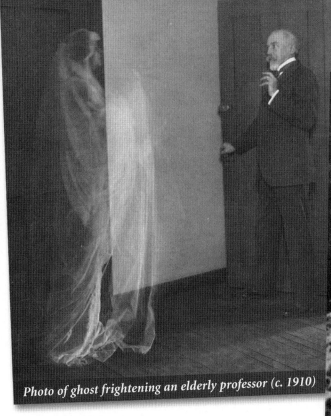

*Photo of ghost frightening an elderly professor (c. 1910)*

*Photo of a UFO taken on 16 January 1958 off the coast of Brazil*

## Lead-in

- Look at the photos. What do you know about these phenomena? Which photos do you think could be genuine?
- Are you the kind of person who believes there must be a logical explanation for everything, or are you prepared to believe in the existence of things which can't be rationally explained?
- How far do you agree or disagree with this quotation?

*'For those who believe, no explanation is necessary. For those who do not, none will suffice.'*

## Reading  (Paper 1 Part 2)

**Before you read**  1  Look at the photo and read the heading and first paragraph of the article.
   1  What is happening in the photo?
   2  What are you going to read about in the rest of the article?
   3  What do you think the writer's attitude to his subject will be?

**Reading**  2  Read the rest of the main text. (Ignore the missing paragraphs at this stage.)
   Then discuss the answers to the questions in Exercise 1.

# People don't want to know how it's done
## The spell-binding world of conjuror Steve Cohen *by Cole Morton*

A mobile phone rings. This is astonishing, not just because it happens in the middle of a highly intimate theatrical performance, but because the person who is making it ring in a most remarkable way is the star of the
5 show. Serious followers of magic know that Steve Cohen is one of the most remarkable mind-readers and conjurors in the world, and this evening 40 people have paid a lot of money to gather in a tiny crowded room at this London hotel to watch him in action.

**1**

10  In the office of the billionaire Mayor of New York, he once asked for a dollar bill. Watched closely by the Mayor, Cohen rubbed the bank note with his fingers until the signature of the Secretary to the Treasury became that of the Mayor himself. Or so he says. The note hangs in a
15 frame on the wall of the Mayor's office, apparently, but I can't go and see it.

**2**

It is, of course, Cohen who is responsible. The thing is, nobody has told him the number to dial. The owner of the phone was just told to visualise the necessary digits, in
20 silence. When it rang, the man jumped out of his seat, literally, and looked shaken. Scared, even.

**3**

He attributes his success to the way he is able to connect with and engage his audience; an approach inspired by the parlour magicians of the nineteenth
25 century. With simple tricks and the intimacy of a small room, Cohen is able to have the audience participate in nearly every part of the act. A believer in the power of persuasion, he is of the opinion that psychology and magic go hand in hand, and I notice he likes to use the language
30 of eastern philosophy in his shows.

**4**

Well, up to a point. Yesterday, when we were talking in his hotel suite, he asked me to visualise a wonderful holiday. I thought of walking along a beach in Mauritius. Then he said 'Take your shoe off,' which suddenly had white sand in it. 35 And a shell. This would be amazing stuff were it not that he was holding the shoe, not me. Any magician worth their top hat ought to be able to smuggle a shell into a shoe while the customer has his eyes half closed thinking about a beach.

**5**

Two women close their eyes and hold out bare arms. He 40 taps one with a feather, lightly, three times — but it's the other one who reacts and swears she has been touched.

Now he takes three wedding rings from volunteers, puts them into a glass tumbler, shakes it and lifts the rings out with a pen. They are interlinked. Amazing! Then he shows 45 us the time on a stranger's watch. A woman is asked to hold the watch in her fist and think of a number. She says 18. When she opens her fist, the hands on the watch have moved back 18 minutes on their own.

**6**

'On a deep level, people don't want to know how it's done,' 50 says Cohen. He's not about to tell anyone, not for all the money in the world. 'Magic works for everybody, from the richest to the poorest. A comedian can make you laugh, music can make you tap your feet, but magic makes you wonder.'

## Gapped text

▶ Task strategies page 168

**3 a** For questions 1–6, you must choose which of the paragraphs A–F below fit into the numbered gaps in the article. Read the task strategies on page 168 before you start.

**b** Read the text before and after question 1 and look at the highlighted words. Which of the paragraphs below fits?

**c** Continue in the same way and complete the task. (Note that in the exam, there is one extra paragraph which does not fit in any of the gaps.)

**A** I don't really believe the story, either, which is why I'm sitting with people who have paid £50 each to be inches away from Cohen's magic fingers. One member of the audience is a magician himself, but even so, he is absolutely astonished when his mobile goes off.

**B** Personally, I don't find it very convincing. For all his talk of spiritual energy, he is essentially only trying to trick us into thinking something supernatural is going on. Anyone who seeks out an exclusive show like this is eager to be fooled, so a combination of quick, skilful moves, distraction, psychological techniques and card-counting must surely do the trick.

**C** It's this last one that wins me round! Now I know why rich and powerful people obsessed with controlling their own lives will pay so much for the existence of the inexplicable. They want the chance to believe in something extraordinary, to see it with their own eyes.

**D** It's tricks like these that focus on our minds that are the most amazing. 'For those who believe, no explanation is necessary. For those who do not, none will suffice,' says Cohen. His shows are always sell-outs, their popularity mainly spread by word of mouth, so he clearly strikes a chord. Cohen says it's not about the money, but his love of entertaining; nevertheless, the magic trade is clearly highly lucrative.

**E** The young red-haired American doesn't go in for the smoke and mirrors or elaborate sets of stadium magicians. He prefers to keep it small and personal and charge for it: the likes of Michael J. Fox and other film stars pay up to $15,000 for him to appear at private functions like this one, which is why he's known in the States as the Millionaire Magician.

**F** Which is why, tonight, I have managed to sustain my scepticism all the way through his skilful card tricks and the one with the silver coin that turns into a brick. After all, this was learned from his uncle at the tender age of six, and so is obviously explicable. However, now things are beginning to get very weird.

## Task analysis

**4** Compare and justify your answers. Discuss:
1 what the highlighted words and phrases refer to in the text.
2 what kind of links you found in the rest of the text.

## Discussion

**5** How far do you agree with these statements from the text?

'People don't want to know how it's done.' (Steve Cohen)

'Anyone who seeks out an exclusive show like this is eager to be fooled.' (Cole Morton)

# Vocabulary

## Using the correct word

Many words that share a similar general meaning can't be used in the same contexts because they don't mean *exactly* the same thing.

**1** Choose the correct word to complete these sentences. You can find one word in each pair in the text on pages 24–25.

1 *well-paid / lucrative*
 a The magic trade is clearly highly .............. . (paragraph D)
 b For two years, he had a .............. job performing in Las Vegas.

2 *number / digit*
 a Nobody has told him the .............. to dial. (line 18)
 b A bank security PIN is usually a four-.............. code.

3 *see / visualise*
 a He asked me to .............. a wonderful holiday. (line 32)
 b It was impossible to .............. how he was doing it.

4 *intimate / close*
 a … not just because it happens in the middle of a highly .............. theatrical performance … (line 1)
 b The partnership between a magician and his assistant is very .............. .

**2** a Complete these sentences using the verbs *trick*, *cheat* or *deceive* in the correct form.

1 Magicians are essentially trying to .............. us into thinking something supernatural is going on. (page 25, paragraph B)

2 If you think you don't need to study, then you are .............. yourself.

3 If a candidate .............. in the exam and is found out, he/she will automatically fail.

b Fill in the table. Then choose the correct word forms to complete the sentences below.

| Verb | Noun – idea | Noun – person | Adjective | Adverb |
|---|---|---|---|---|
| trick | .............. [C] .............. [U] | trickster | .............. | |
| cheat | .............. [U] | .............. | | |
| deceive | .............. [U] deceit | | .............. .............. | .............. .............. |

1 Film makers use a lot of .............................. photography to create special effects.

2 Some effects are quite complex, while others are .............................. simple.

3 The images they create look very real, but appearances can be .............................. .

4 The photograph is supposed to show a ghost, but I'm sure it's just .............................. .

5 Don't do business with Angelo; he's a .............................. and a liar.

6 In his dealings with me, he's been sly and .............................. , telling one lie after another.

7 I trusted him totally, so I didn't see through his lies and .............................. for a long time.

8 .............................. in athletics is becoming more common as more athletes take drugs to improve their performance.

c Have you ever been
 1 tricked into doing something you didn't want to do?
 2 cheated out of some money?
 3 a victim of a deception?

## Ways of touching

**3** a Complete these sentences with the verbs used in the text. They both refer to ways of touching. Can you demonstrate how the actions are different?

1 Cohen .............. the banknote with his fingers … (line 12)

2 He .............. one woman on the arm with a feather. (line 40)

b Use the following verbs in the appropriate form to complete the story below. Use each verb once only.

| rub | tap | touch | hold | scratch |
|---|---|---|---|---|
| press | push | pat | stroke | feel |

Detective Fairley was baffled. The house looked empty, and the owner seemed to have disappeared. He (1)........................ the door bell and waited. No reply. In his hand he was (2)........................ the search warrant the judge had given him earlier. Tired and tense, he (3)........................ the back of his neck as he waited. Then he went to the side of the house and (4)........................ on the window to attract attention. Nothing. He (5)........................ his head, trying to work out what had happened. At the back of the house, he found the door ajar. He (6)........................ it open and went inside, where he found the owner's dog. He (7)........................ its head and (8)........................ its rough fur. The dog was calm; Fairley couldn't understand why.
On the table was a cup of coffee. He (9)........................ the cup, and it was warm. He put his hand on the wall; he could (10)........................ a vibration. Suddenly he heard a sound.

c Finish the story in 50 words. Include some of the following verbs.

| squeeze | punch | grasp | itch |
|---|---|---|---|
| slap | grab | clutch | grip |

▶SRB p17

## Listening 1    Developing skills (Part 1)

**Before you listen**

1   a   Look at the pictures. What do these situations suggest to you?

b   Do you follow any special rituals when:
- you are about to take an exam?
- you are travelling by train or car?
- you are choosing an important number (e.g. a lottery number)?
- you are playing or watching a sport?
- someone wishes you good luck or mentions something unlucky?

**Understanding the main point**

2   ◠ You are going to hear a talk about superstitions. Listen to the speaker's introduction. What is he going to discuss in his talk? Choose from A–C.
   **A** Reasons why people were superstitious in the past
   **B** How people rely less on superstitions nowadays
   **C** Why many people are still superstitious today

**Understanding text structure:**
discourse markers

3   a   Each of these sentences represents one section of the talk. Which order do you think they will come in?
   ☐ **A** People still believe in superstition, even if their rituals don't work.
   ☐ **B** Some types of people are more superstitious than others nowadays.
   ☐ **C** People are superstitious because they tend to hold on to old ideas.
   ☐ **D** On balance, superstition may be a good thing.
   ☐ **E** Some superstitious rituals have become part of polite social interaction.

b   ◠ Listen to check your ideas. Which of the following does the speaker use to introduce each section of the talk?
   a   a rhetorical question (i.e. a question which he goes on to answer)
   b   a marker that indicates sequence of ideas (e.g. *firstly, another,* etc.)
   c   an emphasis marker (that indicates this is the most important point)
   d   a marker that introduces a contrasting idea (e.g. *nevertheless*)

   Section 1 ☐   Section 2 ☐   Section 3 ☐   Section 4 ☐   Section 5 ☐

**Extracting specific information**

4   Read through the examples the speaker used to illustrate each of his main points. Then listen again and complete the sentences with one to four words.

Introduction:   In the USA, (1)..................................... per cent of people have lucky charms.
Section 1:   People throw (2)..................................... over their shoulder if it gets spilt.
   People (3)..................................... if they talk about bad things which may happen.
   People (4)..................................... if they want good wishes to come true.
   People use a (5)..................................... if you wish them good luck.
Section 2:   British people say (6)..................................... if someone sneezes.
Section 3:   People (7)..................................... if good luck charms don't work.
Section 4:   There is an actor who (8)..................................... before a big show.
   One footballer has a ritual way of (9)..................................... before a big match.

**Discussion**

5   Which of the superstitions mentioned are you familiar with? What other examples could you add?

## English in Use 1 (Paper 3 Part 6)

**Lead-in**

1  Look at the photo and discuss these questions.
1  Where is this place?
2  What do you think the monument represents?

**Gapped text**

▶ Task strategies pages 169 and 170

2  a  Read the title and the text below quickly. (Ignore the gaps at this stage.)
1  Who might have built the Sphinx?
2  What might have caused it to be damaged?

b  Look at question 1. Which ways can you think of to complete the sentence?

c  Now look at four possible answers. Which one fits the space?

A  which looks like
B  which some people describe
C  which suggests
D  which might have been

d  Do the task. Read the task strategies on pages 169 and 170 before you start and use the Help clues below if necessary.

For questions **1–6**, read the following text and then choose from the list **A–I** below the best phrase to fill each one. Each correct phrase may only be used once. **Some of the suggested answers do not fit at all.**

# The Mystery of the Sphinx

One of the world's most studied ancient monuments is the Sphinx, which is located close to the Great Pyramid, 16 kilometres from Cairo in Egypt. Carved in ancient times out of a single piece of limestone over 60 metres long and 20 metres high, it weighs hundreds of tons. This extraordinary monument consists solely of the head of a man and the body of a crouching lion, a combination (1)............. strength and wisdom. Over the years, the face has sustained damage. The smile, (2)............. as mysterious, is in fact the result of erosion rather than design, and the nose, which has long since been broken away, was probably the unfortunate victim of invading soldiers' target practice. At one time, there was a serpent on its forehead and a royal beard, a fragment (3)............. in a museum.

But who built this monument (4)............. guarding significant places, is not part of a pair but stands alone? Most Egyptologists agree that it was built by Pharaoh Khafre 5,000 years ago. However, some recent commentators have speculated that it belonged to a much older civilisation, which disappeared in a legendary flood (5)............. everything in the world over 7,000 years ago. They have tried to demonstrate that the weathering of the Sphinx was caused by water rather than wind and sand, and one has even suggested (6)............. on a more ancient site about 12,500 years ago. Whatever its origins, there is no doubt that to the Egyptians, the Sphinx represents the very essence of their country's magnificent culture.

**HELP**

➤ Question 2
Is this part of a defining or non-defining relative clause?

➤ Question 4
What is the function of the comma in this sentence?

➤ Question 6
What time is referred to here, present or past?

A  of which exists
B  which some people describe
C  that was clearly known
D  that is supposed to have destroyed
E  which suggests

F  that it fits in
G  which, no matter how many
H  that it might have been built
I  which, unlike most of the others

3  Compare and justify your answers. Which questions did you find most difficult and why?

**Discussion**

4  Should we try and restore damaged monuments like this, or just keep them as they are?

▶SRB  p19

# Language development 1

▶ Grammar reference page 175

## Review of relative clauses

**1** Find and correct the mistakes with relative clauses in the following sentences.
1 A beautiful part of Britain is Wiltshire, where is the ancient monument of Stonehenge.
2 Stonehenge is a circle of stones which they date back over 5,000 years.
3 The monument, thousands of people visit each year, is 50 metres across.
4 The original purpose of the monument that has not been discovered might have been for sun worship.
5 June 21ˢᵗ, the longest day, is the day on when the stones line up with the rising sun.
6 Little is known about the people, who built Stonehenge, or their beliefs.
7 Some of the stones, they weighed up to 3 tonnes, were carried over 200 kilometres.
8 Modern engineers, who their efforts to repeat this achievement have failed, don't know how the stones were transported.

## Words used with relative pronouns

**2** Mark the option(s) that can fit in each space. There may be more than one.
1 The Bermuda Triangle is an area ........ many ships and aircraft have disappeared.
   **A** which   **B** in which   **C** where   **D** to which
2 The earliest recorded incident occurred in 1870, ........ a thousand people have disappeared there.
   **A** by when   **B** since when   **C** at which point
   **D** by which time
3 A lot of pilots, ........ were very experienced, have got lost there.
   **A** many of whom   **B** some of which   **C** all of them
   **D** whoever
4 Two cases, ........ have been widely reported, are quite mysterious.
   **A** all of which   **B** none of which   **C** both of which
   **D** the result of which
5 Some ships prefer to avoid the Triangle, ........ they have much longer journeys.
   **A** by which time   **B** as a result of which
   **C** at which point   **D** in which case
6 Some people believe ........ they read about such mysteries.
   **A** anything   **B** everything that   **C** all what
   **D** half of which

## Replacing relative clauses

**3** **a** In the following sentences, the relative clauses have been 'reduced' using a present or past participle clause or an infinitive with *to*. Re-express them using relative clauses.
1 Tibet, situated between China and Nepal, is home to the famous yeti.
2 The yeti is a human-like creature said to live in the high Himalayas.
3 People living in the area say it is a common sight.
4 The first person to catch a yeti will become famous.

**b** Reduce these relative clauses with an appropriate structure from Exercise 3a.
1 Many years ago, people who were walking in the mountains claimed to have seen a tall, hairy figure in the distance.
2 However, there was no one who was carrying a camera who could take a photo.
3 A photo of a huge footprint, which was taken in 1951, remains the only real evidence.
4 The hunt for the yeti, which people also describe as being like a giant bear, continues.

**4** Read the following true story. Then combine the groups of sentences using relative and reduced relative clauses.

(1) Miranda Seymour is a well-known writer. She has written many books. Some of the books are biographies. (2) In 1995, she wrote a book about a poet. The poet was called Robert Graves. He had travelled extensively in Egypt. (3) After the book was published, someone gave her an antique gold ring. The ring had belonged to the poet. (4) She started to wear the ring. At this point, strange things started to happen. (5) Her husband left her. She had been married to him for 14 years. After that, she was burgled. (6) The next thing to happen was that her mother was diagnosed with cancer. Her mother had always been healthy. (7) Then Miranda lost her teaching job, and finally her tenant left. He had only just moved in. (8) Miranda looked at the ring. She was wearing it on her finger. (9) That very day she gave it away to a museum. The museum collects objects. They belonged to the poet. (10) Immediately she found a new tenant. He was perfect. (11) Her mother got better. She hadn't had cancer after all. (12) On top of this, she got her job back. She had lost it earlier.

# Writing 1   Planning your writing

**Writing strategy**

Planning your writing in advance will help you organise your ideas in the most logical way and save you time in the exam.

**Writing strategy**

In a formal piece of writing, make sure you have:
- a brief introduction that states the topic or the purpose of writing
- a number of supporting paragraphs that develop the topic
- a conclusion that rounds off the text.

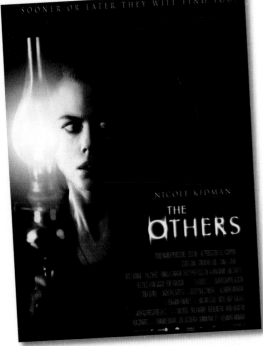

1  a  How do you usually approach a piece of writing? For example, do you:
- start writing the piece immediately?
- make a list of important points to include, and decide on the best order?
- write the whole piece very quickly, then write it out again neatly?
- write brainstorming notes?
- group your ideas into a paragraph plan?
- make a note of useful expressions you can use?

  b  Which approach is most/least appropriate when answering a question in Paper 2 of the exam?

2  In which of these texts would you expect to find an introduction, supporting paragraphs and a conclusion?
1  a magazine article
2  a report for an organisation
3  a personal note
4  a book/film/theatre review
5  a set of directions
6  an informal letter
7  a leaflet

3  a  Read this task. How many paragraphs do you think will be needed?

> Write a review of a 'mystery' film that you have seen (e.g. a ghost story). Give a brief outline of the plot and say what your opinion of the film was.

  b  Look at the brainstorming notes a student made. Why are two points crossed out?

> 'The Others' – spooky ghost story
> see it! – best film of the year
> great acting
> Nicole Kidman (plays Grace –
> husband away at the war)
> ~~NK's 24th film!~~
> simple plot – well-structured
>
> G's two children have mysterious
> illness – are hypersensitive to light
> eerie atmosphere
> slow moving – keeps you in suspense
> three servants – arrive from
> nowhere → strange events
> ~~now released on DVD~~

  c  Decide on the best order for these paragraph topics.
- ☐ Recommendation
- ☐ Plot summary
- ☐ Opinion in detail: acting, direction, music
- ☐ Title/type of film/overall impression

  d  Complete this paragraph plan using the topic headings and notes above.

> *Paragraph 1:*
>
> *Paragraph 2:*
>
> *Paragraph 3:*
>
> *Paragraph 4:*

4  a  Choose a film you have seen with a 'spooky' angle. Plan and write a review of it.

  b  Read the reviews written by other students in the class. Which sounds like the best/worst film?

▶SRB  p20

# 2B It's only logical!

## Listening 2 (Paper 4 Part 1)

**Before you listen**

1 Discuss these questions.
1 Do you regard yourself as lucky or unlucky? For example, do you often win competitions? Are you accident prone?
2 Some people say you 'make your own luck'. Others say you are 'born lucky'. What do you think?

**Sentence completion**

▶ Task strategies pages 170 and 171

2 ⌒ Do the task below. Read the task strategies on pages 170 and 171 before you start and use the Help clues if necessary. Listen to the recording twice.

You will hear the psychologist Robert Wiseman talking about some research he did into why some people believe in the existence of good and bad luck. For questions **1–8**, complete the sentences.

### The Luck Factor

Robert advertised in a ☐ 1 to find the volunteers he needed for his research.

The volunteers wrote ☐ 2 , as well as completing tests and questionnaires.

Robert believes that luck largely depends on how people ☐ *and* ☐ 3 in a particular situation.

In Robert's first experiment, volunteers were asked to count the number of ☐ 4 in a newspaper he gave them.

In the experiment, some people failed to notice a large ☐ 5 which they were meant to read.

Robert says that lucky people often have a ☐ 6 personality, which means they may be more open to chance opportunities.

Robert stresses that ☐ 7 may be just as important as logic in decision-making.

Robert describes 'lucky' people as having a ☐ 8 attitude to life.

**HELP**

➤ **Question 1**
Robert says he advertised in three places: a noticeboard, the local press and a national magazine. Which advert was successful in helping him find volunteers?

➤ **Question 2**
You are listening for something the volunteers wrote. It's not *questionnaires*, as these are mentioned in the sentence.

➤ **Question 3**
In this sentence, Robert is expressing a conclusion. Listen for an expression that signals this.

➤ **Question 8**
Listen for the adjective that Robert uses to describe lucky people.

**Task analysis**

3 Robert Wiseman used clear signals to structure his talk and introduce each point.
EXAMPLE: *The first thing I did* was to recruit some volunteers.

How far did you use these to help you identify the information needed for the task?

**Discussion**

4 Discuss these questions.
1 Wiseman concludes that luck does exist and 'our attitude to life is the key'. How far do you agree? Think of your own experience.
2 Based on his findings, what advice would you give to someone who complains that they 'never have any luck'?

# Speaking (Paper 5 Part 1)

**Asking questions**

1 a Look at these alternative ways of asking questions to find out information about another person. Can you think of any other ways of asking for the same information?

1 a How long have you been living here?
  b How many years have you lived in this place?

2 a What kind of work do you do?
  b What do you do for a living?

3 a Do you have any special hobbies?
  b What do you like doing in your leisure time?

4 a What would you like to be doing in a few years' time?
  b What are your ambitions for the future?

b Now write questions you can ask a partner about these topics. Try not to use the same words as the prompts.
  • Their experience of learning English/another foreign language
  • Things they particularly like about life in this country
  • Places of interest they have visited in this country

c Compare your questions with the class. How many different ways of asking for the same information have you come up with?

**Interacting**

2 a 🎧 Read and listen to these two exchanges. Why is the second a better example of social interaction? Mark useful phrases.

1 **A:** What kind of work do you do?
  **B:** I don't work, I'm a student. And you?
  **A:** Me too. Do you have any special hobbies?
  **B:** Yes, I enjoy playing football. What about you?
  **A:** I like going to the cinema.

2 **A:** What do you like doing in your leisure time?
  **B:** Well, what I enjoy most is playing football. I play regularly for the local team, and in fact we've got a match coming up this weekend.
  **A:** Oh, really! Good luck. To be honest, I'm not actually that keen on football myself. My favourite free-time activity is going to the cinema.
  **B:** Oh, I enjoy that, too. What's your favourite film?

b Work in pairs. Develop a conversation using the questions you prepared in Exercise 1. Make sure you show interest in what your partner says, and encourage them to give more details. Use some of the expressions in the box to help you sound natural.

| Giving answers | Reacting/asking for more information |
| --- | --- |
| *As a matter of fact,* (it's been quite a struggle for me).<br>*No, I'm afraid I don't* (speak another language)*, but* (I've always wanted to learn Spanish).<br>*Yes, I do, actually. In fact,* (it's one of the things I like most).<br>*Well, I suppose* (what I'd really like to do is …) | *Is that* (very far from here)?<br>*What exactly* (can you do there)?<br>*Oh, do you/have you? Does that mean you* (have moved over here permanently)?<br>*That's interesting. I* (have always wanted to go there). |

**Sample answer**

▶ Task strategies pages 171 and 172

**3** You will hear two students doing Part 1 of the test. There are three parts. Read the task strategies on pages 171 and 172 before you listen.

a 🎧 Listen to the first part, in which the examiner asks the candidates some questions. Why are Enrico's answers better than Cécile's?

b 🎧 Listen to the next part, in which the examiner asks the candidates to find out some information about each other.
  1 Why is Enrico's question better than Cécile's?
  2 What could he have done to help Cécile speak more?

c 🎧 Listen to the final part, in which the examiner asks some more questions.
  1 What expression does Enrico use to give himself 'thinking time'?
  2 What should Cécile have done when she was unable to think of an answer?

**Social interaction**

**4** a Work in groups of four and choose a role.
    INTERLOCUTOR: Ask the questions on page 205. Stop the discussion after three minutes.
    CANDIDATES A AND B: Respond to the examiner.
    ASSESSOR: Listen and evaluate the candidates' performance.

  b Change roles so that everyone has a turn at answering the questions.

**Task analysis**

**5** Discuss and evaluate your performance. How well do you think you followed the task strategies?

▶SRB ( p22 )

## English in Use 2 (Paper 3 Part 2)

**Lead-in**

1 Discuss these questions.
1 Have you ever met a complete stranger who knows someone you know?
2 Do you think such a thing is just a coincidence, or can you suggest a more rational explanation?

**Open cloze**

▶ Task strategies page 169

2 a Read the title and the text below quickly and answer these questions. (Ignore the spaces at this stage.)
1 Why, in the view of the writer, is coincidence not surprising?
2 What can you assume if 23 people are together in the same room?

b Do the task. Read the task strategies on page 169 before you start and use the Help clues below if necessary.

For questions **1–15**, complete the following article by writing each missing word in the space. **Use only one word for each space**. The exercise begins with an example (**0**).

### Coincidence

Coincidence is (0) ..when.. two things happen at the same time, in the same place or to the same people in a way which seems surprising. Throughout history, such events (1)............. been thought to be important but to have no logical explanation.

Recently, however, it has been shown that if two strangers sit next to (2)............. other on a plane, more than 99 times (3)............. of a hundred they will be linked by two or more people they have (4)............. common. For example, the cousin of one of the passengers may know (5)............. other's dentist. People won't necessarily discover these links, since in casual conversation no one could ever possibly mention (6)............. of their 1,500 (7)............. so acquaintances, as well as their acquaintances' acquaintances. Also, these days, people know the names of more people than ever before, (8)............. only family members but public figures.

(9)............. of the reasons that we should not be surprised by coincidence is given by mathematicians. They say that 367 people must be gathered – one more (10)............. the number of days in a leap year – to ensure that two of (11)............. share a birthday, but (12)............. we are willing to settle for a 50:50 chance of it happening, only 23 people need to be gathered.

So, no time should (13)............. wasted trying to explain the meaning of coincidences. They just happen. In reality, the (14)............. astonishingly incredible coincidence (15)............. be the complete absence of coincidence.

**HELP**
➤ Question 1
What time period is being referred to?
➤ Question 2
The completed phrase means *one another*.
➤ Question 4
Which preposition completes the fixed expression?
➤ Question 9
How many reasons are given in the next sentence?

**Task analysis**

3 Answer the questions about the task.
1 Which questions test
• articles? • quantity terms?
2 Which questions did you find most difficult, and why?

# Language development 2

▶ Grammar reference page 176

## Use of articles

**1 a** Complete this text using the best form for each space: *a/an*, *the* or *ø* (no article).

Last summer, my family decided at **(1)**............... short notice to go for **(2)**............... one-week holiday in **(3)**............... France. We needed **(4)**............... accommodation with **(5)**............... space for six people. One of our friends has **(6)**............... good knowledge of **(7)**............... country, as he works in **(8)**............... travel industry, so we asked him for **(9)**............... advice. He suggested **(10)**............... area which, he said, usually has **(11)**............... good weather and recommended **(12)**............... hotel which **(13)**............... most people like because **(14)**............... food is excellent.

Within **(15)**............... hour of arriving at **(16)**............... hotel, I bumped into **(17)**............... old friend, Barbara, whom I hadn't seen for ten years. We had been at **(18)**............... school together, and there had been **(19)**............... time when we were very close. But over the years, we had lost **(20)**............... contact.

Over **(21)**............... next week, we spent **(22)**............... hours catching up on all **(23)**............... news. It turned out that not only do we live just **(24)**............... few miles apart, but we even go to **(25)**............... same shops! Barbara has actually visited **(26)**............... office where I work. Both of us have **(27)**............... four children, have taken up **(28)**............... squash and are learning to play **(29)**............... piano!

It was **(30)**............... best holiday I've ever had, and Barbara and I are planning to meet up again in **(31)**............... near future.

**b** Have you got a story to tell about a coincidence?

## Singular, plural or uncountable?

**2** Find and correct the mistakes in these sentences. There may be more than one mistake.

1 The police has not charged the suspect because there isn't an evidence.
2 If you think you're getting a flu, a good advice is: stay in bed and drink lots of fluids!
3 Politics aren't a subject that most people enjoys studying.
4 At school, maths were my favourite subject and athletics were my least favourite.
5 On the flight home, one of my luggages came open, and one of my belongings are missing.
6 Four days are a long time to wait for an appointment.
7 Two per cent are a small pay rise, and I expect at least 80 per cent of the staff is going to go on strike.
8 A number of coincidences has been noted.
9 The number of lucky escapes have increased year on year.

## Determiners, pronouns and quantifiers

**3 a** Mark the correct alternative.
1 *Many / Much* people try their luck on the Lottery.
2 *The most / Most* people never win very *much / many*.
3 I've tried and failed *lots / many* times myself!
4 Recently, *few / a few* of my colleagues and I formed a lottery syndicate.
5 But there's *little / a little* chance of us winning the jackpot.

**b** Mark the correct alternative. There may be more than one correct option.
1 *Each / Every / Both* person in the syndicate chooses two numbers.
2 *Each / Every / Both* of us has our favourite numbers.
3 There are two different games, and we enter *each / every / both*.
4 The draws take place *each / every / both* Saturday and Wednesday.
5 *Each / Every* few weeks, we win a small amount.

**c** What would you do if you won the Lottery?

**4** Complete this text using appropriate quantifiers from the box.

| all the | the whole | both | neither |
|---------|-----------|------|---------|
| no | none | not | either |

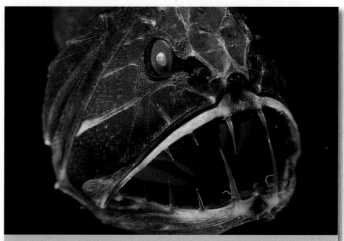

One of the last great mysteries is how creatures live in the deep sea. **(1)**............ the Pacific and the Atlantic are very deep oceans. A recent British expedition could have chosen **(2)**............ ocean to explore, but selected an area of the Pacific near Hawaii. They discovered many interesting creatures, **(3)**............ of which had been seen before. In fact, **(4)**............ one of the new finds was similar to any previous find. Two species of fish were of particular interest. However, **(5)**............ survived being brought to the surface.

Unfortunately, deep-sea research is expensive, and **(6)**............ amount of money is enough, so it will be a very long time before **(7)**............ of the Pacific is explored, let alone **(8)**............ oceans on the planet.

# Writing 2   Leaflet (Paper 2 Part 2)

**Lead-in**

1  a  Look at the extracts from two leaflets.
    1  What is the purpose of each leaflet?
    2  In what way is their style similar/different? How does this relate to their purpose?
    3  What techniques have been used to make the information easy to read?

## YOUNG PERSON'S HILLWALKING CLUB

Founded just five years ago, the Young Person's Hillwalking Club provides adventurous young hikers with an active line-up of challenging walks.

**EVENTS**
**Walks**
As well as local walks, a number of walks are planned each year to such places as:
- the Lake District
- the remote Scottish Highlands

**Activities**
The club offers to members:
- an active social programme, including barbecues and pub crawls
- summer trips – a two-week trip to France is planned for this year

**MEMBERSHIP**
Membership is open to anyone aged 20–40 who's reasonably fit. Simply turn up to one of our walks and join on the day.

b  Discuss these questions.
    1  Do you belong to any clubs or societies (e.g. chess, backgammon, music)?
    2  What makes a good club?

**Understand the task**

▶ Writing reference page 190

2  Read the task below and answer these questions.
    1  What is the PURPOSE of the leaflet and who will read it?
    2  How many PARTS are there to the question? Mark them.
    3  What STYLE will you use for the readership? neutral? persuasive?
    4  What will make it an EFFECTIVE leaflet?

> You are doing work experience in an English-speaking country and helping out in the Leisure and Recreation department of the local city council. You've been given the task of writing a leaflet for local people, telling them about a well-established chess club that meets in the city leisure centre. The council would like to encourage more people to join.
>
> In your leaflet, you should include:
>
> - background information (e.g. when the club was established, who the members are)
> - practical information (e.g. how often it meets, who can join)
> - reasons for joining.
>
> Write the **text for the leaflet** in approximately 250 words.

**Plan your leaflet**

3 Write a plan for your leaflet, following these steps.

a Headings in a leaflet can often be questions, which are then answered in the text. Choose five or six headings for your leaflet from this list, and put them in the order you will use them.

| | | |
|---|---|---|
| Are there any social events? | Why join the club? | How old are the members? |
| Can you use the other recreation centre facilities? | Are there any competitions? | Where and when do we meet? |
| Do we offer coaching? | Who do you contact? | What's the atmosphere like? |
| Who can join? | Who are we? | How good do you have to be? |
| How do you become a member? | What other benefits are there? | Is it open to all ages, and men and women? |
| | When were we established? | |

b Look at the other questions in Exercise 3a. Under which of your main headings will you answer these questions?

c Now make notes under each heading in your plan. You will need to make up the information. Decide what subheadings you could have under each main heading. Will you use bullet points or numbers for the subheadings?

**Language and content**

4 a Compare these two possible openings to the leaflet. Which style is most appropriate for the task and why?

A

The City Chess Club was established in 1904 and is a large, successful club in the centre of the city. Members' ages range from the early teens to near 80.

B

Whether you are a budding Grandmaster or a complete beginner, you will be guaranteed a warm welcome at the thriving and popular City Chess Club.

b Choose a phrase from the table below to complete these sentences. In some cases there is more than one possibility. Then match your sentences with the headings in Exercise 3a.

1 … our coaching programme for juniors.
2 … of all ages and strengths are always welcome.
3 … a small and friendly chess club in the city centre.
4 … join in the many social activities run by the leisure centre.
5 … every Friday at 7.30.
6 … Internet matches with other clubs around the country.
7 … to give advice to less experienced players.
8 … become a member can call us at the following number.

| Giving background information | Giving reasons for joining |
|---|---|
| *… is one of the (most) …* | *We participate in/organise/run …* |
| *We are …* | *The club (regularly) offers/provides (a range of competitive matches for) …* |
| *Our (members) include …* | *One of the most popular (features of our club) is …* |
| **Giving practical information** | *It doesn't matter whether you are …/what level of ability …* |
| *Anyone wishing to (apply) … can/should/…* | *Members have the opportunity to/are able to …* |
| *The club meets …* | *Experienced (players are often on hand) …* |
| *… is open to …* | *New members …* |

**Write your leaflet**

5 Now write your own leaflet, using the ideas and some of the language above. Write your answer in about 250 words.

**Check your leaflet**

6 Edit your leaflet using the checklist on page 188.

▶ Writing reference page 188

▶SRB p25

# Module 2: Review

**1** Rewrite the ideas in italics using the correct form of the word in brackets. Add any other words necessary.

1 Her films *seem simple but they aren't*. (deceive)

.......................................................................

2 *Actually*, I'm quite superstitious. (matter)

.......................................................................

3 *He's very positive* about his job. (attitude)

.......................................................................

4 Who *made all* this mess on the floor? (responsible)

.......................................................................

5 There's always someone *who's available* to help. (hand)

.......................................................................

6 Most people hear about the shows *informally from other people*. (mouth)

.......................................................................

7 There hasn't been an accident yet – *luckily!* (touch)

.......................................................................

8 Many young people feel his films *say things that are familiar and true*. (chord)

.......................................................................

9 What*'s the cause of your success*? (attribute)

.......................................................................

10 His mobile phone *rang* unexpectedly. (go off)

.......................................................................

**2** Complete the sentences by putting one word in each gap.

1 He was accused of ................. during a game of cards.

2 We treat people equally, regardless of their ethnic ................. .

3 Listening to songs in English improves your ................. to speak and understand.

4 We've got an important match coming ................. this weekend.

5 I didn't like his show at first, but his charming personality won me ................. .

6 His telephone number differs from mine by one ................. .

7 My mosquito bites were ................. so much I just had to scratch them.

8 Don't leave me ................. suspense. I need to know.

9 You must be accident-................. – you're always hurting yourself.

10 When there are 366 days in a year, it's called a ................. year.

11 There's no logical ................. for what happened. It's a mystery.

12 Was the ................. King Arthur based on a real king?

**3** Decide which word or phrase best fits each space.

1 'Out of body' experiences are experiences ............ people feel they are outside their bodies looking at the world.
   **A** all of which   **B** through which   **C** in which
   **D** most of which

2 Three days ............ a long time to be unconscious.
   **A** feel   **B** seems   **C** appear   **D** are

3 UFOs, ............ to be spaceships, usually have rational explanations.
   **A** often claimed   **B** which often claim
   **C** whose claims   **D** none of whom claim

4 Only two ............ five people believe in the paranormal.
   **A** from   **B** by   **C** over   **D** out of

5 ............ I've heard about him has been complimentary.
   **A** Whenever   **B** In which case   **C** Everything that
   **D** Where

6 Tom, ............ a condition called 'synaesthesia', hears letters and numbers in terms of colour.
   **A** that suffers from   **B** who was born with
   **C** he has   **D** where

7 ............ show lasts three hours.
   **A** All the   **B** Most   **C** Both   **D** The whole

8 A lot of people have the condition, ............ think of it as a gift.
   **A** most of them   **B** most of who   **C** mostly they
   **D** most of whom

**4** Correct the twelve mistakes with determiners, relatives and subject-verb agreement in this text.

Reincarnation is the belief that, after death, some aspect of every of us lives again in other body, both human or animal. Indeed, most of the tribes avoid eating certain animals because they believe that the souls of their ancestors live in them. Reincarnation was once a belief mainly of the Hinduism and Buddhism, either of whom are Eastern religions. Recently, however, a number of Western belief systems has started to incorporate it into their teachings. Perhaps the reason for this is that it seems to offer explanation for a range of unexplained phenomena, such as the ability of people to regress to a past life under the hypnosis. Of course, reincarnation remains a belief, and there's very few chance that it ever will be proved.

## Overview

- **Reading:** multiple-choice questions (Paper 1 Part 3)
- **Vocabulary:** word formation (nouns); collocation; idiomatic expressions
- **Listening 1:** listening for gist; identifying paraphrase (Paper 4 Parts 3 and 4)
- **Language development 1:** punctuation review
- **English in Use 1:** error correction (spelling and punctuation) (Paper 3 Part 3)
- **Writing 1:** coherence
- **Listening 2:** multiple-choice questions (Paper 4 Part 4)
- **Speaking:** issues and opinions; collaborative task (Paper 5 Part 3)
- **Language development 2:** modals
- **English in Use 2:** register transfer (Paper 3 Part 5)
- **Writing 2:** report (Paper 2 Part 1)

# 10 HEROIC LIONS ONE STUPID BOY

ENGLAND goalscorer Michael Owen weeps on a team-mate's shoulders after our brave lions' tragic World Cup defeat on penalties against Argentina last night. Glenn Hoddle's team fought like heroes after being reduced to 10 men early in the second half because of David Beckham's stupid sending off for aiming a kick at an opposition player. Now he must be kicking himself...

**END OF ENGLAND'S DREAM – PAGES 2,3,4,5 AND SPORT**

## Lead-in

- Look at the newspaper extracts. What do they illustrate about the up- and downside of being a celebrity?
- Discuss these quotations. Which do you agree with?

*'Celebrities occupy the highest tier in our society. They live in the grandest houses, dictate the latest fashions, and enjoy unlimited opportunities. Who wouldn't want to be one?'* (member of the public)

*'Fame? I wouldn't wish it on my worst enemy's dog.'* (Madonna)

### Goal in 93rd minute brings World Cup joy

# ENGLAND SAVED BY BECKHAM

By **Patrick Collins**
CHIEF SPORTS WRITER

IN the final moments of a memorable Manchester afternoon, David Beckham struck a football with venomous power and guile.

The ball soared and swung and exploded into the roof of the Greek net.

Within that crowded half-second, England had qualified for the finals of the World Cup, and the mood of a sombre nation had been lifted to the skies. For at the very moment that Beckham's goal gave England a 2-2 draw against Greece in the 93rd minute, news reached Old Trafford that Germany had drawn 0-0 with Finland in Gelsenkirchen.

That astonishing conspiracy of

*Continued on Page 3*

ON TOP OF THE WORLD: David Beckham celebrates his goal with a pat on the back from Emile Heskey

## Reading (Paper 1 Part 3)

**Before you read**  1 Look at the title and subheading of the article. What do you think the *bizarre contradictions* might be?

**Skimming**  2 Skim the article quickly. (You only need to read the introduction, the first and last sentence of each paragraph and the conclusion.) What is the main topic of each paragraph?

# FAME – who needs it?

## David Gritten reveals the bizarre contradictions of life in the fierce glare of the limelight

Most people assume that being famous is a broadly desirable state – one that often brings power, attention and wealth. Every day, we see photos of celebrities smiling as they walk along red carpets to premieres, or
5 share jokes at glitzy parties. Fame looks like a condition to which one might aspire. However, the film director Nigel Cole tells an anecdote that puts a rather different perspective on fame.

Cole had made a documentary about the wild horses
10 that roam the remote plains of Mongolia, which was presented by Julia Roberts, the world's most famous film actress. For the documentary, she had spent a fortnight living there with a family of horse herders. Roberts, who travels light when the occasion demands, arrived in warm,

15 casual clothes without make-up, carrying one bag. Shooting on the film began. But soon the head of the family complained to Cole that a joke was being played on him. At a relative's flat, he had seen a video of Roberts' film *Pretty Woman*, and this casually dressed woman did not
20 conform to the image he had in his head. 'Apparently, Julia was not haughty enough or glamorous enough to be famous,' says Cole.

How strange is fame of that order! How hard it must be to hang on to one's sense of identity, to inhabit a world in
25 which you are under constant public scrutiny for weight gain or loss, or mere flashes of bad temper. You are surrounded by a retinue of people who may not necessarily be your friends, but whose livelihood depends on you; you are a commodity, a profit centre, so no one
30 wants to get on the wrong side of you. As a result, fame can engender distrust and isolation, meaning that nobody can be taken at face value. It must play havoc with one's sense of self-worth.

Fame does not always have a beneficial effect on one's
35 personality. Pomposity, arrogance and rudeness are qualities that take you far in some areas of the entertainment industry, especially if you are male. Many famous people seem less well-adjusted and more ill-at-ease than 'normal' people, their social skills petrify, and
40 they forget how to have a 'normal' conversation. They tend to be a guarded and defensive breed, perceiving slights where none exist, and being greatly unsettled by small inconveniences. And while none of this is a reason to feel sorry for all celebrities, it highlights an intriguing paradox,
45 since we tend to think of fame as something unconditionally desirable.

Then there are the fans, whose attentions may be welcome at first, but who soon come to seem irritating, not to say irrational in their devotion. Psychologists have concluded that the lower a person's religious conviction, the more likely that person is to idolise a particular celebrity – even, in some cases, behaving in a way he or she believes the hero would approve of. The extraordinary power that certain famous people have over people's imaginations is, arguably, because the people they represent embody a wide array of archetypal traits which have current appeal. This explains why someone like Pierce Brosnan may appear to possess magical qualities to his fans; not because he is a hero in his own right, but because he is the current incarnation of a mythical figure called James Bond.

Perhaps this is why as soon as the illusion fades, the public will turn on their idols. Egged on by the popular press, the public have an insatiable appetite for seeing the famous toppled from their thrones. A fall from grace by a celebrity is a big story, and the fact that the individual is held very dear or much respected as a household name will not temper the mercilessness of the reporting. Celebrity carries with it an odd moral neutrality, and the innocence with which people succumb to the fame virus counts for nothing; once they are famous, their every false move is ruthlessly scrutinised. This is the ugly underbelly of celebrity, the flipside of fame that the non-famous rarely pause to consider.

## Multiple-choice questions

▶ Task strategies page 168

3 Read the magazine article and answer questions 1–5. Mark the letter A, B, C or D. Give only one answer to each question. Read the task strategies on page 168 before you start.

a Look at question 1 and find the paragraph containing the anecdote. What point is the writer making? Mark the part which gives you the answer.

b Read the options (A–D). Each of the options may seem to be saying something which is true, but which one reflects the writer's purpose in telling us this anecdote?

c Continue in the same way and complete the task.

1 The writer uses the anecdote about Julia Roberts to make the point that
   A the most well-known stars find it impossible to disguise their identity.
   B it is sometimes hard for film stars to mix socially with ordinary people.
   C ordinary people have unrealistic expectations of film stars.
   D some famous film stars enjoy taking on different roles in real life, too.

2 In the third paragraph, the writer suggests that the most famous film stars
   A begin to suspect the sincerity of those with whom they work closely.
   B are unable to rely on the support of even their oldest friends.
   C begin to doubt their own ability to sustain the celebrity lifestyle.
   D become less aware of how the general public actually views them.

3 In the fourth paragraph, the writer observes that famous people have a tendency to become
   A self-centred.        C over-sensitive.
   B self-important.      D over-ambitious.

4 According to the writer, famous people are sometimes 'idolised' by certain fans because
   A they set themselves up as role models for others to imitate.
   B they actually encourage this kind of attention at the beginning.
   C they are perceived as having powers that cannot easily be explained.
   D they seem to combine various qualities which the fans view as desirable.

5 What does the writer suggest in the final paragraph?
   A Only the most respected celebrities can survive an attack by the press.
   B Most celebrities will eventually begin to disappoint their fans.
   C Untalented celebrities are unlikely to enjoy lasting fame.
   D Bad publicity can actually increase a celebrity's appeal.

## Task analysis

4 Compare and justify your answers with reference to the text.

## Discussion

5 Discuss these questions.
   1 Look at the answers to the multiple-choice questions again. How far do you agree with the main idea of each paragraph? Can you think of more examples to support these ideas?
   2 To what extent do the media in your country encourage the 'cult of celebrity'?
   3 Do you think the media should be prevented from reporting on the private lives of famous people?

# Vocabulary

## Word formation: nouns

**1** **a** Read these extracts from the text on pages 40–41. What are the verb forms of the highlighted nouns?

1 David Gritten reveals the bizarre contradictions of life in the fierce glare of the limelight (subheading)

2 As a result, fame can engender distrust and isolation, … (para. 3)

**b** Write the nouns of the following verbs and adjectives. Check your spelling in the text.

1 scrutinise (*v.*) (para. 3) ...........................

2 arrogant (*adj.*) (para. 4) ...........................

3 rude (*adj.*) (para. 4) ...........................

4 inconvenient (*adj.*) (para. 4) ...........................

5 attend (*v.*) (para. 5) ...........................

6 devote (*v.*) (para. 5) ...........................

7 imagine (*v.*) (para. 5) ...........................

8 neutral (*adj.*) (para. 6) ...........................

9 innocent (*adj.*) (para. 6) ...........................

**c** ⌒ Mark the stressed syllable in each word in Exercise 1b. What patterns do you notice? For which words does the stress change according to the word class? Listen and check.

**d** Complete these sentences using nouns from Exercise 1b.

Two years ago, a friend of mine landed a role in a popular TV soap opera. In a relatively short time, she has risen from unemployed actress to minor celebrity. The public's identification with the character she plays has been amazing; it's not unusual for people to come up to her in the street and address her as 'Susie', her character's name. She says she doesn't mind the **(1)**............. of regularly being stopped when she is out, but jokes that she now has to pay more **(2)**............. to her appearance!

She has never experienced any **(3)**............. from members of the public, but it's been a different story with journalists. There is no **(4)**............. as far as the press is concerned; they either love you or hate you. Either way, they take pleasure in subjecting every aspect of a star's private life to public **(5)**............. .

My friend doesn't (yet!) have the **(6)**............. associated with some celebrities, but she has certainly lost the naive **(7)**............. she once had.

**e** Discuss these questions.

1 What are the most popular 'soaps' in your country? Why are they popular?

2 How well known are the actors? Would you recognise any of them on the street? What would you do if you did?

## Collocation: adjectives + nouns

**2** **a** Match the sentence halves.

1 The public seems to have an insatiable

2 There is now a vast

3 Each tries to show a different

4 Some like to focus on their religious

5 Other magazines just like to catch them in casual

6 A picture of a star in a bad

7 And a story about their lack of social

8 The favourite target is a household

9 Magazine editors believe that public

10 However, many of the stories in the popular

a convictions or political beliefs.

b skills is worth a fortune.

c array of magazines that focus on celebrities.

d temper is more valuable than a studio shot.

e name behaving badly.

f appetite for stories about celebrities.

g clothes and without make-up.

h perspective on celebrity life.

i press later turn out to be untrue.

j scrutiny is the price of fame.

**b** Use each collocation in a sentence of your own, based on your opinion or experience.

EXAMPLE: *People have an insatiable appetite for gossip. I suppose it's human nature.*

## Idiomatic expressions

**3** **a** Complete the expressions with words from the box.

| face | sorry | joke | far | wrong | power |
|------|-------|------|-----|-------|-------|

1 *To play a* ............. *on someone* is to do something to them for a laugh.

2 *To get on the* ............. *side of someone* is to do something that gives them a bad opinion of you.

3 *To take someone/thing at* ............. *value* is to accept it as it is, without looking for hidden meaning.

4 *To feel* ............. *for someone* is to feel sympathy for them because something bad has happened.

5 *To have* ............. *over someone* is to have influence or authority over them.

6 *To take someone* ............. is to help them to be successful.

**b** Complete these sentences with a suitable phrase.

1 Hard work, talent and ambition can ........................... .

2 Be careful not to ........................... your manager; he could make life difficult for you.

3 Remember that they ........................... you; they can affect whether or not you get promoted.

4 Not everything they say can ........................... .

5 My manager promised me a bigger office, but he was just ........................... .

6 It's impossible not to ........................... the people who work hard, but don't make it to the top.

▶SRB p28

# Listening 1  Developing skills
(Parts 3 and 4)

**Before you listen**

1 Look at the signed photo.
1 Do you recognise this person and why he is famous?
2 Why do you think some people collect autographs?

**Listening for gist**

2 a You are going to hear an interview with a man called Charlie Lane, who collects autographs for a living. The following topics are all discussed in the interview. Number them in the order you think they will be discussed.

☐ Charlie Lane's feelings about his job
☐ Methods Charlie Lane first used to get autographs
☐ How Charlie Lane started collecting autographs
☐ How Charlie Lane's hobby developed

b 🎧 Listen to the recording to check your answers.
1 What helped you confirm your answers?
2 Can you remember any details related to each topic area?

**Identifying paraphrase**

3 a 🎧 Read question 1 and the options. Then listen to the first part of the recording again and choose the correct answer A, B or C.
1 Why did Charlie begin collecting autographs?
   A Because he wanted to please his father.
   B Because he wanted to impress people.
   C Because he wanted to be like his friends.

b Which option above, A, B or C:
1 reflects something that was said in the interview, but doesn't answer the question?
2 is not an accurate reflection of the text?
3 paraphrases the language in the interview and answers the question?

c Look at the extract from the audioscript on page 205 and check your answers.

**Multiple-choice questions**

4 a 🎧 Read questions 2–4 and the options. Then listen to the rest of the recording section by section and choose the correct answer.

2 How does Charlie feel now about his early attempts to get autographs?
   A disillusioned
   B pleased
   C embarrassed
   D proud

3 Charlie's interest in his hobby increased when he found that
   A it created a link with the past.
   B it was a way of making money.
   C it helped him make new friends.
   D it could be a possible career.

4 What is Charlie's attitude now towards his career?
   A He would have preferred to be a musician.
   B He likes the freedom it gives him.
   C He appreciates the financial security it provides.
   D He thinks it will lead to more interesting things.

b Compare and justify your answers with reference to the recording.

**Discussion**

5 Discuss these questions.
1 What do you think are the pros and cons of Charlie Lane's job?
2 What other unusual jobs have you heard about?

# Language development 1

▶ Writing reference page 201

## Capitals and full stops (.)

**1 a** Decide where capitals and full stops are needed in this text.

> people interested in celebrity should visit the popular london attraction madame tussaud's wax museum on marylebone road it features wax images of people from all walks of life: from modern music superstars (eg miss dynamite) and hollywood legends to scientists such as british astrophysicist prof steven hawking avoid saturdays in july and august the winter months are much quieter

**b** What other uses can you think of for capital letters?

## Apostrophes (')

**2 a** Read the sentences (a–e) and answer the questions (1–5) below.
  a We can stay in either Tom's house or Charles' flat.
  b My sister's room is on the left and my brothers' room is on the right.
  c I'd like to go to Prague – it's famous for its architecture.
  d Most actors know that an actor's life is hard.
  e That's a great idea; let's hope it'll work.

  1 What are the main uses of apostrophes?
  2 How do we show possession when a word ends in -s?
  3 In sentence b, how many sisters and brothers does the speaker have?
  4 In sentence c, what's the difference between *it's* and *its*?
  5 In sentence d, what's the difference between *actors* and *actor's*?

**b** Add apostrophes to the text where necessary.

> Madame Tussauds is one of Londons oldest attractions. One of its most popular displays is the Chamber of Horrors. The collection was started in Paris by Marie Tussauds mothers employer, a Dr Curtius. Marie brought Dr Curtius original collection of heads to London in the early 1800s, and its been constantly updated ever since. Its only two minutes walk from Baker Street tube station. But dont forget that the museum shuts at six oclock!

## Commas (,)

**3 a** Read these sentences and work out the rules for commas. Then check in the Writing reference.
  1 Madonna has homes in London, Los Angeles and New York.
  2 If you have the right attitude, you'll make it.
  3 Winning an Oscar is an impressive achievement, isn't it?
  4 Unfortunately, lasting relationships are rare in show business.
  5 Julia Roberts, whose best known film is *Pretty Woman*, has been married twice.

**b** Add commas to these sentences where necessary.
  1 I'll ask Robbie to give you a ring if I see him.
  2 An autograph collector needs a notebook a couple of pens a camera and a lot of patience.
  3 Tell me what are you going to do next?
  4 What's the film that got ten Oscars last year?
  5 I managed to get a ticket believe it or not.
  6 Pierce Brosnan the actor who played James Bond is Irish.

## Speech marks (' ')

**4 a** Read the examples. What do you notice about the use of capitals, commas and full stops with direct speech?
  1 Fred Allen once said, 'A celebrity is a person who works hard all his life to become known, then wears dark glasses to avoid being recognised.'
  2 'I don't know who he is,' she said, 'but he looks great!'

**b** Add quotation marks and appropriate punctuation to this dialogue.
  A table for two said the celebrity in a quiet corner preferably
  Sorry sir replied the waiter we're full
  Do you know who I am asked the surprised celebrity
  No sir said the waiter but if you ask your mother I'm sure she'll tell you

## Other punctuation

**5 a** Find examples of the following items in Exercises 1 and 2 above. What do you think is their function?
  ● colon (:)  ● semi-colon (;)  ● dash (–)

**b** Punctuate these sentences using each form of the punctuation in Exercise 5a once.
  1 To be successful, you need three things talent, determination and good luck.
  2 I'd like to see the show again in fact, I'm going to book tickets tomorrow.
  3 Katie is a great actress she has sensitivity and a good voice.

# English in Use 1 (Paper 3 Part 3)

### Lead-in

**1** Discuss these questions.

1 The two people in the photo are married. Do you know who they are?
2 What difficulties do you think celebrity couples face?

### Error correction

▶ Task strategies page 169

**2** **a** Read the title and the text below. (Ignore the mistakes at this stage.)

1 Why is it harder being a celebrity today than 50 years ago?
2 Why was it difficult for Joanne Woodward?

**b** Read the instructions. What do you have to do in this type of error correction task?

**c** Look at the examples (00) and (000). What kind of errors are shown?

**d** Do the task. Read the task strategies on page 169 before you start and use the Help clues below if necessary. Note that in the exam, there is a maximum of one mistake in a line.

In most lines of the following text, there is **either** a spelling **or** a punctuation error. For each numbered line, write the correctly spelt word or show the correct punctuation. **Some** lines are correct. Indicate these lines with a tick (✓). The exercise begins with three examples (**0**), (**00**) and (**000**).

## CELEBRITY COUPLES – A MARRIAGE THAT SURVIVED

| | |
|---|---|
| Unfortunately, lasting relationships are rare in Hollywood. If both | **0** ✓ |
| partners are well-known film stars in the public eye the hole | **00** whole |
| time, it is difficult to keep a marriage stable A show-business | **000** stable. |
| career is very unpredictable, and this makes a steady home life | **1** |
| difficult. Now, with celebrity gossip readily availible on the Internet, | **2** |
| the presures have become even more intense. However, one | **3** |
| film-star couple, Paul Newman, and Joanne Woodward, who | **4** |
| first met each other in 1952 have survived all the difficulties. | **5** |
| Woodward, though, confesses she found combineing family life | **6** |
| and her husbands' popularity hard, particularly when the smash-hit | **7** |
| movie *The Hustler* opened three years' after they wed. 'These | **8** |
| days people are lovely and gracious and tend to treet me and Paul | **9** |
| like elder statesmen' she said recently. 'But when I was young | **10** |
| and we had young children, it was dreadful. I hated it when | **11** |
| photographers would shove me aside to aproach Paul while I | **12** |
| was trying to protect the children. She also admits to being | **13** |
| uncomfortable with some of Paul's acheivements. But despite the | **14** |
| sacrifices the couple, especialy Woodward, have made, their | **15** |
| partnership has endured and is an example for others to follow. | **16** |

**HELP**
➤ **Question 3**
Which word needs a double consonant?
➤ **Question 7**
Does this sentence make sense? How many husbands has she got?
➤ **Question 10**
Which rule about punctuating direct speech is being broken here?

### Task analysis

**3** Discuss these questions about the task.

1 How many mistakes did you identify correctly?
2 What are the most difficult types of mistakes to spot?

### Discussion

**4** What do you think is the secret of a lasting relationship?

# Writing 1  Coherence

▶ Writing reference page 200

## Writing strategy

In the exam, you are assessed on your ability to produce well-organised pieces of writing with a logical sequence of ideas. Make sure

- your introduction states the topic clearly
- each new paragraph has *one* main idea, stated in a topic sentence
- the main idea is supported by *relevant* details
- the details are presented in a logical sequence
- the details are connected by linking devices.

1  Compare these two paragraphs. Which paragraph fulfils the requirements listed in the Writing strategy?

**A**

Fame is nothing new. Alexander the Great is supposed to have started the cult of celebrity in the 4th century when he placed his own image instead of the image of the gods on his empire's coins. And then in the early 19th century, the fame of the revolutionary English poet Lord Byron attracted crowds of adoring women to his poetry readings. However, it was not until the 20th century, and the growth of the mass media, that we had celebrities who were famous, not because they were talented or powerful, but just because they caught the public attention in some way.

**B**

If you want to become famous, you need to think positively. The reason I want to be famous is not only because of the attention everyone would give me but because it would help make me richer. If I wanted to become famous, I would decide how I was going to achieve it. The most important message to myself would be 'Never give up!' I would set myself a small number of daily priorities and make sure I started to reach my goals. You have to believe that you deserve success. Famous people have to be a bit ruthless and only think about themselves.

2  Read the information about ways of organising details in a paragraph. Decide how the coherent paragraph in Exercise 1 is organised.

### Methods of organising the details

1  Example/illustration: provide a list of examples or an illustration to support the main idea.
2  Time order: present the details in the order in which they happened.
3  Comparison/contrast: the details show how things are similar or different.
4  Emphatic order: the supporting details are listed with the least important first and the most important last. The reader is most likely to remember the last thing read.

3  Rewrite the incoherent paragraph in Exercise 1 to make it coherent.
   1  Decide what the main idea is, and write a topic sentence.
   2  Cross out any irrelevant details.
   3  Decide on a logical order for the supporting details.
   4  Use appropriate linking devices to connect the ideas.

4  a  Plan and write your answer to this task.

   Write a description of a famous person who you admire, explaining why you admire them.

   b  Exchange your answer with a partner. Is your partner's answer well organised? Are the ideas well linked?

 ▶SRB  p31

# 3B What I believe in

## Listening 2 (Paper 4 Part 4)

### Multiple-choice questions

▶ Task strategies pages 170 and 171

1 🎧 Listen and do the task below. Read the task strategies before you start and use the Help clues if necessary.

You will hear five short extracts in which different people are talking about protests they have taken part in. For questions **1–10**, choose the correct answer, **A**, **B** or **C**.

**Speaker 1**

1 What is the **first speaker's** job?
  A a nurse
  B a fire fighter
  C a teacher

2 He has gone on strike to protest about
  A excessive working hours.
  B lack of training opportunities.
  C inadequate levels of funding.

**Speaker 2**

3 Why did the **second speaker** decide to go on a march?
  A She was persuaded to do so by somebody else.
  B She realised that it might influence a policy.
  C She felt deeply committed to the issues.

4 What was her impression of the event?
  A It was surprisingly well attended.
  B It was not very well organised.
  C It was a waste of time going.

**Speaker 3**

5 Through his action, the **third speaker** hoped to
  A make a company change its policy.
  B draw attention to an unrelated issue.
  C get an ugly piece of equipment removed.

6 How does he feel now about what he did?
  A delighted by the level of attention it received
  B frustrated not to have achieved his aims
  C justified in the form of protest he chose

**Speaker 4**

7 Why did the **fourth speaker** protest about a proposed building development in her town?
  A She objected to losing a recreational area.
  B She doesn't approve of the type of building.
  C She thinks the town needs other kinds of development.

8 What was the reaction of other townspeople to her protest?
  A They viewed it negatively.
  B They were indifferent to it.
  C They were supportive of her.

**Speaker 5**

9 Why did the **fifth speaker** take part in student protests?
  A He believed passionately in the issues.
  B He regarded it as part of the lifestyle.
  C He had pressure put on him by others.

10 How does he feel now about what he did?
  A He's embarrassed by it.
  B He's amused by it.
  C He's proud of it.

HELP
➤ Questions 5/6
The questions focus on the speaker's aims (Q5) and what he achieved (Q6). The text is also divided into these two points. Which comes first?
➤ Question 9
Listen for the speaker's reasons at the time.
➤ Question 10
Listen for his feelings *now*.

### Task analysis

2 Compare and discuss your answers.
  1 What did you hear in the text that made you choose the options you did? Why are the other options not correct?
  2 In this part of the paper, are you listening for gist (the general idea the speaker is expressing) or detail (one fact that the speaker mentions)?

### Discussion

3 Do you think all five of these protests were acceptable? What level of protest would you regard as unacceptable?

A

B

C

LOUD AND PROUD

## Speaking (Paper 5 Part 3)

**Vocabulary:
issues and opinions**

**1 a** Match these different forms of protest to the pictures.

1 signing a petition
2 handing out leaflets
3 holding a meeting
4 taking part in a march
5 writing in to a newspaper

**b** Mark the correct preposition in these phrases.

1 to have an influence *on / in*
2 to have a say *in / on*
3 to change people's minds *in / about*
4 to put forward your views *in / on*  } something/somebody
5 to express your opinion *on / in*
6 to generate publicity *for / to*
7 to put pressure *at / on*
8 to (make someone) back *down / away* on
9 to force people to come *at / to* a compromise *about / with*  } something
10 to contribute *to / with*

**c** Answer these questions. Use expressions from Exercises 1a and 1b.

1 What do you think the people in the pictures are protesting about?
2 Why are they doing it? What do you think they hope to achieve by their actions?
3 What impact might their protest have?

**2** Complete these extracts from news articles, using words and phrases from Exercise 1 in the correct form.

A

Twenty thousand protestors **(1)**............................ along the city's main street yesterday, hoping to **(2)**............................ politicians' **(3)**........................... about this sensitive issue. However, it would appear that the government has already come to a decision and is unlikely to **(4)**........................... on the issue.

B

Local residents **(5)**........................... in the village hall last night, at which everyone had the opportunity to **(6)**........................... the proposed new bypass.

C

Campaigners stand in the street every day; they **(7)**........................... leaflets to members of the public in order to **(8)**........................... the subject, and they ask people to **(9)**........................... . They hope that if they get enough signatures, it will **(10)**........................... the government to reconsider its policy on this important issue.

**Sample answer**

▶ Task strategies pages 171 and 172

**3 a** Read the task strategy for Part 3 on page 172.

**b** 🎧 Look at the pictures again. Listen to the examiner's instructions and answer the questions.
1 What TWO things do you have to do?
2 How long have you got to do it?

**c** 🎧 Listen to two people doing the task. Do you agree with their conclusions?

**d** How successfully did they carry out the task? Did they follow the advice in the task strategies?

**Useful language:**
discourse markers

**4 a** Listen to the sample answer again. Which of the words or phrases in the box below is used to:
1 qualify something you or someone else has just said?
2 emphasise that what you are saying is correct or true?
3 add something else to something you or someone else has said?
4 introduce disagreement?
5 change the subject/move on?

| | | | |
|---|---|---|---|
| *Of course,* | *Besides that,* | *Not only that,* | *Mind you,* |
| *Anyway,* | *Well, actually,* | *As a matter of fact,* | |
| *As well as that,* | *Anyhow,* | *Having said that,* | |

**b** Read the conversation. One expression in each set can't be used in the context. Cross it out.
A: Have you heard how much our team are paying for this young footballer they've been after? It's ridiculous.
B: I agree. Nobody's worth that much! (1) *Anyway, / Mind you, / Having said that,* we certainly need a good striker if we want to win the league this year.
A: True. But how will he cope with having all that money and fame at the age of 19? (2) *Besides that, / Not only that, / Having said that,* it'll put a lot of pressure on him to get the goals.
B: You're right. It'll be hard.
A: (3) *Mind you, / Actually, / Having said that,* he <u>is</u> being paid to do something he loves. We should be so lucky!

**Collaborative task**

**5 a** Work in pairs and do the task in Exercise 3. Time yourselves. Remember to follow the task strategies.

**b** Tell the class briefly which method you have chosen and why.

**Task analysis**

**6** Did you:
• speak for the full four minutes?  • listen and respond to each other's points?

# Language development 2

▶ Grammar reference page 177

## Necessity, prohibition, advice, permission

**1  a  Rewrite the sentences using modal or semi-modal verbs.**

1  You are not allowed to demonstrate here.
2  I think the best thing for you to do is to go on strike.
3  It's essential that we have a vote before we call a strike.
4  It's not essential to send all these letters today.
5  I think it's too late to protest now – why didn't you protest before?

**b  Complete the second sentence so it means the same as the first.**

1  I can't give you my decision until I have spoken to the staff.
   I ................................. to the staff before I give you my decision.
2  You can go on strike even if you are not in a union.
   You .................................. to go on strike.
3  The only way to show we were serious was to go on strike.
   We .................................. in order to show we were serious.
4  The police closed the road, even though it wasn't necessary.
   The police .................................. the road, but they did anyway.
5  I joined the protest because I had a day off that day.
   I .................................. to work that day so I joined the protest.
6  The police told us to move on, but we decided to ignore their orders.
   We .................................., but we decided to ignore the orders of the police.
7  I expected Gary to be back hours ago.
   Gary .................................. hours ago.

**c  Answer these questions.**

1  What things do you have to do every day in your studies or work? Which things do you most/least enjoy doing?
2  Is there anything you should have done this week but haven't? Explain why not.

## Ability, possibility/probability, deduction

**2  Find and correct the mistakes in the following sentences.**

1  Harry started collecting last year, and so far he can raise £10,000 for charity.

2  We couldn't get to meet the minister yesterday, but eventually we could speak to him on the phone.
3  Jack could photocopy the leaflets at the office yesterday, but he forgot.
4  They say there can be nearly half a million people on the march tomorrow.
5  Why not come with us on the demo? You could enjoy it.
6  The damage might be caused by the people who were demonstrating.
7  You must know there was going to be trouble when you saw the crowds.

## Intention, willingness, characteristics

**3  Complete the sentences using *will, won't, would* or *shall.***

1  The new stadium .............. hold at least 50,000 spectators.
2  When I was at school, my friends and I .............. often hang out in the school playground until it was dark.
3  I don't know what's wrong with the car. It just .............. start.
4  It .............. start raining just as we're about to go out, .............. it?
5  I'll pick you up at eight o'clock, .............. I?
6  .............. you mind giving me a hand with my homework?
7  What's the matter? Why .............. you talk to me?
8  She .............. insist on wearing the most outrageous clothes. I think she does it to annoy her parents.
9  I .............. have thought you'd be pleased that I've bought a new car!
10  You .............. do as I say, whether you like it or not!

## Alternatives to modals

**4  Rewrite the following sentences using one of the structures below. Which structures are formal?**

| | | |
|---|---|---|
| be required to | be + *to*-infinitive | had better |
| be under no obligation to | | be advisable to |
| feel obliged to | be forbidden to | |

1  Visitors must report to reception on arrival.
2  You don't have to answer the following questions.
3  I should phone home and tell them that I'm going to be late.
4  I thought I had to invite my cousins to our wedding.
5  All library books must be returned by the end of term.
6  Mobile phones must not be used in this area.
7  You should take out insurance when travelling abroad.

## English in Use 2 (Paper 3 Part 5)

*Singer Robbie Williams at the 10th Rights of the Child convention*

**Lead-in**

1  In what ways can entertainers help charities?

**Register transfer**

▶ Task strategies pages 169 and 170

2  a  Read both texts quickly.
   1  What is unusual about the band mentioned in the text?
   2  How is the style of the second text different from the first?

   b  Do the task.

The Marketing Director of a large charity is writing a report about the value of entertainers to their charity. Read the following email from the Marketing Manager to the Marketing Director. Use the information in it to complete the numbered gaps in the report. The words you need **do not occur** in the email. **Use no more than two words for each gap**. The exercise begins with an example (**0**).

**EMAIL**

Recently, much more of the money that we need to keep our charity alive has come from the entertainment industry raising money for us. For a long time now, entertainers have given shows on stage without asking for a fee, whilst others have recorded songs for a particular occasion and given us the royalties, and some have gone on TV and asked ordinary people for money. Other entertainers have backed us more indirectly – like sending us things they own for us to auction.
But one band has just done something even better and pledged to give a tenth of everything they earn for charities like us to share. It's great that the band should be so generous – and we're delighted to accept. I reckon they earned £5 million in just one year last year, which means that the amount going to charity will be £500,000. On top of that, they are arranging a money-spinning tour round the States for later this year, although they haven't yet decided precisely where they are going to play.

**REPORT**

In recent years, an (**0**) increasing amount of the money that is required to ensure (**1**)............................ of our charity has been provided by entertainers raising money on our (**2**)............................ . For a number of years, singers and comedians (**3**)............................ at concerts and shows free (**4**)............................ , recorded special songs and donated their earnings to us, or made TV appeals to the general (**5**)............................ . Others have given us their (**6**)............................ in less direct ways, for example, by providing some of their (**7**)............................ to be sold at charity auctions.

However, recently one group has gone (**8**)............................ all the others and is donating a tenth of all their income to be divided among a range of charities (**9**)............................ ourselves. We, of course, (**10**)............................ this generous act. It is estimated that the band earned £5 million in the last year (**11**)............................ , raising £500,000 for good causes. (**12**)............................ , a lucrative tour of the US is being arranged for later this year, although the (**13**)............................ for the concerts is yet to be decided.

**HELP**

➤ Question 1
You need a noun here.

➤ Questions 2/4/5
These are fixed expressions.

➤ Question 7
Which noun means *things they own*?

➤ Question 9
What is a more formal expression for *like* here?

➤ Question 10
Think of a suitable verb.

## Task analysis

3  Answer these questions about the task.
   1  Which text contains more passive constructions?
   2  Which gaps required a single noun to replace a phrase?

## Discussion

4  Discuss these questions.
   1  Do you know of any celebrities or organisations that donate to charity in your country?
   2  Do you think everyone should give money to charity on a regular basis?
   3  How can people be encouraged to do so?

## Writing 2   Report (Paper 2 Part 1)

**Lead-in**   1   Think of some ways to raise money for charity (e.g. by taking part in a sponsored walk). Which do you think are the most effective?

**Understand the task**

▶ Writing reference page 191

2   Read the task below and answer these questions.
1   WHO are you? WHAT do you have to write? WHO will read it? (Look at the instructions for the task.)
2   What is the PURPOSE of your piece of writing?
3   What POINTS have you been asked to include? (Look at the note.)
4   What INFORMATION does the pie chart contain?
5   What STYLE will be appropriate for your writing?
6   What will make the reader think it's a WELL-WRITTEN report?

*Coinstar machines give users the option to donate their loose change to charity.*

You are working in Britain, and in your spare time you help a charity organisation which raises money for disadvantaged children. Recently, you organised a fund-raising day for the charity, and the Director of the charity has asked you to write a report for the Board of Governors describing the day, and making recommendations for what to do next year. Read the note below, on which you have made some notes, and the pie chart you have prepared. Then, using the information **carefully**, write the report requested by the Director.

Yes, a good time was had by all. Not too many problems.

I'm glad the fund-raising day went so well and you managed to raise so much money. It sounds as if it was fun.
I was wondering whether you could write a report, providing an overview of the day, and saying who was involved, how they raised the money and what recommendations you would make for a similar event next year.

More than last year.

About 50, mostly students from the university – they were great! + a few friends from work.

Greater variety of activities, e.g. sponsored runs, street parties (?!), etc.; providing collectors with special badges – some people thought we weren't genuine!

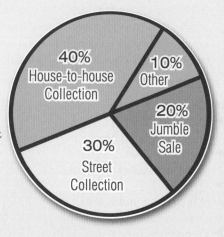

40% House-to-house Collection

10% Other

20% Jumble Sale

30% Street Collection

Now write your **report** to the Board of Governors as outlined above (approximately 250 words). You should use your own words as far as possible.

**Plan your report**    3    Write a plan for your leaflet, following these steps.

    a    Choose the best heading for paragraphs 1 and 2 of your report from these options.
         **Paragraph 1:** Foreword / Introduction / Prologue
         **Paragraph 2:** Summary / Overview / General impression

    b    Mark the information you will select from the input. Decide how many more paragraphs you will need to cover all the points in the task.

    c    Choose the best headings for your paragraphs from this list.

| | | |
|---|---|---|
| Suggestions | Participation | Raising money |
| Proposals | Recommendations | Methods of fund raising |
| Conclusions | How the money was raised | |

    d    Make notes of what you will include under each heading in your plan. Think about these points:
         • What is the aim of paragraph 1?
         • In paragraph 2, how can you give a general picture without repeating the detail needed for paragraphs 3–5?

    e    Think of a suitable title for the whole report.

**Language and content**    4    a    Look through the phrases below. Some of them are in the passive voice. Why is the passive often used in reports?

    b    Write an opening sentence for each of the paragraphs in your plan, using some of the phrases. You can change the words in brackets if you wish.

| | |
|---|---|
| **Introduction** | *The main purpose/principal aim of (this report) is to …*<br>*(This report) is intended to …*<br>*(This report) describes/discusses/provides …* |
| **Generalising** | *In the main … / In general … / On the whole …*<br>*It seems that everyone …* |
| **Talking about specifics** | *(This year) it was decided …*<br>*(Collections) were carried out …*<br>*(Assistance) was provided by …*<br>*(Volunteers) included …*<br>*(The total raised) exceeded …*<br>*(A campaign appeal) was launched (to) …*<br>*The largest part of (the sum raised came from) …*<br>*(A large amount of money) was raised by …* |
| **Concluding and making recommendations** | *To sum up … / To summarise …*<br>*In short … / In conclusion …*<br>*In the light of (this year's experience), …*<br>*In my view, in future, we should …*<br>*It is recommended that …*<br>*My recommendations are as follows: …* |

**Write your report**    5    Now write your report in about 250 words, using some of the language above. You can use some key words from the input, but you should reword phrases as far as possible.

**Check your report**    6    Edit your work using the checklist on page 188.

▶ Writing reference page 188

# Module 3: Review

**1** Decide which word or phrase best fits each space.

1 There is a ........ array of goods on sale in the shops.
**A** wide **B** plentiful **C** significant **D** substantial

2 Tickets for the show were selling at three times their face ........ .
**A** worth **B** price **C** value **D** cost

3 Some stars have got an awful temper, and you shouldn't get on the ........ side of them.
**A** negative **B** opposite **C** wrong **D** bad

4 Working for charity should have a beneficial ........ on Bob's ego.
**A** control **B** outcome **C** affect **D** effect

5 Sometimes you have to ........ your principles.
**A** get away with **B** make off with
**C** stand up for **D** send out for

6 We ........ a campaign to help the homeless.
**A** launched **B** founded **C** established
**D** originated

7 These days, many fashion designers are ........ names. Everyone knows them.
**A** usual **B** household **C** regular **D** everyday

8 Someone ........ a cruel joke on him when they said he was going to become famous.
**A** made **B** cracked **C** executed **D** played

9 Some of the speeches ........ , and I got bored.
**A** went on a bit **B** turned out somewhat
**C** hung about a little **D** came across slowly

10 She ........ a very important role in a new TV drama.
**A** served **B** occupied **C** landed **D** adopted

**2** Complete the second sentence so that it has a similar meaning to the first.

1 It's breathtaking how arrogant some politicians can be.
The ................................................. is breathtaking.

2 She was jealous of how popular her husband was.
She was jealous of her ........................................... .

3 Switzerland stayed neutral throughout both World Wars.
Switzerland preserved ..................................... throughout both World Wars.

4 He contradicted himself a lot.
There were ................................................. in what he said.

5 They have remained partners for a long time.
Their ................................................. a long time.

6 It's inconvenient getting a fine, but nothing more.
Getting a fine is an ..................................... , but nothing more.

7 She feels very isolated by her fame.
Her fame gives her a ..................................... .

8 He was proud he had achieved so much.
He was proud of his ..................................... .

9 She'd never expected that so many fans would be so devoted to her.
She'd never expected so ..................................... so many fans.

10 Can you sign this form?
Can you ..................................... on this form?

**3** Complete the sentences with an appropriate verb form.

This exercise is based on the case of Major Charles Ingram and his wife, Diana, who were convicted of cheating in the quiz show *Who Wants to be a Millionaire?*

1 'You ............ listen carefully to four alternative answers,' said the quiz-show presenter.

2 '............ I phone a friend?' 'OK. What's your friend's name?'

3 A man in the audience coughed on the right answer. The contestant must ............ heard it.

4 The director didn't believe the man ............ be getting all the questions right without help.

5 He thought the man coughing might have ............ helping the contestant.

6 Sometimes the man didn't ............ to cough. The contestant knew the answer anyway.

7 They ............ have been mad doing this with so many people watching!

8 The director thought he'd ............ report his suspicions to the police.

9 The contestant wasn't ............ to persuade the court he hadn't cheated.

10 He knew he ............ have lied, but he did anyway.

**4** Correct the ten punctuation mistakes in this text.

*All the President's Men*, directed by Alan Pakula and starring Robert Redford and Dustin Hoffman is about two young reporters' from the *Washington Post* who after a lengthy investigation, discover that president Nixon had been lying to the nation about a break-in that occurred in the Democratic Party offices in the Watergate Hotel. Pakulas' film praised by everyone for it's acting, won many plaudits from the critics, including Vincent Canby, the film critic of the *New York Times* who said, 'In my view, no film has come so close to being such an accurate picture of american journalism at its best.

# MODULE 4
## Life's rich tapestry

## Overview

- **Reading:** multiple matching (Paper 1 Part 4)
- **Vocabulary:** idiomatic expressions; emphasis; prepositions
- **Listening 1:** identifying the topic; listening for information (Paper 4 Part 4)
- **Language development 1:** word-formation review
- **English in Use 1:** word formation (Paper 3 Part 4)
- **Writing 1:** making your writing interesting
- **Listening 2:** multiple-choice questions (Paper 4 Part 3)
- **Speaking:** relationships; long turn (Paper 5 Part 2)
- **English in Use 2:** gapped text (Paper 3 Part 6)
- **Language development 2:** noun clauses
- **Writing 2:** competition entry (Paper 2 Part 2)

## Lead-in

- What do you think is the relationship between the people in the photos? How do you know?
- How well do you think they get on?
- In your experience, is it easier to get on with people who are similar to or different from yourself?
- What relationships are most important to you at this point in your life?

# 4A Making choices

## Reading (Paper 1 Part 4)

### Before you read

1 Look at the photos and the headings of the article to find out what it's about. Can you predict any answers to the question in the subheading?

### Skimming

2 Read through each text quickly. What seem to be the most important 'ingredients' for a successful working partnership?

### Multiple matching ▶ Task strategies page 168

3 For questions 1–16, answer by choosing from the five people (A–E). Some of the choices may be required more than once. Before you start, read the task strategies on page 168 if necessary. The first question has been done for you.

| Which person states the following? | | | |
|---|---|---|---|
| We have a good effect on one another. | **1** ....D.... | | |
| Arguing about things can be beneficial. | **2** ............ | | |
| We are able to be totally honest with each other. | **3** ............ | | |
| I'm impressed with his breadth of experience. | **4** ............ | | |
| I believe our relationship was destined to be. | **5** ............ | | |
| We each specialise in different aspects of the business. | **6** ............ | **7** ............ | |
| People don't always treat us in the same way. | **8** ............ | | |
| We make sure our responsibilities don't overlap. | **9** ............ | | |
| We sometimes have trivial arguments. | **10** ............ | | |
| Neither of us is self-important. | **11** ............ | | |
| It's important to have someone to discuss things with. | **12** ............ | | |
| We help each other to keep events in perspective. | **13** ............ | | |
| We often compromise on big decisions. | **14** ............ | | |
| We feel we are working towards the same objectives. | **15** ............ | **16** ............ | |

4 Compare and justify your answers. What parallel phrases did you find?

## Discussion and vocabulary

5 Discuss these questions.
  1 Look back at texts B, C and D. According to the writers, how are they different from their partners?
  2 Think of someone you get on well with. In what ways are you similar or different?

# Two's company

**What are the special ingredients which underpin certain working relationships and make them so successful?**

## A Ian Hislop, political editor and comedian, talks about his writing partner, cartoonist Nick Newman

Nick and I were at school together, and I was very envious that he could be funny as well as being able to draw so well – most of us had only one skill.

He's very, very good company, he makes me laugh more than anyone I know. The best thing about working with him is that it doesn't feel like work at all. Although, working so closely together, it can feel a bit like a marriage at times – squabbling about who left the top off a pen, that sort of thing.

I don't think there's any rivalry between us, although I think that Nick gets irritated if my so-called celebrity status means I sometimes appear to be the one chosen to do a particular job. I can't imagine a situation where we're ever not working together a lot of the time. If you've known somebody for that long, you've the right to say 'That's not funny' without one of us feeling crushed by it. It saves a huge amount of editing!

## B Domenico Dolce talks about his co-designer, Stefano Gabbana

We first met as assistant designers in the same studio in Milan. I believe in life's pre-planned events and the fact that we were meant to work together, but Stefano laughs at me and says I'm talking superstitious nonsense.

We are quite opposite in many respects, though at work we have a common purpose and do most things together. We help each other out, because Stefano dislikes the business side of things, and I would rather stay in the background when it comes to public relations. We have different design strengths, too. I am good at tailoring, the cut on a jacket, for example, whereas he has more of an eye for the visual look of things.

When it comes to reaching an agreement on issues that matter, we tend to have an equal say. We take a cocktail approach – if he wants a dress to be red and I want it to be white, we might have a whole series of heated discussions and then it will end up pink! I think it's healthy to have a bit of confrontation in a relationship like ours.

## C Mark Sainsbury talks about Samuel Clark, with whom he co-owns a successful restaurant

Our parents were friends, and we've been on holiday together for as long as we can remember. I was also responsible for introducing Sam to his wife, Samantha. When they started going out, we all decided we would set up a restaurant together. Sam and Samantha are now the chefs, and I am the rest of the operation.

Sam and I are very different, but our relationship is full of respect. I care about all the non-cooking details, if the mirrors are polished, that sort of thing; I prefer to do things thoroughly and well. Mark would be hopeless at that. He's also too thin-skinned to deal with customers – he'd find it very hurtful when they were rude, whereas it doesn't bother me at all. However, he's absolutely brilliant with the chaos in the kitchen and at dealing with the unexpected, which would throw me completely. So we support and balance each other really effectively.

But our relationship hasn't been a complete bed of roses. What helps us to get on is a very clear demarcation of the areas we're in charge of; we don't tend to tread on each other's toes.

## D Tim Bevan talks about Eric Fellner, co-chairman of the film company that produced *Four Weddings and a Funeral* and *Captain Corelli's Mandolin*

Film production is a lonely occupation, and it's much better doing it as a duo. We discuss most matters. It's crucial to have a partner who you can bounce ideas off. We haven't had an argument in ten years, and we see or speak to each other every day, although, funnily enough we hardly ever see each other socially.

In this business, you can be the greatest person one minute and losing millions the next. Through the highest of highs and lowest of lows, we help each other to be objective about things, without giving up or getting above ourselves.

Character-wise, we couldn't be more different. I'm very pro-active and probably more aggressive in attitude, whereas Eric is much more cautious. He can sometimes make me less impatient, and I can make him less hesitant, so we bring out the best in each other. He's very good socially with people, fair-minded, with an extremely good sense of humour, which you need in this game.

## E Ken Livingstone, Mayor of London (2000–), talks about Bob Kiley, Commissioner of Transport for London (2001–05)

We needed someone to improve London's ailing Underground network, and I was one of the team which interviewed Bob by satellite in New York for the job of Commissioner for Transport. It's not a good way of doing an interview, but he was outstanding, he was our choice by a mile, and now we work together on a regular basis.

When we first met, we hit it off from the word go; you sense immediately if the chemistry's working. You go out for a meal with Bob, and he's got all these stories to tell. He has known all the main people in American politics in the last 25 years, and the diversity of things he has done is quite incredible. However, despite all this, he doesn't take himself too seriously; he's not pompous or 'full of himself'. I like to think we have this in common.

We see or talk to each other ten to twelve times a week. We have had cross words, but not very often. He also knows what being a mayor involves, and I know a fair bit about transport, so we work together very well. Basically we share the same vision and trust each other absolutely. I'm never going to let him go!

# Vocabulary

## Idiomatic expressions

**1 a** Mark the three idiomatic expressions in this extract from the text on page 57. What do they mean?

*'When we first met, we hit it off from the word go; you sense immediately if the chemistry's working.'*

**b** Read the definitions of some more expressions from the text. Mark the correct word in each expression.

1 If someone talks about themselves a lot, we say they are *full of / filled with / complete in* themselves.

2 When you get annoyed with someone, you might *make / give / have* cross words with them.

3 If you are able to laugh at yourself, it means you don't *think of / take / believe* yourself too seriously.

4 When you offend someone by interfering in something they are responsible for, you are treading on their *shoes / feet / toes*.

5 To say a situation is not always happy, easy or comfortable, you can say it is not always a *bunch / bed / basket* of roses.

6 If you're able to enjoy things that are funny, or you can make people laugh, you have a good *skill / feeling / sense* of humour.

7 If you are good at noticing things, you have a good *sight / eye / vision* for something.

8 A discussion, argument or debate that is full of angry and excited feelings is a *hot / heated / heavy* discussion.

9 When you assist someone who is busy or has problems, you help them *up / over / out*.

**c** Which of the personal characteristics in Exercise 1b apply to you or someone you know?

## Expressions that give emphasis

**2 a** Look at the phrases that give emphasis in these extracts from the text. Mark the best meaning.

1 It doesn't bother me at all. (extract C)
I am *very upset / not upset*.

2 He was our choice by a mile … (extract E)
He was *a bit / much* better than the other candidates.

3 I know a fair bit about transport … (extract E)
I know *quite a lot / a great deal* …

4 … we trust each other absolutely … (extract E)
We consider each other to be *very / 100%* trustworthy.

**b** Use each expression from the box once only to complete the text below.

> at all   barely   absolutely   by a mile   quite
> a bit of   a fair bit of   full of

'One of the strangest relationships I have is with someone I can **(1)**............... communicate with. For many years, I have imported products from a supplier in China called Mr Wu. At the beginning, it was **(2)**............... difficult – I spoke no Chinese, and he spoke no English, so we had to use interpreters. But now that we've been working together so well for so long, I trust him **(3)**............... .

I'm a busy man, and I do **(4)**............... of business elsewhere, but Mr Wu is the best supplier I have **(5)**............... . Although I'm **(6)**............... a perfectionist, I know that when I place an order with him, I don't need to worry about it **(7)**............... .

I can be **(8)**............... confidence that the order will arrive exactly when Mr Wu says it will!'

**c** What type of words are the expressions in Exercise 2b used with? Where do they fit in the sentence (e.g. before/after a noun/adjective/clause)?

## Prepositions

**3 a** Complete the spaces in this text with the correct preposition. Mark the completed phrase.

One of the most successful rock bands of all time is the Rolling Stones, still touring **(1)**............... a regular basis after 40 years **(2)**............... the business. They have had a huge effect **(3)**............... many other groups. One reason for their success is that there isn't any rivalry **(4)**............... the band members. Mick Jagger, who some people say is 'full **(5)**............... himself', loves the publicity and dealing **(6)**............... the media, whereas Charlie Watts prefers to stay **(7)**............... the background. There have been the occasional arguments, but these should be kept **(8)**............... perspective.

**b** Can you think of any more examples of successful partnerships?

SRB p39

## Listening 1 Developing skills (Part 4)

**Before you listen**

1 Decide which four of the following qualities are essential in a good sales manager and complete this sentence.

A good sales manager must be …

*adaptable approachable caring creative decisive enthusiastic experienced independent knowledgeable organised resilient a team builder*

**Identifying the topic**

2 🎧 You are going to hear a radio programme called *Moral Issues*, which looks at decisions people make that affect the lives of others. Listen to the first part of the programme and answer the questions.
1 What is the choice that Tom Wilkins has to make?
2 How many people are involved in his decision?
3 What is each one's area of responsibility?

**Listening for information**

3 a 🎧 In the programme, the people involved are interviewed separately. Read through the notes below. Then listen to the next part of the programme and find one strong point and one weak point for each of the employees.

| STRONG POINTS | |
|---|---|
| A has relevant knowledge | |
| B has experience in different departments | Mike .............. |
| C is well organised | Joanne .............. |
| D has useful contacts | Jason .............. |
| E is good at making decisions | Carol .............. |
| F shows initiative | |

| WEAK POINTS | |
|---|---|
| G is not very well qualified | |
| H has the lowest sales figures | Mike .............. |
| I does not find team-building easy | Joanne .............. |
| J does not like having to adapt | Jason .............. |
| K sales figures have declined recently | Carol .............. |
| L joined the company most recently | |

b Compare your answers and give more detail to support each point. Listen again if necessary.

c Match the notes above to these extracts from the recording.
1 … if it's a 'last in first out' scenario, I'm definitely for the chop.  Jason, L
2 it all works like clockwork
3 I really dread the thought of what will happen with these changes.
4 I've pretty well got it at my fingertips now …
5 The team's figures have taken a bit of a knocking …
6 I am ready to try out new ideas …
7 … everyone who's anyone knows me in the business.
8 at the bottom of the league as regards sales

**Discussion**

4 a Work in groups. Decide which two of the four sales managers – Mike, Joanne, Jason or Carol – you would make redundant, and which two you would retain. Give reasons.

b Compare your choice with other groups.

c 🎧 In the programme, Tom finally gives and justifies his choice. Listen to the last part of the recording to see who Tom decided to make redundant. Do you think he made the right choice?

# Language development 1

## Word formation

In Paper 3 Part 4, you have to form a word from a given stem to fill in gaps in a text. You may have to make up to four changes. These may involve:

- adding a suffix, e.g. *fortunate* (adj.) → *fortunately* (adv.); *simple* (adj.) → *simplify* (v.); *write* (v.) → *writing* (n.)
- adding a prefix, e.g. *fortunately* → **un**fortunately; *large* (adj.) → **en**large (v.)
- making an internal spelling change, e.g. *deep* (adj.) → *depth* (n.); *thief* (n.) → *theft* (n.)
- making a word plural, e.g. *responsible* (adj.) → *responsibility* (n.) → *responsibilities*

Forming new words from a stem often involves a spelling change. In the exam, your spelling must be accurate.

## Adding suffixes

**1 a** Form words with a different word class by adding suffixes. Pay attention to spelling. Use your dictionary if necessary. There may be more than one answer.
  1 Make these verbs into adjectives.
    *amuse   collapse   depend   differ   hesitate   influence   please   produce*
  2 Make these nouns into adjectives.
    *affection   aggression   danger   energy   envy   fun   history   hope   success*
  3 Make these verbs into nouns.
    *amuse   confront   decide   defend   discover   participate   persist   please   save*
  4 Make these adjectives into nouns.
    *accurate   cruel   confident   diverse   happy   jealous   lonely   popular   tolerant*
  5 Make these nouns and adjectives into verbs.
    *beauty   deep   general   legal   popular   strength   wide*

  **b** Complete the table with examples from Exercise 1a. Which suffixes add a recognisable meaning to the word?
    EXAMPLE: *-ible/-able* = that can be, fit to be

| Change | Suffixes | Examples |
|---|---|---|
| 1 verb → adjective | *-ing* | *amusing* |
| 2 noun → adjective |  |  |
| 3 verb → noun |  |  |
| 4 adjective → noun |  |  |
| 5 adjective → verb |  |  |
| 6 noun → verb |  |  |

## Making internal spelling changes

**2** Make these words into nouns by making a spelling change.

| | | | | |
|---|---|---|---|---|
| *broad* | *choose* | *die* | *fly* | *high* |
| *long* | *prove* | *strong* | *succeed* | |

## Adding prefixes

**3** Look at the table of prefixes and their general meaning. Add more examples from the list.
  *appear   arrange   conformist   cook   danger   date   develop   drawn   education   exist   populated   power   print   reversible   rich   school   secure   worker*

| Prefix | General meaning | Examples |
|---|---|---|
| un-, im-, in-, dis-, irr-, non- | not, the opposite of | *unbelievable, non-fiction* |
| mis- | wrong(ly) | *misunderstand* |
| co- | together, with | *co-production* |
| en-, em- | cause to be, make into | *enlarge* |
| re- | again, in a different way | *replace* |
| under- | not sufficient | *underpaid* |
| over- | too much | *overpaid* |
| pre- | before | *prefix* |

## Word families

**4** A good way of increasing your vocabulary is to make a note of other forms of a word you know, or a new word you come across. Use your dictionary to help you complete these word families.

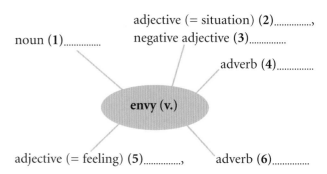

noun (**1**)............
adjective (= situation) (**2**)............,
negative adjective (**3**)............
adverb (**4**)............
**envy (v.)**
adjective (= feeling) (**5**)............,
adverb (**6**)............

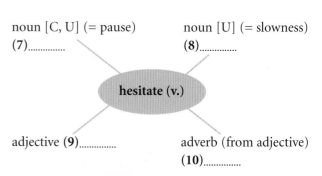

noun [C, U] (= pause) (**7**)............
noun [U] (= slowness) (**8**)............
**hesitate (v.)**
adjective (**9**)............
adverb (from adjective) (**10**)............

▶SRB  p40

# English in Use 1 (Paper 3 Part 4)

**Lead-in**

1 Are you a decisive shopper, or the opposite? Give examples.

**Word formation**

▶ Task strategies pages 169 and 170

2 a Read the title of each text to identify the topic. Then read them through quickly, without looking at the words on the right. Which descriptions in the texts match you best?

b Do the task. Read the task strategies on pages 169 and 170 before you start and use the Help clues if necessary.

For questions **1–15**, read the texts below. Use the words to the right of the texts to form **one** word that fits in the same numbered space in the text. The exercise begins with an example (**0**).

CATALOGUE EXTRACT

## A store with a difference

At the best of times, it's difficult to choose presents for people. It's even more difficult when you are on a (**0**) restricted budget and people give the (**1**)............... of having everything they need. Maybe it is 'the thought that counts', but to avoid making (**2**)............... decisions and (**3**)............... buying things people have already got, it is best to choose one of two policies. Either you can carry out some kind of (**4**)............... of what the people need and want, in which case you will be thought of as a (**5**)............... individual who really cares for them. Alternatively, you can buy some (**6**)............... object you like on a whim, and the (**7**)............... of your choice will bring a little joy into their lives. For fantasy shoppers like you, we have some truly amazing gifts.

| | |
|---|---|
| (**0**) | **RESTRICT** |
| (**1**) | APPEAR |
| (**2**) | DISASTER |
| (**3**) | INTEND |
| (**4**) | INVESTIGATE |
| (**5**) | CONSIDER |
| (**6**) | IMAGINE |
| (**7**) | ORIGINAL |

**HELP**

➤ Question 2
Which suffix is needed to make this noun into an adjective? What spelling change do you need to make?

➤ Question 3
Do you need a positive or negative word?

MAGAZINE EXTRACT

## What kind of shopper are you?

When you go into a food store, are you someone who (**8**)............... carries a shopping list and never gives in to (**9**)..............., or are you the kind of shopper who only chooses things on the spot? Most of us are probably somewhere between the two. There are those of us who like to think of ourselves as (**10**)............... individuals, who carefully make (**11**)............... between brands and prices, only to go and buy (**12**)............... large quantities of something we don't really need because we notice we can make (**13**)............... savings. Or we are the kind of shopper who hunts through the organic fruit and vegetable sections trying to think of a balanced meal to cook, when our (**14**)............... is aroused by the dessert counter, and before we know it, our trolley is full of (**15**)............... foods we know we should avoid.

| | |
|---|---|
| (**8**) | VARY |
| (**9**) | TEMPT |
| (**10**) | DISCERN |
| (**11**) | COMPARE |
| (**12**) | EXCEPT |
| (**13**) | SUBSTANCE |
| (**14**) | CURIOUS |
| (**15**) | HEALTH |

**HELP**

➤ Question 10
Which suffix is needed to make this verb into an adjective?

➤ Question 11
Is this singular or plural?

➤ Question 12
Is an adverb or noun required here?

➤ Question 15
Do you need a positive or negative meaning?

**Task analysis**

3 Answer the questions about the task.
1 Which questions required both a suffix and a prefix?
2 Which questions required a spelling change?

# Writing 1  Making your writing interesting

1 a Read the introductory paragraphs A and B, which are from two different texts. For each paragraph, decide:

   1 what kind of text it is from      3 who it is aimed at.
   2 the purpose of the text

**A**

As they grow up, children are faced with a multitude of choices, whether it is which people to have as friends, how to spend money, which university to go to, or, perhaps most importantly of all, which career to pursue. As teachers, we need to help children develop the skill of making these decisions for themselves, and one way of doing this is by getting them from a very young age to take more responsibility for what happens in the classroom.

**B**

The worst are the 'control freaks', who won't allow us, their children, to choose anything for ourselves, let alone make any of the immensely difficult decisions that need to be made in life. They say we are too immature, too easily led astray by our friends or influenced by what we watch on TV. Maybe we are. But if we don't get the chance to decide things for ourselves, it's hardly surprising if, when we get older, we turn into unthinking rebels, unwilling to do anything sensible.

## Writing strategy

In certain types of writing, such as articles and reviews, you need to use techniques that capture and hold your reader's interest to the end. For example, you should:

• use a catchy title to attract attention (e.g. *Two's company*, page 57)
• make sure your opening paragraph makes the reader want to carry on (e.g. *A mobile phone rings. This is astonishing …* page 24)
• use a range of interesting vocabulary.

b Choose the most appropriate opening sentence for each paragraph above from these choices. Why is the other sentence not appropriate?

   **A** 1 As a wise old philosopher once said, 'It is the choices we make – not luck – that determine our future.'
       2 Knowing how to make an informed choice is a crucial skill in life.

   **B** 1 Why is it that when we are struggling to grow up, our parents so often fail to realise the effect they have on us?
       2 In the social sciences, 'bad parents' are sometimes thought of as parents who have little interest in their child's ability to make good decisions.

c Match the sentences you chose to the following descriptions.

   a a factual statement of the topic      d a quotation
   b a rhetorical question                 e a technical definition
   c a surprising/controversial statement

d Which of these other ways of making writing interesting are illustrated in the less formal paragraph?

   • intensifying adverbs                    • lively expressions
   • adjectives                              • specific details
   • mixture of short sentences and long sentences   • direct speech

2 a Which text, A or B, is this second paragraph from?

Children should be given the chance to discuss options and fully inform themselves of the consequences of the choices they make. Advice and guidance need to be given, but the child should be given the freedom to accept or reject them so that they feel the final decision is theirs. In the event of a poor decision being made and the child realising the consequences of failure, the adult's role is to be sympathetic and not belittle the child in any way.

b Rewrite the paragraph in a suitable style for the other text. You might want to use some of these informal expressions.

| |
|---|
| *what we need is …    weigh up the pros and cons    talk things through* *take on board    make something ours    get it wrong* *make a mess of something    make (someone) feel small* |

c Now write a final paragraph in the same style.

# 4B Human nature

## Listening 2 (Paper 4 Part 3)

### Multiple-choice questions

▶ Task strategies pages 170 and 171

1 🎧 Do the task below. Read the task strategies on pages 170 and 171 before you start and use the Help clues if necessary. Listen to the recording twice.

You will hear an interview in which the psychotherapist Kate Holt is talking about the influence of the family on a child's personality. For questions **1–6**, choose the correct answer **A**, **B**, **C** or **D**.

1 In Kate's opinion, what accounts for personality differences between siblings?
   A Every person is born with a nature which is unique.
   B Each child is exposed to a unique set of experiences.
   C Children are influenced by people from outside the family.
   D Parents adopt varying approaches to child-rearing over time.

2 Kate says that, compared to younger siblings, the oldest child in a family will often
   A be under greater pressure to do well in life.
   B receive more parental love and affection.
   C develop a more cautious personality.
   D become more ambitious in later life.

3 What does Kate describe as the typical traits of younger siblings?
   A They tend to be less successful in academic subjects.
   B They tend to be closer to their father than their mother.
   C Their main priority is to establish a distinctive identity.
   D Their interests often closely reflect those of their parents.

4 According to Kate, the extent to which a child is affected by the birth of a younger sibling depends on
   A the personality of that sibling.
   B how close the children are in age.
   C the number of children in the family.
   D how the parents deal with any problems.

5 In Kate's view, a child will go on to develop successful adult relationships if it
   A inherits certain social skills.
   B is taught to control its emotions.
   C is cared for by a variety of people.
   D has a good model of behaviour to follow.

6 Kate thinks the most valuable contribution a psychotherapist can make is to
   A enable people to recognise patterns of behaviour they need to change.
   B help people develop a more effective range of parenting skills.
   C allow people to discuss why they behave in the way they do.
   D give advice to people who want to change their lives.

**HELP**
➤ Question 1
Kate tells us what different people think about the issue, but she uses the phrase *My own view is* to indicate which is her opinion.
➤ Question 2
Listen for what Kate says the oldest child typically does.
➤ Question 4
Listen for what Kate says the effect is mainly due to.

### Task analysis

2 Compare and justify your answers. Why did you rule out the other options? Look back at Exercise 3b on page 43.

### Discussion

3 Read through the task again. Based on your own experience, how far do you agree with the opinions expressed?

## Speaking  (Paper 5 Part 2)

**Vocabulary:
relationships**

**1 a Which of the photos do you think the following sentences refer to? There could be more than one possibility.**

1 They obviously have a very close relationship.
2 They probably spend a lot of time together.
3 I should think they're quite bossy.
4 He's totally dependent on her for everything.
5 They're completely engrossed in what they're doing.
6 It looks as if the parent is very caring.

**b Make more sentences about the people in the photos and how they might feel towards each other. Use some of the expressions below.**

*responsible for   inseparable from   protective towards   enthralled by
furious with   devoted to   resentful towards*

**2 a Choose the correct alternatives in these extracts of people talking about their families.**

1 I grew up in quite *an intimate / a tightly-knit* family. There's always been a *strong / tight* bond between me and my brother. As children, we relied on *each other / the other* for support, and we have a lot of *same interests / interests in common*.
2 In my country today, the *extended / increased* family is less common. That means parents have to pay more for childcare, so *single / only* children like me are not as unusual as they used to be.
3 My older sister and I were always squabbling as children. I was very envious *of / at* her because she was my father's favourite. We get *on / by* well now, but there's still a lot of sibling rivalry between us.
4 My parents had high *aspirations / expectations* of me. I was a very *conscientious / conscious* student at school because I didn't want to *let down / disappoint* them.
5 I'm the black *sheep / ox* of the family. I rebelled against my parents right from the *go / start*, refused to do *as / that* I was told and just did what I wanted to do. We do *have / speak* cross words quite often, but I think a bit of confrontation is *unhealthy / healthy* in any family.

**b Rewrite the phrases in italics with expressions from the box, making any changes necessary.**

| *fall for* | *get his own way* | *get on with* | *take after* | *see eye to eye* |
|---|---|---|---|---|
| *run in the family* | *hit it off* | *fall out* | *lose touch* | *look up to* |

1 My brother *is very similar to* our father.
2 Children shouldn't be allowed to *do exactly what they want* all the time.
3 I've always *respected* my father for what he's achieved.
4 My sister and I never *agree* about anything.
5 Her talent for music *is inherited*.
6 Unfortunately, when I left school, I *didn't keep in contact* with my old friends.
7 When my best friend and I first met, we *liked* each other immediately.
8 I *started to love* Tom the moment I met him.

**c Talk about your family and friends, using words and expressions from Exercises 2a and 2b.**

Task strategies pages 171 and 172

**Sample answer**

3 a Check the task strategy for Part 2 on page 172 before you listen.

b 🎧 Look at the photos again. Listen to the examiner's instructions. What TWO things does the task involve?

c 🎧 Listen to someone doing the task. Which pictures does she talk about? Do you agree with what she says?

d Did she deal with both parts of the task? How successfully did she follow the task strategies?

**Useful language: expressing probability and certainty**

4 Listen again to the candidate's answer and complete the sentences.
In the photo of the mother with the baby, (1).......................... a feeling of tenderness.
How (2).......................... these relationships change? Well, (3).......................... , at some point the baby is going to become less dependent on its mother, and therefore that relationship is (4).......................... change.
With the father and son, the child (5).......................... become interested in other things … So if they don't have common interests, that (6).......................... their closeness.

**Long turn**

5 a Work in pairs. You are each going to do the task in Exercise 3, using a different pair of photos.
STUDENT 1: Talk about photos C and D.
STUDENT 2: Talk about photos E and F on page 205. (Student 1 should look at them while you are talking.)

b Look at photos C–F again and talk together about who you think has the closest relationship. Take about one minute for this.

**Task analysis**

6 Did you:
- use as wide a range of language as you could, or did you 'play safe'?
- *both* give your opinions in Exercise 5b?

▶SRB  p43

# English in Use 2 (Paper 3 Part 6)

**Lead-in**

1 Discuss these questions.
1 How would you define intelligence?
2 Do you believe we can develop our intelligence? If so, how?

**Gapped text**

▶ Task strategies pages 169 and 170

2 a Read the text and decide whether these sentences are *True* or *False*. Ignore the gaps for now.
1 Intelligence refers to ability in one area.
2 Identical twins have the same level of ability.
3 Studying can make your brain larger.

b Do the task. Check the task strategies on pages 169 and 170 before you start and use the Help clues below if necessary.

Read the text and then choose from the list (**A–I**) below the best phrase to fill each of the spaces. Each correct phrase may only be used once. Some of the suggested answers do not fit at all.

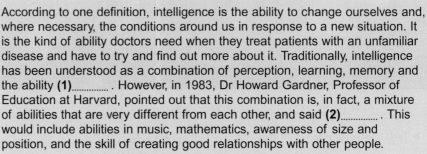

## Understanding intelligence

According to one definition, intelligence is the ability to change ourselves and, where necessary, the conditions around us in response to a new situation. It is the kind of ability doctors need when they treat patients with an unfamiliar disease and have to try and find out more about it. Traditionally, intelligence has been understood as a combination of perception, learning, memory and the ability **(1)**............. . However, in 1983, Dr Howard Gardner, Professor of Education at Harvard, pointed out that this combination is, in fact, a mixture of abilities that are very different from each other, and said **(2)**............. . This would include abilities in music, mathematics, awareness of size and position, and the skill of creating good relationships with other people.

How far intelligence is something we are born with and can't change is **(3)**............. . Some of them argue that while intelligence might be in our genes, it is nevertheless affected by our environment. Studies on twins would seem to show **(4)**............. , and because identical twins are almost the same in this respect, in tests they show the same degree of intelligence. But the results do not rule out the possibility that we can improve our intelligence, so **(5)**............. is open to debate.

Indeed, there is evidence that learning and studying can help improve a person's brain structure, and that dietary supplements, and even exercise, can make a beneficial change in the balance of chemicals in the brain. In a recent study, it was even found **(6)**............. of taxi drivers in London grew larger to help them store a detailed mental map of the city.

**HELP**

➤ **Question 2**
You need to read the next sentence to exclude possible options.

➤ **Question 3**
Read the next sentence. Who does *them* refer to?

➤ **Question 5**
Not all the options can be followed by *is* and still make sense.

A how we should interpret them
B that being in the job is difficult
C to solve problems
D that part of the brains
E what the effects of premature birth are
F that intelligence is largely due to the physical size of the brain
G what scientists have been trying to discover for years
H that what we needed was a theory of multiple intelligences
I how they all disagree

**Task analysis**

3 Answer the questions about the task.
1 Which questions, if any, did you find difficult and why?
2 Which of the correct answers were noun clauses?
3 What clues helped you with the answers (e.g. grammar, vocabulary, punctuation, reference words)?

**Discussion**

4 Which ideas in the text do you agree/disagree with?

# Language development 2

▶ Grammar reference page 179

## Noun clauses

> Noun (or nominal) clauses are groups of words that function like a noun in a sentence. We can always refer to a noun clause using *it* or *that*. Sometimes a noun clause can be replaced by a noun or pronoun.

**1** Read the text below and mark further examples of:

1 *that* clauses
   a) following a noun   b) following an adjective
   c) as object of a verb

2 clauses beginning with a question word
   a) as subject of the sentence   b) following *be*
   c) following a preposition

3 *-ing* or *to*-infinitive clauses
   a) as subject   b) following *be*
   c) following a noun or adjective

> Multiple Intelligence (MI) theory suggests that people learn differently. What is good for one learner might not be good for another. One feature of the theory is how it identifies eight different pathways to learning. Using words might help one learner, whereas another might benefit from the use of music, pictures or movement. How you teach should depend on who you are teaching, not what you are teaching. If the goal is to help learners get the most from a lesson, it is important to adopt a variety of approaches. There is evidence that more people are becoming aware of MI theory, and it is encouraging that more teachers are adopting its ideas, although some still have no desire to change their approach. To achieve the best results for everyone must be the aim of all schools, but whether or not the ideas become uniformly adopted remains to be seen.

**2** Mark the correct word in each pair. In some cases both are possible.

1 Neurologists have been able to identify *which / what* areas of the brain are associated with intelligence.

2 It is clear *how / that* there is a link between brain size and intelligence.

3 It has already been proved *that / when* you can improve your intelligence.

4 *It is highly likely / There's a strong likelihood* that a child's early environment affects their intelligence.

5 Many people are interested in knowing *how far / whether* intelligence is affected by diet.

6 *To identify / Identifying* intelligence levels in young children is hard.

7 The effect of teaching on learning is *that / what* researchers have been trying to establish for a long time.

8 *That / What* we learn now will have consequences for education in the future.

**3** Complete the text with a suitable word in each gap.

> I'm interested to know (1).............. I can improve my memory. I'm always forgetting (2)............ I've left things or (3)............ people are when they call. When I arrange a meeting, I never remember (4).............. day it is, let alone (5).............. or not I've got the right time. It's lucky (6).............. people usually call to remind me (7)............... time to meet.
> The other day, a friend asked me (8).............. I wanted to go to the cinema with her. I couldn't decide (9).............. to join her or not, as I had no idea (10).............. I had seen the film or not. It seemed likely (11).............. I had seen it, but it didn't matter as I couldn't remember (12)............. the ending was anyway. (13).............. people put up with me I've no idea.
> Recently I read about (14).............. you can improve your memory by eating some type of oil. The only problem is (15).............. I can't remember (16)............... it is called!

**4** Rewrite these sentences using a suitable noun clause.

1 It is human nature that parents want what is best for their children.
  It is human nature for ........................... what is best for their children.

2 There is debate about how parents should bring up children.
  ........................... should ........................... children is the subject of debate.

3 All the conflicting information we receive these days is very confusing.
  It is easy ........................... by all the conflicting information we receive these days.

4 It's hard to know who to turn to for the best advice.
  ........................... for the best advice is hard.

5 Understanding that every child is a genius in a different way is important.
  ........................... that every child is a genius in a different way.

6 Parents can easily ignore their children's emotional needs.
  It is easy ........................... their children's emotional needs.

7 It's a mystery to me why some people have children.
  ........................... is a mystery to me.

**5** Use noun clauses to complete these sentences in a way that is true for you. Then compare your answers with a partner.

1 It is easy/hard/impossible for me …

2 My main worry is how/when/whether …

3 I love/hate things that …

4 I can never remember how/where …

5 I think … is a useful/clever way …

6 Whether or not I … depends on …

# Writing 2 Competition entry (Paper 2 Part 2)

**Lead-in**

1 a  Have you ever entered a competition? If so, did you win?

b  For a competition, people may have to submit a piece of writing, which is then judged. What do you think the judges will be looking for in each of these text types? Will it be the same thing for each?
- a story
- an article
- a review of a book, film, etc.
- a description of a person or a place

**Understand the task**

▶ Writing reference page 192

2  Read the task below and answer the questions.
1  How many PARTS are there to the question? Mark them.
2  What is the PURPOSE of the text (e.g. to inform, to entertain)? Who will the READER be?
3  What KIND OF TEXT will you write? Choose the most appropriate text type from the list in Exercise 1b.
4  What STYLE will be appropriate?
5  What will make yours a GOOD competition entry?

You have seen the following notice for a competition in an in-flight magazine.

**COMPETITION**

**The Importance of a Good Memory**

Some people find it easy to remember things; others find it much more difficult. How important is it to have a good memory in life, and what problems does a bad memory cause? What suggestions can you make to help people improve their memory? Send us your ideas.

The best entry will be published in a future issue, and the winner will receive two free tickets to Vienna.

Write your **competition entry** in approximately 250 words.

**Plan your entry**

▶ Writing strategy (planning) page 30
(coherence) page 46

3 a  Make notes under these headings.
1  Why a good memory is useful in life (e.g. for passing exams)
2  How a poor memory makes life difficult (e.g. missing appointments, needing to leave reminder notes everywhere)
3  Ideas for improving your memory (e.g. building up a visual picture)

b  Your answer should probably have four to five paragraphs. Look at the paragraph plans below, which show alternative ways to approach your entry. Decide which approach you will follow. Then select the best ideas from your notes above and write your paragraph plan.

**Plan A**
**Paragraph 1:** Introduction
**Paragraph 2:** Why a good memory is useful + examples
**Paragraph 3:** How a poor memory makes life difficult + examples
**Paragraph 4:** Suggestions for improving your memory
**Paragraph 5:** Concluding remarks

**Plan B**
**Paragraph 1:** Introduction
**Paragraph 2:** Compare benefits of having a good memory with problems of having a bad memory
**Paragraph 3:** Suggestions for improving your memory
**Paragraph 4:** Concluding remarks

## Language and content

▶ Writing strategy (interest) page 62

**4 a** In more informal articles, the writer addresses the reader directly and uses colourful and descriptive language. What other techniques and types of language can you use?

**b** Which of these do you think would make a good opening sentence for each paragraph in plan B? Why?

**Paragraph 1**

a Some people are lucky enough to be able to remember facts, figures, names and faces, and they never forget appointments.

b Are you one of those lucky people with a good memory, someone who can remember everyone's name at a party and never forgets an appointment?

**Paragraph 2**

a Having a good memory is useful at all stages of your life.

b You always want to remember things – it doesn't matter how old you are, does it?

**Paragraph 3**

a For example, when you want to remember someone's name, you should try to concentrate on it and use it as often as possible in conversation.

b But don't worry – the idea that there is nothing we can do about a bad memory is wrong.

**Paragraph 4**

a In short, we might have a naturally poor memory, but there are ways of improving it and remembering things we never thought possible.

b So as you can see, it is up to you to take responsibility for improving your memory.

**c** Choose expressions from this list for your main paragraphs. Then complete the sentences for your answer.

| | |
|---|---|
| **Introducing the topic** | *Whether you (are at college) or (in a job), a good memory is …*<br>*We are all familiar with (the drawbacks of a bad memory): …* |
| **Giving examples** | *Being able to remember (facts) helps us to …*<br>*Another advantage/disadvantage of (a good/bad memory) is …*<br>*And of course, …* |
| **Comparing and contrasting** | *Those of us lucky enough to have (a good memory) …, whereas the rest of us …*<br>*On the other hand, (if you suffer from a poor memory) …* |
| **Making suggestions** | *How (we remember things) can depend on (a number of things, such as) …*<br>*If (you want to be able to remember) …*<br>*One/Another thing you can do (to improve your memory) is …* |
| **Summing up** | *Anyway, in a word, …*<br>*So, as you can see, there is still hope (for all of you who) …* |

## Write your competition entry

**5** Now write your own competition entry, using some of the ideas and the language above. Don't forget to think of a title. Write your answer in approximately 250 words.

## Check your answer

▶ Writing reference page 188

**6** Edit your article using the checklist on page 188.

# Module 4: Review

## 1 Decide which word or phrase best fits each space.

1 My mother has a ......... for a bargain
A big nose   B fast foot   C good eye   D keen sense

2 I don't like being dependent ......... anyone.
A towards   B on   C with   D in

3 They both have red hair – it ......... the family.
A runs in   B comes from   C started out with
D is down to

4 His brother is ......... older than her.
A every bit as   B a bit much   C not a bit
D a fair bit

5 Carl feels very protective ......... Gabriel.
A for   B with   C towards   D for

6 They work together, but they don't always ......... in
each other.
A bring out the best   B give their best
C know best   D look their best

7 They all support each other – they're a very .........
family.
A extended   B immediate   C tightly-knit
D nuclear

8 He's just helping us ......... in the office on a
temporary basis.
A along   B off   C on   D out

9 My boss ......... himself very seriously.
A takes   B looks after   C seems   D is pleased with

10 Just do ......... you're told!
A how   B as   C what   D like

11 He's very good at using charm to ......... .
A get in touch   B get a word in   C get his own way
D get away from it all

12 The first time they met, they didn't ......... at all.
A have cross words   B tread on their toes
C have a heated discussion   D hit it off

## 2 Rewrite each sentence using the word in brackets so it has a similar meaning. Do not change the word in any way.

1 I was impressed how wide his experience was.
(*breadth*)

...........................................................................

2 He had no brothers or sisters. (*only*)

...........................................................................

3 It was really hard to decide. (*tough*)

...........................................................................

4 All the brothers are very close. (*bond*)

...........................................................................

5 She lost her job because of the cutbacks.
(*redundant*)

...........................................................................

6 He has such a high opinion of himself. (*full*)

...........................................................................

7 Why aren't they friends any more? (*fallen*)

...........................................................................

8 In the end, I always do what I want. (*way*)

...........................................................................

## 3 Complete the text with the correct form of the words on the right.

In his in-(1).......... study of the subject,
the psychologist David Keirsey has
declared there are four main types of
human temperament.
**Artisans** are highly (2)........... and
(3)........... people. This type includes
(4)........... artists and (5)........... .
**Guardians** are cautious people, whose
greatest (6)........... lies in upholding
family values. They are solid citizens
who would, quite (7)..........., support
social institutions against any (8)...........
ideas that (9)........... their existence.
**Idealists** have a great (10)........... in the
need to remove (11)........... . They see it
as their (12)........... to help us (13)...........
our (14)........... through cooperation.
**Rationals** like to understand how
things work. They make their (15)...........
through the power of reason.

1 DEEP
2 ENERGY
3 PRODUCE
4 INFLUENCE
5 ACT
6 HAPPY
7 HESITATE
8 CONFORM
9 DANGER
10 BELIEVE
11 CONFRONT
12 RESPONSIBLE
13 RICH
14 LIVE
15 DISCOVER

## 4 Correct the errors in the use of noun clauses.

1 To decide who to live with is the most important
choice we make in life.

2 Some people really know how dress in order to
show their personality.

3 If you want to understand a person, look at which
their life choices are.

4 It's always difficult to decide what spend our
money on.

5 I know how if our choices reflect our personality,
they turn out to be better choices.

6 It's interesting what decisions based on the
opinions of others are usually wrong.

7 The question is how far or not we really have a
choice in any particular situation.

8 It's easy saying that we don't have a choice.

9 What means is that we don't want to choose
between the different alternatives.

10 It's a strong likelihood therefore we don't really
register them as choices.

▶ Exam Practice 2

# Global issues

## Overview

- **Reading:** gapped text (Paper 1 Part 2)
- **Vocabulary:** idiomatic expressions; collocation; confusable words; words for eating/drinking
- **Listening 1:** listening for gist; identifying key information; sentence completion
- **English in Use 1:** lexical cloze (Paper 3 Part 1)
- **Language development 1:** modifying gradable/ungradable adjectives
- **Writing 1:** selecting and ordering information
- **Listening 2:** sentence completion (Paper 4 Part 1)
- **Speaking:** the environment; collaborative task (Paper 5 Parts 3 and 4)
- **English in Use 2:** register transfer (Paper 3 Part 5)
- **Language development 2:** conditionals
- **Writing 2:** an article (Paper 2 Part 1)

## Lead-in

- What global issues do the photos illustrate?
- What aspects of 'globalisation' do you consider beneficial? negative?
- Read the following quotation. How far do you agree with it? What 'alternatives' can you think of?

  *'Greed and envy demand continuous and limitless economic growth of a material kind, without proper regard for conservation, and this type of growth cannot possibly fit into a finite environment. We must therefore study ... the possibilities of evolving an alternative system which might fit the new situation.'*
  (E.F. Schumacher, economist, 1973)

# 5A In the slow lane

## Reading (Paper 1 Part 2)

**Before you read**  1  Look at the title and subheading of the article below.
1  What do you think *the globalisation of urban life* means?
2  Why do you think the members of the 'League of Slow Cities' are against it? What do you think they want to put in its place?
3  In what ways do you think they might achieve their goals?

**Reading**  2  Read the main text to find the answers to the questions in Exercise 1. (Ignore the missing paragraphs for the moment.) How accurate were your predictions?

• • • • • • • • • • • • • • • • • • • • • • • • • • • • • • • • • • • • •

# Life in the slow lane

• • • • • • • • • • • • • • • • • • • • • • • • • • • • • • • • • • • • •

*Members of the League of Slow Cities are fighting against the globalisation of urban life. Carl Honoré reports.*

Even on a normal working day, Bra seems like the perfect place to get away from it all. Locals linger over coffee at pavement tables, watching the world drift by. Everyone has time to say a warm 'Buongiorno'. And no wonder. Bra and
5 three other Italian towns signed a pledge in 1999 to turn themselves into havens from the high-speed frenzy of the modern world.

| 1 |
|---|

The movement was first seen as an idea for a few people who liked to eat and drink well, but now it has become a
10 much broader cultural discussion about the benefits of doing things in a more human, less frenetic way. Yet true to their culinary roots, Slow Cities place great emphasis on the enjoyment of food and wine, the fostering of conviviality and the promotion of unique, high-quality and specialist foods.

| 2 |
|---|

15 An old town on a hillside, Bra lies just outside the area where Italy's finest wine is produced. As such, it might be considered of marginal interest, but here is where the concept of Slow Cities comes into its own. While neighbouring towns enjoy exalted reputations for wine and white truffles, Bra's
20 celebrity is founded on more down-to-earth things like fresh vegetables, local cheese and sausage. It is all about developing local specialities and improving the quality of life, epitomised by their symbol, the snail, which is slow and tastes good. And just as Slow Food's seal of approval has been
25 a badge of distinction in Italy for some time, the designation *Città Slow* has also become a mark of quality.

| 3 |
|---|

Slowly but surely, Bra is working through the 55 manifesto pledges. In its historic centre, the city has closed some streets to traffic and banned supermarket chains and
30 lurid neon signs. Small family-run businesses – among them shops selling handwoven fabrics and speciality meats – are granted the best commercial real estate. City Hall subsidises building renovations that use building materials typical of the region. Hospital and school canteens now
35 serve traditional dishes made from local organic fruit and vegetables instead of processed meals and produce from distant suppliers. It is quality, not quantity that counts.

| 4 |
|---|

Despite their longing for kinder, gentler times, though, Slow City campaigners are anxious not to come across as
40 regressive. Yes, the movement aims to preserve traditional architecture, crafts and cuisine. But it also celebrates the best of the modern world. A Slow City asks: Does this improve our quality of life? If the answer is yes, then the city embraces it. And that includes the very latest technology.
45 'Being a Slow City does not mean turning the clock back,' explains Sibille. 'We want to strike a balance between the modern and the traditional that promotes good living.'

| 5 |
|---|

Nevertheless, the Slow City movement still has a long way to go. Efforts to curb noise pollution in Bra are thwarted by
50 people's fondness for shouting into mobile phones and disturbing the peace. As in other Slow Cities, cars and scooters speed through the streets of Bra that are still open to them. 'I'm afraid people continue to drive badly here,' sighs Sibille. This is the area of life where it is hard to make people slow down.

| 6 |
|---|

55 In the town hall in Bra, Sibille is in high spirits. 'It's a long-term process, but bit by bit we are making Bra into a better place to live,' she says. 'When we are finished, everyone will want to live in a Slow City.' This may be going a little too far. *Città Slow*, after all, is not for everyone.
60 Nevertheless, the movement's core idea – that we need to take some of the speed and stress out of urban living – is feeding into a global trend.

• • • • • • • • • • • • • • • • • • • • • • • • • • • • • • • • • • • • •

## Gapped text

▶ Task strategies page 168

3  For questions 1–6, you must choose which of the paragraphs A–G below fit into the numbered gaps in the article. There is one extra paragraph which does not fit in any of the gaps.

a  Read the text on each side of question 1. Mark pronouns and other words that could refer to items in the missing paragraph.
   • What could *The movement* refer back to?
   • What do you expect to read about in the missing paragraph?

Look through the extracted paragraphs to find the one that fits in terms of topic and language links.

b  Continue in the same way and complete the task. Check the task strategies on page 168 and use the Help clues below if necessary.

A  The people of Bra certainly seem happy to work towards this ideal combination of two worlds. Even the young are responding. The pool hall in Bra has turned down the pop music in deference to the Slow ethos. 'Instead of gulping down a Coke in a loud bar, some of my young customers are learning how nice it can be to sip local wine in a place where the music is low,' says the owner.

B  They were inspired by the Slow Food crusade, which began a rearguard action against fast food in Italy in the mid-1980s, with little expectation of success. But people soon cottoned on to the idea that traditional products were being displaced by cheap, mass-marketed food, and they gathered to the 'Slow' banner in droves.

C  To win it, aspiring cities and their mayors are required to implement specific plans, such as cutting noise and traffic; increasing green spaces and pedestrian zones; backing local farmers and the shops, markets and restaurants that sell their produce; promoting technology that protects the environment; preserving local aesthetic and culinary traditions; and fostering a spirit of hospitality and neighbourliness.

D  At the very least, though, *Città Slow* has opened up another front in the worldwide battle against the culture of speed. By 2003, 28 Italian towns were officially designated Slow Cities, with another 26 working towards certification.

E  There are others. Even as life gets sweeter in Bra, many locals still find work too hectic. 'It's all very well for politicians to talk about slow this and slow that,' says the owner of a leather-goods shop. 'But if I want a decent standard of living, I have to work very, very hard.'

F  Again in keeping with Italian custom, and to guard against overwork, every small food shop in Bra closes on Thursdays and Sundays. City Hall now opens Saturday mornings, to allow people to deal with bureaucratic tasks at a more leisurely pace. 'We are slowly recreating a more traditional way of looking at life,' says Sibille.

G  It's about much more than long lunches, though. Every aspect of urban life is now recast – pleasure before profit, human beings before head office, slowness before speed. 'It is not easy to swim against the tide,' says Bruna Sibille, deputy mayor of Bra. 'But we think the best way to administer a city is with the slow philosophy.'

**HELP**
➤ Question 2
   Look for a paragraph that links back to *the enjoyment of food*.
➤ Question 3
   Look at the sentences on each side of the gap. Which paragraph fits the topic and contains examples of *manifesto pledges*?
➤ Question 4
   Look for a paragraph that refers back to traditional ways of doing things.

## Task analysis

4  Compare and justify your answers. What grammatical or lexical links helped you?

## Discussion

5  a  List all the Slow City manifesto pledges mentioned in the article. Which ideas have been or are being implemented in your town/city? Which ones would you like to see implemented?

   b  Find expressions in the text that relate to these categories. Then explain the benefits of the slow life, using some of the expressions to help you.

| The Slow City way of life | The globalisation of urban life |
| --- | --- |
| *linger over coffee* | *high-speed frenzy* |

# Vocabulary

## Idiomatic expressions

**1 a** Mark the idiomatic expressions in this extract from the text on pages 72–73. What do they mean?

> 'Being a Slow City does not mean turning the clock back,' explains Sibille. 'We want to strike a balance between the modern and the traditional that promotes good living.'

**b** Match the sentence halves and mark the idiomatic expressions. They are all used in the text.

1 It's important to relax and get away
2 The police should arrest people who disturb
3 Governments have a long way
4 Not many people are ready to swim
5 The concept of healthy eating is slowly
6 For most things in life, it is quality,
7 Summer is terrible because tourists come
8 It's hard to strike the right

a the peace by having noisy parties.
b but surely catching on with the public.
c against the tide and refuse to buy cars.
d not quantity that counts.
e balance between work and life.
f from it all on a regular basis.
g in droves to visit my town.
h to go before they achieve equality for all.

**c** How far do you agree with the statements in Exercise 1b?

## Choosing the correct word

**2 a** Mark the correct verb in each set.

1 As part of its campaign to *proceed / promote / provoke* a healthy lifestyle, the government is getting tough on smoking.
2 They have *decided / wished / pledged* to reduce the number of smoking-related illnesses within ten years.
3 Some organisations want them to *censor / ban / bar* smoking in all public places.
4 However, this would be a difficult policy to *implement / do / carry off*.
5 In addition, everything the government does to *bring down / curb / crack down* smoking reduces the income they receive from tax on cigarettes.
6 This *equalises / epitomises / expands* the type of dilemma many governments face.
7 On the one hand, they must protect citizens and *cut / slice / chop* health-care costs.
8 On the other hand, they need to *serve / reserve / preserve* people's rights and freedoms and maintain tax income.

**b** What is your opinion on this issue?

## Expressions that are easily confused

**3** Complete the sentences in each pair with the correct expression. What is the difference in meaning?

1 *standard of living / cost of living*
   a It is high rents that make the ............................ so high in this city.
   b The ............................ in this country has improved dramatically over the last few decades.
2 *lifestyle / way of life*
   a The traditional ............................ in some villages hasn't changed for years.
   b Living in the city, I had a very hectic ............................ .
3 *living* (n.) */ livelihood*
   a He was a taxi driver who lost his ............................ when cars were banned from the city centre.
   b He makes his ............................ as a tour guide.
4 *alive / living* (adj.)
   a He's had so many accidents, he's lucky to be ............................ .
   b He is one of our greatest ............................ poets.
5 *lifetime / lifelong*
   a William hasn't been the same since the death of his ............................ friend.
   b He has spent his ............................ fighting against injustice.
6 *outlive / live out*
   a After Jack retired, he decided to ............................ the rest of his days in a quiet country village.
   b Jack is so fit and healthy I'm sure he'll ............................ the rest of his family.

## Words for eating and drinking

**4 a** Look at this extract from the text and mark the verbs that describe ways of drinking. What is the difference in meaning?

> 'Instead of gulping down a Coke in a loud bar, some of my young customers are learning how nice it can be to sip local wine in a place where the music is low.'

**b** Match the verbs on the left to appropriate completions on the right. When might you eat or drink in these ways?

| | | | |
|---|---|---|---|
| 1 | munch | a | a biscuit/sandwich |
| 2 | suck | b | a fizzy drink from the bottle |
| 3 | swig | c | a drink through a straw |
| 4 | wolf down | d | a glass of water in one go |
| 5 | nibble at | e | an apple |
| 6 | pick at | f | food or drink quickly and greedily |
| 7 | guzzle | g | your food |
| 8 | chew | h | your dinner |
| 9 | drain | i | your food carefully before swallowing |

►SRB  p50

## Listening 1    Developing skills (Part 1)

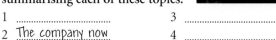

**Before you listen**

1   Do you recognise this logo and slogan? What do you know about the company?

**Listening for gist**

2   a   🎧 You are going to hear a man talking about the company. The talk covers four main topics. Listen and write three or four words summarising each of these topics.

1   ....................................    3   ....................................
2   The company now    4   ....................................

b   Each of these sentence openers was used to introduce a new topic in the talk. Match them to one of the topics you listed in Exercise 2a.
a   *However, it's not all been plain sailing.*
b   *Nike has responded to these accusations by …*
c   *Well, the company's grown hugely since then, and is currently …*
d   *Originally, when it was started up …*

**Identifying key information**

3   a   🎧 Words or phrases giving key information are often stressed by the speaker. Listen to the first part of the talk again and underline the **three** words or phrases in the list below that are stressed.

| | | | |
|---|---|---|---|
| *manufacturer* | *changed* | *logo* | *Blue Ribbon Sports* |
| *was called* | *Nike* | *student* | *goddess* |

b   For sentence completion tasks, you often need to understand what reference words such as nouns or pronouns refer to. Can you remember what the highlighted words refer to in these extracts from the recording?
1   Originally, when it was started up in the USA in the 1960s, the company was called Blue Ribbon Sports.
2   She got a fee of just $35 for designing it, and it's been used by Nike ever since.

c   Now use your answers to Exercises 3a and 3b to help you to complete these gapped sentences.

The sports goods manufacturer [          1          ] was known as Blue Ribbon Sports in the 1960s.

In 1971, a student produced the [          2          ] which is still used by Nike today.

**Sentence completion**

4   a   🎧 Read through the sentences below. Then listen to the rest of the recording and complete each sentence with a word or short phrase.

Nike produce most of its [          3          ] in developing countries.

Campaigners have accused Nike of human rights violations and providing unsatisfactory [          4          ] for employees.

In response, Nike has now set up a code of conduct for its manufacturers, including a ban on [          5          ]

The Indonesian project called [          6          ] shows how Nike can benefit the global community.

b   Compare and justify your answers with reference to the recording.

**Discussion**

5   In what other ways may multinational companies be a positive or negative force?

# English in Use 1 (Paper 3 Part 1)

**Lead-in**

1 In what ways can a country benefit from tourism? What are the possible disadvantages?

**Lexical cloze**

▶ Task strategies page 169

2 a Read the title and text quickly. What is the problem? What solutions are proposed by the organisation Tourist Concern?

b Do the task. Read the task strategies on page 169 before you start and use the Help clues below if necessary.

For questions **1–15**, read the text below and decide which answer **A**, **B**, **C** or **D** best fits each space. The exercise begins with an example (**0**).

## Making tourism a benefit

The growth of cheap and readily (0) B air travel has helped turn tourism into one of the world's largest (1)......... . But behind the image projected by the glossy brochures, there is a less positive (2)........ to the situation. In Goa, for example, indigenous peoples have been displaced to (3)........ way for hotels and golf (4)........ , and local fishermen have been (5)........ access to the beaches from which they set off for work. One (6)........ study has shown that 60 per cent of foreign capital (7)........ in tourism in developing countries returns to first-world countries, and although tourism often provides employment, much of it is low-skilled and very (8)........ paid.

Recently, however, a British organisation, Tourism Concern, surprised everyone by mounting an (9)........ vigorous campaign for tourism which respects the rights of local people. They argue that local people are at present (10)........ near as involved as they should be in decisions about how to (11)........ their area for tourism. (12)........ , they believe tourists should be actively encouraged to use what is often perfectly satisfactory accommodation offered by local communities, and to fly with airlines (13)........ in the host countries. This would (14)........ that jobs are provided at all (15)........ and that capital does not disappear out of the country.

| | | | |
|---|---|---|---|
| 0 A known | B available | C suitable | D convenient |
| 1 A industries | B trades | C productions | D deals |
| 2 A face | B section | C edge | D side |
| 3 A leave | B make | C get | D move |
| 4 A pitches | B grounds | C courses | D courts |
| 5 A rejected | B denied | C disallowed | D stopped |
| 6 A comprehensive | B inclusive | C complete | D total |
| 7 A provided | B placed | C speculated | D invested |
| 8 A hardly | B weakly | C poorly | D roughly |
| 9 A extensively | B extremely | C utterly | D actually |
| 10 A no one | B nothing | C nobody | D nowhere |
| 11 A grow | B inflate | C reproduce | D develop |
| 12 A Nevertheless | B Despite this | C Furthermore | D On the contrary |
| 13 A based | B created | C stood | D laid |
| 14 A promise | B agree | C undertake | D ensure |
| 15 A heights | B planes | C levels | D steps |

**HELP**

➤ **Question 1**
Which word collocates with *tourism*? We often talk about *the tourist …*

➤ **Question 3**
Which word completes the fixed expression with *way*?

➤ **Question 4**
All of these are used with sports, but only one is used in golf.

➤ **Question 8**
Only one of these collocates with *paid* to mean *badly*.

**Task analysis**

3 Which questions test these combinations?
1 adverb + adjective  2 adjective + noun

**Discussion**

4 Polls carried out by tour operators suggest that the demand for 'responsible tourism' is growing. Answer the questions on page 206, then compare your answers with the poll findings at the bottom of page 207.

# Language development 1

▶ Grammar reference page 180

## Modifying gradable and ungradable adjectives

**1** **a** Look at the highlighted words in this extract from the text on page 76 and answer the questions below.

> 'A British Organisation, Tourism Concern, surprised everyone by mounting an *extremely vigorous* campaign for tourism which …'

1 What is the function of the adverb?
2 What other adverb(s) would fit here?
3 Why is *absolutely* not possible?

**b** Tick (✓) the sentences that use modifying adverbs correctly. Correct the others.
1 It is totally obvious that tourism has many drawbacks.
2 It is absolutely important that the local people and the environment are protected.
3 The ecosystem of these islands is very unique.
4 Residents are deeply divided about the expansion of tourism.
5 Some of the islanders have become completely rich as a result of tourism.
6 But many are somewhat furious about what is happening.
7 They have formed an association which is dead opposed to further development.

**2** Some adverbs are used in combination with certain adjectives only. Complete the text by choosing the adverb that collocates with the adjective in bold.

Until recently, progress on the tiny African islands of São Tomé and Príncipe has been (1)................... slow. For many years, the islands have been (2)................... **dependent** on foreign aid. With the discovery of oil, however, life for the 140,000 inhabitants is about to become (3)................... **different**.

Not all the changes are likely to be (4)................... **beneficial**. The islanders are (5)................... **attached** to their unspoiled beaches and rainforest, and some people worry that the islands' (6)................... **balanced** environment will become (7)................... **polluted**. The government has drawn up (8)................... **publicised** plans on how the new income from the (9)................... **valuable** discovery will be spent on improving education and health, for which funds are currently (10)................... **inadequate**.

A few residents remain (11)................... **opposed** to the development, fearing that the consequences will be (12)................... **disastrous**. However, the majority are looking forward to becoming (13)................... **wealthy** in the near future.

| | | |
|---|---|---|
| 1 A totally | B painfully | C absolutely |
| 2 A heavily | B bitterly | C most |
| 3 A highly | B seriously | C utterly |
| 4 A heavily | B entirely | C perfectly |
| 5 A completely | B seriously | C deeply |
| 6 A perfectly | B totally | C painfully |
| 7 A highly | B totally | C heavily |
| 8 A entirely | B widely | C deeply |
| 9 A seriously | B heavily | C highly |
| 10 A terribly | B totally | C heavily |
| 11 A bitterly | B painfully | C widely |
| 12 A painfully | B utterly | C deeply |
| 13 A highly | B perfectly | C seriously |

**3** **a** Complete the text below using an appropriate adverb from box A and adjective from box B. Use each word once only.

A

> absolutely  fairly  totally  completely  terribly
> really  somewhat  very  pretty  quite  slightly
> almost  virtually  rather  a bit  relatively

B

> empty  tedious  irate  pleased  cheap  unique
> alarmed  perfect  similar  furious  unusual
> delighted  identical  relieved

My uncle was (1)................... when a restaurant belonging to a well-known global chain opened next door to his. The prices at the new place were (2)................... compared to his. The following week, his restaurant was (3)................... as his regular customers went to try the new restaurant.

After a couple of weeks, however, he was (4)................... when his business started to return. Now both restaurants co-exist happily together. Cautious people tend to choose the chain, knowing that the decor will be (5)................... to others they have visited and that the production-line food will be (6)................... . Others prefer my uncle's place, as his personal style of decoration is (7)..................., and his food, based on his family's secret recipes and odd mix of ingredients, is (8)................... .

**b** Compare your answers with other students. How many different combinations are possible?

**4** Complete these sentences with your own ideas.
1 I feel perfectly safe when …
2 My town/area/region is heavily dependent on …
3 It's painfully obvious that we need …
4 I think that it is totally unacceptable to …
5 I would be bitterly disappointed if …
6 I find it completely incomprehensible that …

# Writing 1   Selecting and ordering information

## Writing strategy

In Paper 2 Part 1, you have to process information from different texts and combine it into a single piece of writing.
- Read the input carefully and mark the points you need to include.
- Ignore irrelevant information.
- Make a paragraph plan before you start writing.

1   You recently visited Australia and went on a tour to Uluru (part of the Kata Tjuta National Park). A friend has sent you a cutting from the local paper, which is critical of the way the Anangu are managing the site.

a   Read the newspaper cutting, your notes on the itinerary you received from the tour promoter, and the extract from a government report.

> Why are the Anangu people making it so difficult for tourists to climb Ayers Rock? After all, they benefit from tourism, and it is in their interests to increase visitor numbers to the rock. Yet they have had the airstrip and Resort Camp removed from the park area around the rock, and now they're planning to get rid of the car park so as to discourage climbers. Surely this is not a sensible policy?

The Anangu (who've been there over 20,000 years!) call it Uluru. They should have a greater role in promotion/tour organisation. The big profits go to outsiders!

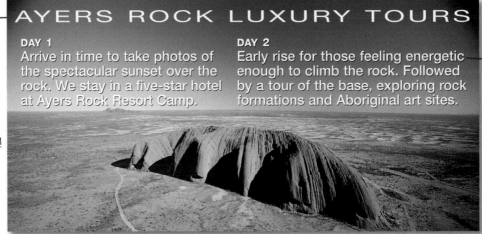

## AYERS ROCK LUXURY TOURS

**DAY 1**
Arrive in time to take photos of the spectacular sunset over the rock. We stay in a five-star hotel at Ayers Rock Resort Camp.

**DAY 2**
Early rise for those feeling energetic enough to climb the rock. Followed by a tour of the base, exploring rock formations and Aboriginal art sites.

The Anangu never climb it. It's a sacred site. We should respect their ancient traditions. Ban climbing!

## Summary of key points

- 24% of household income for the Anangu comes from tourism – mainly low-paid seasonal work around the site.
- Visitor numbers to Uluru are currently 400,000 a year. This is low compared with many other National Parks, and numbers could be increased.

- Last year, vandalism and litter were reduced, but there was an increase in water pollution and destruction of wild plants.
- A Culture Centre has been built, which aims to educate visitors about aspects of the Anangu culture, and the spiritual importance of the area to their people.

b   Answer these questions, and mark the parts that give you the information.
1   Why is Uluru important to the Anangu people?
2   What benefits does tourism bring them? What problems does it cause?
3   Do you think the Anangu want to encourage or discourage tourism to Uluru?
4   What does the government want?
5   What does the writer of the newspaper article want?
6   What's your opinion, according to your notes on the itinerary? What do you think should happen?

▶ Writing reference page 193

2   Prepare to write a letter to the newspaper editor, saying why you disagree with the criticisms expressed and putting forward your views.

a   Decide what information in the input you can use to support your opinion, then write a paragraph plan.

b   Compare and discuss your plan with a partner. Have you selected the same information from the input? Is all the information relevant?

3   Write your letter.

# 5B A fight for survival

## Listening 2 (Paper 4 Part 1)

**Before you listen**

1 a You are going to hear a talk about the history of Easter Island in the Pacific, which is famous for its large stone statues. Look at the photo and answer the following questions.
   1 Why do you think these ancient statues were built?
   2 What do you think might be the link between the statues and the collapse of the society that built them?

   b Read through the sentences in the listening task below. What answers do they give to the questions above?

**Sentence completion**

▶ Task strategies pages 170 and 171

2 🎧 Do the task below. Read the task strategies on pages 170 and 171 before you start and use the Help clues if necessary. Listen to the recording twice.

You will hear the environmentalist Ian Stein giving a talk about the history of Easter Island in the Pacific. For questions **1–8**, complete the sentences.

### The Statues of Easter Island

Ian describes Easter Island as one of the most [ 1 ] islands in the world.

The local people built stone platforms called *ahu*, mostly near the island's [ 2 ]

The position of the statues suggests that they were regarded as providing [ 3 ], as well as being objects of worship.

The job of constructing the statues was made easier by the ready availability of food such as fish, [ *and* 4 ]

The islanders built larger and larger statues as [ 5 ] between rival tribes increased.

The method chosen for the [ 6 ] of the statues contributed to the loss of trees on the island.

By 1600, a great deal of wood was already being used as a result of an increase in the island's [ 7 ]

The first European explorers found the surviving Easter Islanders living in [ 8 ] on very limited resources.

**HELP**
➤ Question 2
   *Fields* and *villages* and *coast* are mentioned, but which were the platforms near to?
➤ Question 5
   You are listening for an abstract noun – what kind of things could increase *between tribes*?

**Task analysis**

3 Compare and justify your answers.
   1 What signals helped you identify the information you needed?
   2 What kind of words were mainly needed in the gaps (e.g. verbs, nouns, adjectives)?

**Discussion**

4 Discuss these questions.
   1 What measures could the islanders have taken to prevent disaster? Why didn't they?
   2 What relevance does this story have to the present day?

## Speaking (Paper 5 Parts 3 and 4)

**Vocabulary: the environment**

1 a Look at the photos and say what important environmental problem you think each one illustrates.

b Put the words and phrases into five groups relating to each of the problems you identified.

| | |
|---|---|
| *become pest/disease resistant* | *global warming* |
| *bio-degradable materials* | *health hazards* |
| *bio-diversity* | *improve flavour/nutrition* |
| *build-up of greenhouse gases* | *incinerate/recycle waste* |
| *contaminate water supplies* | *lead to/run the risk of* |
| *deforestation* | *famine/drought/flooding* |
| *destroy the ozone layer* | *loss of natural habitat* |
| *dispose of/dump (waste/rubbish)* | *pollute (the atmosphere)* |
| *DNA technology* | *spray crops with pesticides* |
| *extinction* | *trigger allergies* |
| *genetically modified crops* | *use up/run out of/conserve resources* |
| *give off/emit (carbon dioxide/ toxic fumes)* | *wipe out/kill off (animals/fish/birds)* |

c Match these captions to the photos and complete them using words and expressions from Exercise 1b in the correct form.

1 *Waste should be disposed of carefully or (1)........................... rather than dumped. Greater use of (2)........................... materials will help to (3)........................... the world's natural (4)..........................., and benefit the environment.*

2 *Cars (5)........................... poisonous gases, which (6)........................... the atmosphere, and cause illnesses and allergies.*

3 *The (7)........................... of greenhouse gases has led to (8)..........................., which is likely to cause more frequent droughts, (9)........................... and (10)............................*

4 *Although some farmers welcome the idea of (11)........................... crops, as they will reduce the use of conventional (12)..........................., there is concern about potential (13)........................... to people and animals.*

5 *(14)........................... in many parts of the world has led to (15)........................... and the (16)........................... of many species.*

d Which of the issues in Exercise 1c do you think is most worrying?

Ⓒ

Ⓓ

Ⓔ

STOP NOW
BEFORE IT'S
TOO LATE!

## Sample answer

▶ Task strategies pages 171 and 172

**2 a** Check the task strategy for Part 3 on page 172 before you start.

**b** 🎧 Look at the photos again and listen to the examiner's instructions. What TWO things does the task involve?

**c** 🎧 Listen to two people doing the task.
1 Do you disagree with anything they say about each problem?
2 What is their conclusion?

**d** How successfully did they carry out the task? Did they follow the advice in the task strategies?

## Useful language: intensifying expressions

**3 a** Listen to the sample answer again and complete these sentences with between one and four words.
1 The more we tamper with food, .............. risks we run with our health.
2 There are more .............. roads being built every day.
3 I don't think we're doing .............. enough to restrict traffic in our cities.
4 Our summers seem to be getting .............. all the time.
5 The situation seems to be .............. as it was years ago.
6 I don't think that the problem of waste disposal is .............. as bad as they make out.
7 I'd say air pollution is .............. the most serious problem on a day-to-day basis.

**b** Which statements above do you agree/disagree with?

## Collaborative task

**4 a** Work in pairs and do the task in Exercise 2. Time yourselves. Remember to follow the task strategies.

**b** Tell the class briefly which problem you have chosen and why.

## Developing the discussion

▶ Task strategy page 172

**5** Work in pairs. Take turns to ask and answer these questions. Read the task strategy for Part 4 on page 172 before you begin.
1 What do you think are the most important environmental issues where you live?
2 What achievements have there been in dealing with them?
3 What new government policies would most benefit the environment?
4 How far do you think genetically modified crops are a benefit? a danger?

▶SRB  p55

## English in Use 2 (Paper 3 Part 5)

**Lead-in**

1 Discuss these questions.
   1 Have you ever experienced weather conditions like the ones in the photo?
   2 What precautions would you take if a blizzard was forecast in the area where you lived?

**Register transfer**

▶ Task strategies pages 169 and 170

**HELP**

➤ Question 3
Which word completes the phrasal verb?

➤ Question 4
Does *substantial* mean *a lot* or *a little*?

➤ Question 9
What's a less formal way of saying *it's recommended*?

2 a Read both texts quickly and answer these questions.
   1 How did your ideas in Exercise 1 compare with the advice in the leaflet?
   2 How is the style of the second text different from the first?

   b Do the task. If necessary, check the task strategies and use the Help clues.

   Read the following government leaflet about how to survive severe weather in winter. Use the information to complete the numbered gaps in the magazine article. The words you need **do not occur** in the leaflet. **Use no more than two words for each gap**. The exercise begins with an example (**0**).

**LEAFLET**

## SEVERE WINTER WEATHER

*Please take time to read this leaflet.*

**Precautions**
• As part of your preparations for a possible blizzard, ensure that there are sufficient ready-made meals in your house, as well as adequate stocks of fuel.
• Should your area be unfortunate enough to be battered by a blizzard, postpone all car journeys until there is a substantial improvement in the weather.
• Stay indoors, except in an emergency situation.

**Driving**
• Drivers on a journey should immediately seek refuge from the blizzard.
• It is generally recommended that drivers remain inside a stationary vehicle which is unable to move, then make contact with the Local Authority (Emergency Department) on their mobile phones and indicate their location.

**Dress**
It is advisable to wear layers of loose clothes to retain body heat and aid air circulation.

**MAGAZINE ARTICLE**

Once again, the government is urging us to get everything ready (0) in case there's a blizzard. We should check that we (1).............. pre-prepared food and fuel indoors. (2).............. our district is unlucky enough to be hit by a blizzard, we should put (3).............. any car journeys until the weather has got a (4).............. . Indeed, we shouldn't even go outdoors (5)............. is absolutely necessary.

For those drivers already (6)............. road, the government's advice is to look for a place to (7)............. from the bad weather at (8)............. . Usually, it's a (9)............. not to leave the car when we're stuck, but to use a mobile phone to get (10)............. with the people in the emergency department of our Local Authority and let them know where (11)............. .

Finally, the government's advice on dress is to avoid tight clothes and wear one layer on top of the other, to (12)............. the heat of our bodies while (13)............. air to move around.

**Task analysis**

3 Answer these questions about the task.
   1 Did you use the words around the gaps to help you find the right part of the leaflet to get the information from?
   2 Which questions required a conditional structure?

# Language development 2

▶ Grammar reference page 180

## Review of conditionals

**1 a** Read these sentences and match the conditions 1–4 to the concepts a–d.

1 The farmers might be happier if we had more rain.
2 The windows rattled if the wind blew strongly.
3 If it hadn't stopped raining, the town would have been flooded by now.
4 If it snows tonight, I'm staying at home tomorrow.

a Events that can occur at any time; *if* can be replaced by *when*
b Possible or likely events/situations
c Events/situations that are unlikely to happen, or contrary to known facts
d Unreal/impossible past situations

**b** Mark the correct form in each pair.

1 If it *snows / will snow* again this week, the match on Saturday *can / could* be cancelled.
2 If it *rains / had rained* during the night, the ground *was / might be* too wet to play.
3 It was a good holiday, but if it *was / had been* sunnier, I would *enjoy / have enjoyed* it more.
4 If there *is / was* an avalanche warning, I *won't / should* go near the mountain.
5 If the typhoon *hit / had hit* the island, everything *had been / would have been* destroyed.
6 If a giant hailstone *hit / hits* you, it *would / would've* hurt!

## Mixed conditionals

**2 a** What two different conditional patterns are combined in these sentences?

1 If I was afraid of lightning, I wouldn't have gone out in the storm.
2 If we had listened to the forecast, we wouldn't be in trouble now.

**b** Complete these sentences with the correct form of the verbs in brackets and a modal verb where appropriate.

1 If the inhabitants of Easter Island ............. (*not destroy*) their forests, their descendants ............. (*still live*) there today.
2 If humans ............. (*not be*) so competitive, the islanders ............. (*not build*) so many statues.
3 The island ............. (*not be*) so interesting for tourists today if the islanders ............. (*not erect*) the statues.
4 If we ............. (*not use*) so many chemicals, we ............. (*not kill off*) so many plants and animals.
5 If we ............. (*invest*) more in finding alternatives to oil, we ............. (*not be*) so dependent on it now.

**c** Complete the following sentences with as many results as you can think of in the present and past.

1 If cars ............. (*not invent*), …
2 If we ............. (*have*) one World Government, …

## Alternatives to *if*

**3 a** Rewrite these sentences using the words given in brackets. Make any changes necessary.

1 If economic conditions don't deteriorate again, air travel will continue to grow. (*unless*)
2 The total number of flights will only decline if fares rise steeply. (*not … unless*)
3 Many people will continue to fly even if the price of tickets goes up. (*whether … or not*)
4 Targets for reducing atmospheric pollution can be met, but only if air travel is dramatically reduced. (*provided that*)
5 Most people are in favour of new airports, but not if they are built near their own homes. (*as long as*)
6 A new airport might already have been built if it had not been for opposition from local groups. (*but for*)
7 People should protest, because if they don't, the new airport will go ahead. (*otherwise*)

**b** Discuss these questions.

1 Is the issue of airports one that concerns people where you live?
2 Are you in favour of/against more airports?

## Omission of *if*

**4 a** Compare the sentences in each pair. What are the differences in form and register?

1 a If you should need assistance, please do not hesitate to contact me.
 b Should you need assistance, please do not hesitate to contact me.
2 a If I had known this would happen, I would never have agreed to your proposal.
 b Had I known this would happen, I would never have agreed to your proposal.
3 a If it wasn't for the fact that he is under 18, we would prosecute.
 b Were it not for the fact that he is under 18, we would prosecute.

**b** Complete these sentences with a suitable word: *had, should, were.*

1 ............. we known you were having difficulties, the company would have been happy to help.
2 ............. the alarm sound, please vacate the room immediately.
3 ............. James not to apply, the consequences would be unimaginable.

## Writing 2 Article (Paper 2 Part 1)

**Lead-in**

1 **Discuss these questions.**
1 Is litter a problem where you live? Who/What causes it?
2 What suggestions can you make to deal with the problem?

**Understand the task**

▶ Writing reference page 192

2 **Read the task and answer these questions.**
1 WHO are you and WHAT are you going to write?
2 What is the PURPOSE of your piece of writing?
3 What POINTS have you been asked to include by the editor?
4 What INFORMATION do the other pieces of input contain?
5 What STYLE will be appropriate?
6 What will make the reader think it's a WELL-WRITTEN piece?

You are studying at a college in Britain and are the student representative on the Health and Safety Committee. Recently the principal launched a campaign against litter in the college. She organised a Clean-up Day and introduced some new policies to help keep the college clean. Since then, the editor of the student newspaper has asked you to write an article for the paper describing what happened on Clean-up Day and outlining the response to the principal's policies.

Read the email from the editor, the poster about the Clean-up Day, and your own notes about the campaign. Then, using the information **appropriately**, write the article (approximately 250 words). You should use your own words as far as possible.

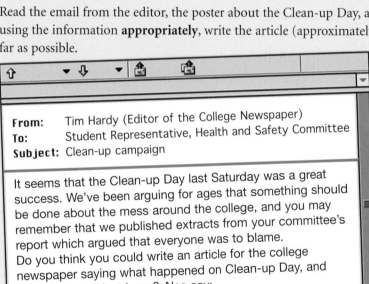

**From:** Tim Hardy (Editor of the College Newspaper)
**To:** Student Representative, Health and Safety Committee
**Subject:** Clean-up campaign

It seems that the Clean-up Day last Saturday was a great success. We've been arguing for ages that something should be done about the mess around the college, and you may remember that we published extracts from your committee's report which argued that everyone was to blame.
Do you think you could write an article for the college newspaper saying what happened on Clean-up Day, and what the effect has been? Also say:
– what the principal's most popular new policy is;
– which of her measures are unpopular (if any).
Many thanks.

**CLEAN-UP DAY**
**VOLUNTEERS NEEDED!**

Help us:

• clean up the college – rubbish bags and rubber gloves provided!

• distribute leaflets about how to keep our college clean!

*Free buffet supper for all volunteers!*

✓ Successes

Clean-up Day – people feel more positive about a clean college

Extra bins – encourage people not to drop litter on the ground

No smoking – most popular policy – even smokers hated seeing cigarette ends everywhere!

✗ Failures

Leaflets – only led to more litter being dropped!

Fines for dropping litter – far too high – will never work

## Plan your article

▶ Writing strategy (planning) page 30
(coherence) page 46

**3 a** Mark the information you will select from the input.

**b** Make a paragraph plan. Your article will need between four and six paragraphs, including:

- an attention-grabbing introduction (e.g. a question or a surprising statement)
- a suitable conclusion (e.g. light-hearted/inspiring/brief and to the point).

Here are some ideas for paragraph topics (not necessarily in an appropriate order):

- The effect of the Clean-up Day
- The policies which work
- The policies which don't work
- Clean-up Day and the reason for it

**c** Make notes of what you will include in each paragraph. Will you mention the newspaper campaign? If so, in which paragraph?

**d** Which of these would make the best title for your article and why?

**A**
> **The pros and cons of the principal's anti-litter campaign**

**B**
> **The big clean-up campaign!**

**C**
> Litter louts beware!

## Language and content

**4 a** Read the sentences (1–6) below and match them with the ways of keeping the reader's attention listed (a–f). In some cases, there is more than one possibility.

1 'More bins, please!' was one of the comments we received.
2 Don't forget to keep the emails coming in.
3 What a transformation!
4 We issued rubbish bags and rubber gloves and set you to work.
5 Amazingly, the most popular policy has been the smoking ban, even among smokers.
6 What you don't like, though, is the introduction of fines.

a addressing the reader directly
b emphatic structures
c direct speech
d exclamations
e creating a vivid picture
f surprising information

**b** Decide which of these expressions you could use in your article. Match them to the paragraphs in your plan in Exercise 3.

| | |
|---|---|
| **Addressing the reader** | *Have you ever wondered (what the college would be like if) … ?* <br> *If the answer is (yes) … , you (should have) …* <br> *As you know, (our paper has been campaigning) …* <br> *Some (courageous volunteers) among you …* <br> *You were also (critical of) …* <br> *Doesn't it just make everyone feel (positive about) … ?* <br> *From now on, let's …* |
| **Giving your own opinion** | *We know from (the many emails we received) …* <br> *If we are going to (make our college) …* <br> *Not (an easy task) …* <br> *(Small reward), perhaps, for …* <br> *It's clearly been a good idea to …* <br> *For the first time that any of us can remember, …* |
| **Conveying information** | *On the (day itself) …* <br> *The (editor) has received …* <br> *Judging from the emails we've received, …* <br> *The idea was that …* |

## Write your article

**5** Now write your article, using the ideas and some of the language above. Write your answer in about 250 words.

## Check your article

▶ Writing reference page 188

**6** Edit your work using the checklist on page 188.

▶SRB p60

# Module 5: Review

## 1 Decide which word or phrase best fits each space.

1 Some forms of illness are ........ food allergies.
   A suffered from   B sparked off   C triggered by
   D developed through

2 Not long after I'd cast my line into the river, a fish started ........ my bait.
   A wolfing down   B nibbling at   C draining
   D sucking away at

3 The company became a worldwide success, but it hadn't all been ........ .
   A plain sailing   B effective measures
   C perfectly satisfactory   D a pushover

4 I love sitting in a café watching the world drift ........ .
   A away   B apart   C off   D by

5 Hi-tech factories ........ the spirit of the age.
   A stand for   B personify   C epitomise   D mean

6 The company went broke trying to ........ their rivals.
   A do out of   B outdo   C do without   D do up

7 There is ........ evidence to suggest that the world is getting hotter.
   A ample   B lavish   C overflowing   D a load

8 You'll never make ........ as a writer – it's too competitive.
   A your occupation   B your livelihood
   C employment   D a living

9 He took off his shoes ........ local custom.
   A with respect to   B in deference to   C regarding
   D taking into account

10 There's been a meeting to ........ trade between the two countries.
   A carry on   B engage in   C promote   D conduct

11 He wasn't really eating his dinner, he was just ........ .
   A munching it   B swigging it   C chewing it over
   D picking at it

12 Residents have been mounting an extremely ........ campaign against a new supermarket.
   A vital   B vigorous   C wholehearted   D eager

## 2 Complete the sentences with a word or phrase.

1 Some new fashions take a long time to ........................... with the public.

2 Unless they are protected, some animal species will soon be ........................... .

3 You should avoid inhaling the fumes ........................... by paint.

4 I bought a remote farmhouse in Scotland to get ........................... it all.

5 The president ........................... the risk of being assassinated every time he goes out.

6 He's a real non-conformist, who loves to ........................... against the tide.

7 A young hooligan was arrested for ........................... the peace.

8 Customers are allowed to linger ........................... their coffee until midnight.

9 Inevitably, many poorer countries are still ........................... on foreign aid.

10 There's a long way to ........................... before we eradicate the disease entirely.

## 3 Find and correct the ten mistakes with modifiers and conditionals.

As people are becoming more weight conscious, the major fast-food chains are now offering healthy options as an alternative to traditional burgers and chips. However, if customers didn't complain, there probably wouldn't now be salads on the menu at all. Some customers have been terribly delighted with these new additions, while others have been bitterly upset. Were you one of the ones deeply attached to burgers and chips, don't worry, they're still on the menu.

But for this change of strategy, the fast-food chains' profits will decline even further. The effect on profit margins has been heavily beneficial. What people don't realise is that when you eat a Caesar salad from a fast-food chain, you'd often consume just as many calories as you would if it is a plate of burger and chips! It's utterly obvious that if people simply eat less, there wouldn't be the current obesity crisis.

## 4 Complete the second sentence so that it has a similar meaning to the first.

1 Racism will decline if we make a concerted effort to fight it.
   Provided ........................................................... .

2 Many people are suspicious of genetic modification of food, even if it's safe.
   Whether or not ........................................................... .

3 There'll be a severe water shortage in a few years if nothing is done about climate change.
   Unless ........................................................... .

4 Globalisation might not have spread so quickly if the Soviet Union hadn't collapsed.
   Had ........................................................... .

5 There will always be pollution if we carry on burning fossil fuels
   As long as ........................................................... .

6 There'll need to be more immigration into western Europe if the population carries on declining.
   Should ........................................................... .

7 We wouldn't know what's going on in some countries if it weren't for the Internet.
   But for ........................................................... .

8 If the poor are not to get poorer and the rich richer, we have to have fair-trade policies.
   ........................................... . Otherwise, ........................................... .

# MODULE 6
## Looking forward, looking back

### Overview

- **Reading:** multiple matching (Paper 1 Part 4)
- **Vocabulary:** expressing opinions about the future
- **Listening 1:** predicting; noticing cues, examples and distractors; note completion (Paper 4 Part 2)
- **English in Use 1:** open cloze (Paper 3 Part 2)
- **Language development 1:** emphasis: cleft sentences
- **Writing 1:** cohesion; linking devices
- **Listening 2:** note completion (Paper 4 Part 2)
- **Speaking:** feelings and reactions; long turn (Paper 5 Part 2)
- **English in Use 2:** gapped text (Paper 3 Part 6)
- **Language development 2:** -*ing* or infinitive after verbs
- **Writing 2:** guidebook entry (Paper 2 Part 2)

### Lead-in

- What is the ideal of beauty in your culture? Has it changed compared with the past?
- How far do you agree with the quotations? Give reasons and examples.

  '*Beauty is only skin deep.*' (proverb)

  '*The emphasis should not just be on achieving a superficial beauty, but on discovering things that satisfy both body and soul. To do this successfully, we need to look back at past practices and values, as well as forward to the "wonder cosmetics" of the new millennium.*'

## Reading (Paper 1 Part 4)

**Before you read**    1   Look at the magazine article opposite. How would you answer the questions in the title and subheading?

**Scanning and skimming**    2   a   Look at the list of names in the multiple-matching task below. Scan the article to find how often they are mentioned. Write the appropriate letter (A–E) next to each name. Then skim each section to find out:
    1   the topic area(s) each researcher talks about
    2   the main point they make about it.

     b   Compare your ideas in Exercise 1 with those of the researchers.

**Multiple matching**    3   For questions 1–16, choose your answers from the list of people (A–E). You may choose any of the people more than once.

▶ Task strategies page 168

     a   Look at the two parts of the text that are highlighted. They both refer to *drug companies*, but only one of them answers question 1. Why is the other not correct?

     b   Now complete the task. Check the task strategies on page 168 before you start if necessary. Compare your answers when you have finished.

---

| A | Dr Sally Hancock | C | Dr David Murphy | E | Professor Steve Timms |
| --- | --- | --- | --- | --- | --- |
| B | Professor Susan Cullis | D | Dr Daniel Green | | |

**Which scientist**

| | |
| --- | --- |
| warns about drug companies making false claims? | **1** ............ |
| regrets some people's increasing obsession with appearance? | **2** ............ |
| is pessimistic about reversing a current trend? | **3** ............ |
| has good news for a certain sector of the male population? | **4** ............ |
| believes that some facial features will remain distinctive despite other changes? | **5** ............ |
| is confident that science will help solve a problem that is getting worse? | **6** ............ |
| feels optimistic about potential life expectancy in some parts of the world? | **7** ............ |
| predicts that it will be easier to conceal evidence of ageing? | **8** ............ **9** ............ |
| suggests that there is no short cut to the ideal body shape? | **10** ............ |
| observes that people in some parts of the world are getting physically more alike? | **11** ............ |
| paints a negative picture of young people's future health prospects? | **12** ............ |
| points to a link between a physical disability and certain types of activity? | **13** ............ |
| says that making skin look more youthful will not require a medical operation? | **14** ............ |
| predicts that people will take daily medication to prevent one common condition? | **15** ............ |
| is confident that one existing form of preventive treatment will be used more effectively? | **16** ............ |

---

**Discussion**    4   Discuss these questions.
    1   Which of the possible developments discussed in the article do you think are positive? Which do you feel worried or concerned about? Give reasons.
    2   What area of medical research would you choose to put most money into?

How will we look 100 years from now? Surely we'll all be fitter and more beautiful? Surely not fatter and uglier? We weigh up the latest research.

Science fiction is full of descriptions about how humans might look in the future. It may seem rather far-fetched to think we will have electronic arms and legs, laser vision or be able to fly, as the genre would have us believe. But amongst all these flights of fancy, are there any clues to how our bodies could really look 100 years from now? We interviewed five medical researchers to find out.

One thing is certain, according to **Dr Sally Hancock**, a lecturer in medical sciences. 'Every ten years that go by will mean people in some parts of the world can hope to survive, on average, for an extra couple of years. Which means that a century from now, it'll be the norm to get to the age of 100 if you live in

redundant, too, as in the much longer term we will be putting drugs in our eyes as part of our morning routine to prevent short-sightedness. However, he observes, sadly, 'I fear that, rather than changing our attitudes, advances in science will mean that many people will become even more obsessed by physical perfection and youth.'

**Dr David Murphy** also believes that in the not-too-distant future we will all be able to change our appearance as we wish. 'Although it won't happen overnight, it is likely that at some stage, all people will have to do in order to avoid going grey is to apply a treatment regularly to the roots of the hair. In the very long term, it will also be possible to change hair colour in the same way.'

Professor of genetics **Steve Timms** points out that globalisation is already changing the way we look. 'In Africa, different peoples still look strikingly different, and you can pinpoint where somebody comes from, but you haven't been able to say that in Europe for some time.

# Is this the body of the future?

certain places. If you take care of your health, you might even still be around at 135 years old.'

That's fine, but what shape will we be in? **Professor Susan Cullis**, a medical researcher, does not hold out much hope for us in this area. 'The last 20 years have shown a startling rise in the number of vastly overweight people in the western world, and I can't see any evidence that this pace is going to slow down. Even if it does, the majority of people living there will be obese in 100 years. Those under 20 will continue to be the worst affected, and this will lead to weight-related diseases and premature deaths. In my opinion, obesity will have a bigger impact than anything on how we look, live and die. Yet, as more of us become overweight, expect body ideals to move even further towards the increasingly unattainable – the very thin.'

University professor **Dr David Murphy** is sceptical of any notion of miracle cures, even in 100 years' time. 'Don't be fooled by what the pharmaceutical companies say. However much money they pump into this area, there will never be a drug that allows you to eat what you like and not get fat. The same is true of a "fitness" cure. A drug can only reinforce what you do by yourself. That is not to say there aren't genes for body shape, fitness and so on, but the benefits of exercise on body and mind are so complex that I don't believe drugs will ever be able to replicate these advantages.'

'Drugs will, however, have quite an impact in other areas,' predicts **Dr Daniel Green**, vice-chairman of a research company. 'Men may get fatter, but shiny heads will one day be a thing of the past. There is very promising research going on into growth treatments, using hormones, and I am optimistic that there will be a cure for baldness within a generation. Glasses will be

Everyone seems to be merging together in a kind of "global melting pot", and this process will escalate. Facial appearance and skin colour will be part of this merging, and photographic technology has given geneticists some insight of the "average" face of the future, although some characteristics seem to prove resistant to this – a "strong" nose, for example.'

'Whatever shade it may be, people's complexion will definitely look smoother and more wrinkle-free in 100 years' time,' says **Susan Cullis**. 'The main reason is simply a growing awareness in many parts of the world of the damage caused by the sun. People will continue to become ever more meticulous with the sunscreen. Meanwhile, researchers employed by big corporations are working on a new generation of drugs which they are confident will be able to repair some of the damage already caused. It will also be possible to stop our existing tissue from deteriorating, thus making face-lifts and other cosmetic surgery unnecessary.'

'Technology, in the form of laser treatment, will also help people to avoid the need to wear spectacles,' adds **Sally Hancock**. 'More and more of us, and not just the old, are destined to become short-sighted, as we spend more time reading and doing things on screen. The condition has reached epidemic proportions in some parts of the world, but cheaper and more effective laser technology will make glasses and contact lenses history, long before the relevant preventive drugs become widely available.'

And so we have it. The perfect human of the future. The science may be difficult to predict, but what about people's reaction to it? Do we really want to be perfect? In any case, in a brave new world of near perfect people, perhaps it will be those who are imperfect that are regarded as the most attractive.

# Vocabulary

## Expressing opinions about the future

| A | B | C |
|---|---|---|
| 1 I'm confident/optimistic that | obesity will reach epidemic proportions | a century from now. |
| 2 I predict that | living to 100 will have become the norm | in 100 years' time. |
| 3 I fear that | we will be able to change our appearance | in the (very) short/long term. |
| 4 It seems far-fetched to think that | at will | within a generation. |
| 5 I don't hold out any/much | hair loss will be cured | at some stage. |
| hope that | no one will look their age | one day. |
| 6 I can't see any evidence that | we are going to achieve the perfect body | in the near/not-too-distant |
| 7 I (don't) think/believe that | a cure for cancer will be found | future. |
| 8 In my opinion, it is highly | exercise will become unnecessary | overnight. |
| (un)likely that | laser technology will make glasses and | within a decade. |
| 9 I'm sceptical of claims that | contact lenses history | very soon. |

**1** **a** Make statements about the future using an expression from columns A, B and C. Then compare your ideas with other students.

   **b** Use expressions from above to discuss when you think some of the following could happen.
- a cure for malaria
- a cure for the common cold
- face transplants
- human cloning
- an eat-anything pill
- an effective headache cure
- animal organ transplants

## Using the correct word

**2** **a** Read the extract and mark the correct verb in each set.

> For years, people have dreamt of a product that would prevent skin ageing. In most adults, the quality of their skin starts to **(1)** *deteriorate / decline / slip* after the age of 45. Pharmaceutical companies have **(2)** *pushed / pumped / punched* huge amounts of money into research, but so far have been unable to **(3)** *diagnose / pinpoint / place* the exact cause. Although they have had some success in the laboratory, they have been unable to **(4)** *replicate / indicate / imitate* the results in real life.
>
> Studies **(5)** *point to / build up / make out* a link between diet and skin quality, and this now seems to be the best way forward for most people, **(6)** *returning / reversing / restoring* a trend to seek the solution in science. Changing your diet might be a simpler and cheaper solution than **(7)** *applying / adding / installing* a costly chemical treatment to your skin. People just need to **(8)** *measure / weigh / think* up what is more important: that bar of chocolate or a perfect complexion.

   **b** What other aspects of health can be improved by diet?

## Word formation: suffixes

**3** **a** What does the suffix *-free* mean in this sentence from the text on page 89?

   *'People's complexion will definitely look smoother and more wrinkle-free in 100 years' time.'*

   **b** Complete the following sentences with adjectives formed from the nouns in the box and the suffix *-free*.

| | | | |
|---|---|---|---|
| *debt* | *fat* | *interest* | *lead* |
| *rent* | *sugar* | *tax* | *trouble* |

   1 The company doesn't owe any money to anyone; it is .............. .

   2 I don't have to pay my friend to stay in his flat; I can live there .............. .

   3 The company is offering .............. loans to attract new customers.

   4 As part of my fitness campaign, I'm sticking to .............. drinks.

   5 There was very little traffic today, so I had a .............. journey to work.

   6 Money you win on the lottery is .............. , so you get to keep it all.

   7 Air quality has improved since the introduction of .............. petrol.

   8 Food labelled '95% ..............' sounds much better than 'contains 5% fat'.

   **c** How many more words can you think of that can combine with *-free*? Check in your dictionary. Mark any examples you find in English-language publications and advertisements. Add them to your vocabulary notebook.

 ▶SRB p61

# Listening 1   Developing skills (Part 2)

**Before you listen**   1   Look at the photo, which shows a new piece of apparatus developed for people to use while playing computer games. What do you think its purpose is? How might it work?

**Predicting**   2   In Part 2 of the Listening paper, you will hear the recording only once. It is therefore vital to use the task to help you predict what you're going to hear. Look at the notes below and answer these questions.
1   What are the two main sections of the talk about?
2   What two general types of information will be given in each section?

## WHAT'S IN STORE?

### Modern lifestyles
**Problems**
– people not as (1)............................ nowadays, so obesity is increasing
– people feel more (2)......................... than in the past

**Possible solutions**
– (3).......................... to keep personal records and to set goals
– computer games that provide exercise (with a (4).......................... instead of a gamepad)

### Ageing population
**Problems**
– not enough young people to take care of growing number of old people

**Possible solutions**
– (5)......................... to allow continued independence
– computer-based (6)........................., e.g. games, chats
– drugs and special (7)......................... to slow or stop ageing process

**Noticing cues, examples and distractors**   3   a   🎧 Listen to the first part of the recording and complete questions 1 and 2 in the exam task.

b   Listen again and identify in the recording
1   a phrase meaning *lifestyle*.
2   two examples of how people are *less active*.
3   a phrase which means *obesity is increasing*.
4   a word meaning *more*.
5   a phrase meaning ... *than in the past*.

c   The speaker uses the words ... *greedy than previous generations*. Why is *greedy* not the correct answer to question 1?

d   To help you, the information you need may be repeated during the recording, using different words.
1   How often did you hear a reference to the topic of question 2?
2   Was the word in the same form each time?
3   Which word form did you need for question 2?

e   Now look at the tapescript on page 206 and check your answers.

**Note completion**   4   🎧 Listen to the rest of the recording and complete the notes for questions 3–7 in the exam task. Then compare and justify your answers.

**Discussion**   5   Discuss these questions.
1   In your opinion, what are the best ways to avoid stress?
2   Which of the innovations discussed do you think are the most useful?
3   Can you suggest other ways to help old people remain independent as long as possible?

## 6A

## English in Use 1 (Paper 3 Part 2)

**Lead-in**

1 Discuss these questions.
1 How many hours a night do you sleep on average?
2 Would you like to be able to manage on less sleep?

**Open cloze**

▶ Task strategies page 169

2 a Read the title and the text below quickly and answer these questions. (Ignore the spaces at this stage.)
1 What is *narcolepsy*?
2 What benefits would the new drug have?

b Do the task. Check the task strategies on page 169 before you start and use the Help clues if necessary.

For questions **1–15**, complete the following article by writing each missing word in the space. **Use only one word for each space**. The exercise begins with an example (**0**).

### A New Cure for a Sleeping Disorder

People are becoming increasingly aware of a medical condition known (**0**) as. narcolepsy, which causes sufferers to fall asleep anywhere at any time of day. It is not just (**1**)............... own safety (**2**)............... is at risk. (**3**)............... man, who worked as a builder, fell asleep at the top of a ladder and could easily have fallen and killed both (**4**)............... and anyone passing by.

For years, (**5**)............... had any idea what caused narcolepsy, and nearly (**6**)............... sufferers were given drugs which had serious side effects. Recently, however, researchers at Stanford University and the University of Texas have come to (**7**)............... conclusion that the problem is (**8**)............... to an insufficient quantity of a chemical called orexin in the brain. (**9**)............... this discovery has led to is the development of a new drug which appears to have (**10**)............... side effects at all.

Neither group (**11**)............... researchers has been slow to realise the potential of (**12**)............... a drug. Not only would it help narcoleptics, but it could be used to help certain groups of workers, (**13**)............... surgeons and soldiers, to stay awake. The very latest trials, carried (**14**)............... on a group of young volunteers, have even shown that, (**15**)............... addition, the drug can improve many other aspects of mental functioning, including memory.

**HELP**
➤ Question 3
Which determiner is needed here? Look at the relative clause that follows: is it defining or non-defining?
➤ Question 4
What kind of pronoun is needed here?
➤ Question 14
What particle does this phrasal verb require?

**Task analysis**

3 Which questions test:
1 determiners and articles?
2 pronouns?
3 a structure which gives emphasis to a sentence?

**Discussion**

4 Discuss these questions.
1 What kind of people, other than surgeons and soldiers, would benefit from a drug that kept them awake?
2 Would you use such a drug?

# Language development 1

▶ Grammar reference page 181

## Emphasis with *What, The thing that, The place where, The reason why,* etc.

**1 a** The information in this sentence can be expressed in different ways for emphasis.
*Dr Christiaan Barnard performed the world's first heart transplant in South Africa in 1967.*

Which piece of information is emphasised in sentences 1–4 below?

| | | |
|---|---|---|
| 1 The person who performed the first heart transplant | | Dr Christiaan Barnard. |
| 2 What Dr Christiaan Barnard did *or* The thing that Dr Christiaan Barnard did | **was** | (to) perform the first heart transplant. |
| 3 The year (that/when) Dr Christiaan Barnard performed the first heart transplant | | 1967. |
| 4 The place where the first heart transplant was performed | | South Africa. |

**b** Rewrite the sentences to emphasise the parts in italics, using the words given.
1 The most cosmetic surgery is performed in *Brazil*. (country)
2 Many people have cosmetic surgery *to improve specific facial features*. (reason)
3 I'd really like to change *the shape of my nose*. (What)
4 You need *to take more exercise*. (What)
5 Companies are most keen to develop *a drug that prevents obesity*. (thing)
6 My sister has always wanted *to look like a movie star*. (All/ever)

**c** Complete these sentences so they are true for you. Then compare with the class.
1 If I had cosmetic surgery, the thing that I'd most like to have done is …
2 What I'd quite like to change …
3 The reason why I would never have cosmetic surgery is …

**2 a** Sentences 1, 3 and 4 in Exercise 1a can be re-expressed as follows. Complete the sentences with the correct information.
1 Dr Christiaan Barnard was the person who …
3 ……………… was the year when …
4 ……………… was the place where …

**b** Can you complete these sentences with the correct information?
1 Crick and Watson were the scientists who discovered the structure of *the atom / DNA / the malaria virus* in 1953.
2 Gene splicing was the invention in *1970 / 1973 / 1979* that started genetic engineering.
3 *1978 / 1981 / 1984* was the year when the first test-tube baby was born.
4 *Melbourne / San Diego / Edinburgh* is the city where Dolly the sheep, the first cloned mammal, was born.

## Emphasis with *It + be*

**3 a** Look at the examples of another type of structure used to emphasise different parts of a sentence.

| | | |
|---|---|---|
| It was | Dr Christiaan Barnard | that/who performed the first heart transplant. |
| | in 1967 | that the first heart transplant was performed. |
| | in South Africa | |

**b** Re-express the sentences starting with *It + be* for emphasis.
1 The Danish geneticist Wilhelm Johannsen coined the term *gene*, not Gregor Mendel. (*It was …*)
2 Obesity rather than cancer is now the major cause of death in the UK. (*It is …*)
3 The link between cigarette smoking and cancer was only identified in the 1950s. (*It wasn't until …*)
4 The last time we had a holiday abroad was three years ago. (*It was …*)
5 I didn't realise I'd left my passport behind until I got to the airport. (*It was only when …*)
6 You're always stressed out because you work so hard. (*It's …*)
7 We can only overcome stress if we identify its causes. (*It is only by …*)

**c** Complete these sentences so they are true for you. Then compare with the class.
1 It's … that I find most stressful in my everyday life.
2 What I do to relax is …
3 The only thing that works for me is …

# Writing 1   Cohesion

## Writing strategy

In the exam, you are assessed on your ability to produce well-constructed sentences and paragraphs which link together well and contain no unnecessary repetition. Make sure you use cohesive devices to connect your ideas.

▶ Writing reference page 200

**1 a Read the sentences and decide what the highlighted reference links refer to. Then check your ideas in the Writing reference.**

1  There are several ways of slowing the ageing process. One method is to replace worn body parts. Another is to avoid excessive sunlight.

2  Tania joined a gym last month. In fact, she's been going there every day since then, which is why I never see her these days.

3  Are you one of those people who eat a lot of meat because they believe it will help them lose weight? If so, you are one of millions following such a diet.

4  Helen doesn't believe in plastic surgery, and neither do I.

**b  Complete this text using expressions from the box.**

| such as | finally | prevent ageing | such claims |
|---------|---------|----------------|-------------|
| what's more | secondly | their | neither do | that's why |
| the ones | whatever | which | this aim | first |

These days, some people believe that, (1)................ your lifestyle, in order to stay young-looking you need to use anti-ageing creams or take antioxidants. (2)................ , there are even unscrupulous health-food manufacturers that maintain that (3)................ food supplements can help to reverse the ageing process. Personally, I don't believe in (4)................ at all, and (5)................ most scientists – at least, not (6)................ I've read.

In fact, I think the best way to (7)................ is to take care of yourself. There are several things you can do to achieve (8)................ . (9)................ , you should eat sensibly, (10)................ means including lots of fresh fruit and vegetables in your diet. (11)................ , you should get regular exercise, (12)................ going for a long daily walk. (13)................ , I believe you need to keep your mind active. (14)................ I'm learning a foreign language!

**2 a  Read the extracts from this leaflet advertising a health club. Mark examples of repetition.**

### INTRODUCTION

We appreciate that the last thing many of you have time to do is to keep fit. However, keeping fit is the key to maintaining a healthy body and the key to maintaining a healthy mind. Because we want you to keep fit, we've created a luxury club that offers a convenient and enjoyable way to achieve your personal fitness goals. It doesn't matter what your personal fitness goals may be. There is another thing. We pride ourselves on offering a welcoming atmosphere, a welcoming atmosphere in which you can feel relaxed and at ease.

### FACILITIES

Once inside this urban paradise, you will find a range of facilities. The facilities are all free to members. Why not take a dip in the heated pool? Or why not enjoy a snack by the poolside? Or perhaps you'd prefer a strenuous workout? If you would like a strenuous workout, the Club offers a large variety of state-of-the-art exercise machines, state-of-the-art exercise machines which will challenge the fittest among you.

We think our club is the best in the city and, we're pleased to say, our members also think it's the best in the city.

**b  Now rewrite the extracts to make them more cohesive and avoid repetition.**

**3  Plan and write an information leaflet about a gym or fitness club in your town or city. Make up the information if necessary.**

▶ Writing reference page 190

 ▶SRB pp64–65

# 6B Unveiling the past

## Listening 2 (Paper 4 Part 2)

**Before you listen** 1 Look at the photos and discuss these questions.
1 Dogs are often called 'man's best friend'. Do you agree with this?
2 How much do you know about the origin of the domestic dog?

**Note completion**

▶ Task strategies pages 170 and 171

2 ∩ Do the task below. Read the task strategies on pages 170 and 171 before you start and use the Help clues if necessary.

You will hear part of a radio talk about the history of the domestic dog. For questions **1–8**, complete the notes. **Listen very carefully, as you will hear the recording ONCE only**.

### The history of the domestic dog

First two animals to be domesticated: – dogs
– [_____] 1

Age of oldest dog fossil found to date: [_____ *years*] 2

Area of the world where dogs were
first domesticated: [_____ 3]

How dogs helped humans at first: – hunting
– [_____ 4]

How dogs spread around the world: [*with* _____ *people* 5]

What dogs were probably first traded for: [_____ *and* ____ 6]

What happened to dogs from around 1500:
– introduction of [_____ *programmes* 7]
– new role as [_____ 8]

**HELP**

➤ **Question 1**
Be careful. Two different time periods are mentioned, but only one answers the question.

➤ **Question 3**
Listen for an area of the world – two are mentioned, but only one is correct.

➤ **Question 7**
Listen for the year: the answer comes soon after it. The key word is also repeated.

**Task analysis** 3 Compare and discuss your answers. What clues in the recording helped you to identify the information you needed?

**Discussion** 4 Discuss these questions.
1 What are the most popular pets in your country?
2 What are the advantages and disadvantages of companion animals for the following people: children, elderly people, people who like to travel, disabled people?

# Speaking (Paper 5 Part 2)

**Vocabulary:
feelings and reactions**

**1 a Look at the photos and discuss these questions.**

1 What do the photos have in common?

2 Judging by their expressions and body language, how do you think the people are feeling? Do they look *stimulated* and *involved*, *fed up* or *indifferent*?

**b Match one or more of the reactions to people in the photos.**

1 I wish I'd found out about this place before, it's great.

2 I'm bored out of my mind – when can we go home?

3 This is much more interesting than I'd expected.

4 This is fun – I'm really getting a lot out of it.

5 I think this has put me off museums for good.

6 This kind of museum is great – it really brings history to life.

**c How would you feel and react in these situations?**

**2 a Explain the difference between the following terms.**

1 admission fee   voluntary donation   season ticket

2 an exhibit   an exhibition   an exhibitor

3 a guide   an attendant   a curator

4 an event   an incident   an experience

5 a catalogue   a guidebook   a brochure   an audio guide

6 wander (around)   trudge (along)   stride

**b Complete the text using appropriate words from Exercise 2a.**

Last week, I went with a friend to see an **(1)**................... of vintage clothing at the local museum. I've got a **(2)**..................., which means I can go as often as I like, but you have to pay extra when it's a special **(3)**................... like this. I'm particularly interested in the history of fashion, and we spent at least two hours **(4)**................... around the show. I'd love to have bought the **(5)**................... to keep, but it was too expensive. We did hire an **(6)**..................., though, which explained a lot of the background. The **(7)**................... in each room were very knowledgeable, too.

**Sample answer**

▶ Task strategies pages 171 and 172

**3 a** ∩ Look at the photos again and listen to the examiner's instructions. What TWO things does the task involve?

**b** ∩ Listen to someone doing the task. Which two photos does he talk about? How far do you agree with what he says?

**c** How successfully did the speaker follow the task strategies? Did he deal with both parts of the task? Did he include anything irrelevant to the task?

## Useful language: ways of adding emphasis

▶ Language development 1 page 93

4 a To emphasise a point, you can:

   A use stress and intonation    C use intensifiers/modifiers
   B change the normal word order    D use an auxiliary verb

   Look at these extracts from the recording and mark an example(s) of emphasis in each sentence. Decide which category (A, B or C) each example belongs to.

   1 The girls are actually *doing* something.
   2 … is becoming much more popular
   3 What I don't like about interactive exhibits is …
   4 It's not just the fact that it's …
   5 So I do think that places where …

   b Complete the second sentence so it is more emphatic than the first.

   1 I really don't know why so many people are interested in fossils.
     Why ........................................ I just don't know!
   2 The cost of admission put me off going to the exhibition.
     It was ........................................ to the exhibition.
   3 I particularly enjoy doing hands-on activities.
     What I ........................................ doing hands-on activities.
   4 I couldn't care less about going on the museum trip.
     I'm not ........................................ bothered about going on the museum trip.

## Long turn

5 Work in pairs.

   TASK 1    a STUDENT A: Do the task in Exercise 3. (About one minute)
     STUDENT B: Look at the photos and listen to your partner, then answer this question: 'Which museum would you find most interesting?' (About 20 seconds)

   TASK 2    b STUDENT B: Look at the photographs on page 206 and do the task. (About one minute)
     STUDENT A: Look at the photos on page 206 and listen to your partner, then answer this question: 'Do you think that life has got better or worse today?' (About 20 seconds)

## Task analysis

6 How well do you think you carried out the tasks? What areas are you best at (e.g. timing, fluency)? Where do you need to improve?

## Discussion

7 Discuss these questions.

   1 How important do you think it is for young people to be aware of the past?
   2 Which areas of the past are you most interested in? Why?
   3 To what extent do schools have responsibility for making students aware of their historic and cultural heritage?
   4 Should all museum admission fees be abolished? Would this make a difference to the numbers of visitors?

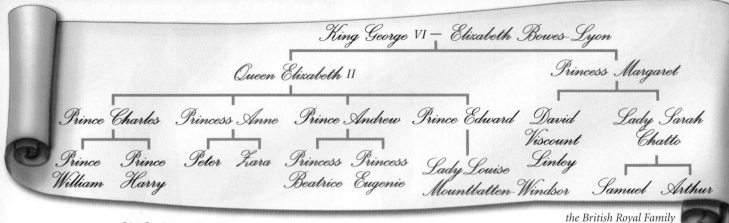

*the British Royal Family*

# English in Use 2 (Paper 3 Part 6)

**Lead-in**

**1** Discuss these questions.

1 How much do you know about your family history?
2 Why do you think some people spend time and money trying to trace their family tree?

**Gapped text**

▶ Task strategies pages 169 and 170

**2 a** Read the text. Ignore the gaps for now. What do you learn about genealogy?

**b** Do the task. Check the task strategies before you begin.

Read the text and then choose from the list (**A–I**) below the best phrase to fill each of the spaces. Each correct phrase may only be used once. **Some of the suggested answers do not fit at all**.

## Tracing your family tree

Genealogy, the history of a family from the past to the present, is one of the most popular subjects on the Internet. Although genealogy has always been conducted professionally for serious legal and financial reasons, as a hobby it began to take off in the 1990s when people started to use the Internet to share information.

Before embarking on genealogy as a hobby, though, you are advised **(1)**............... it is you want to find out about your family and what you will do with the information. Then go from what you know already and work backwards. You should undertake **(2)**............... about as many of your relatives as possible: their date and place of birth, marriage, death and burial. You are encouraged **(3)**............... and talk to relatives and their friends, since a breakthrough often hangs on a single conversation. It's important that you remember **(4)**..............., including a note of where the information came from, for some of the clues will not be obvious at first sight.

After that, you should visit a local records office or reference library **(5)**..............., including wills and tax records. You might also want to join a Family History Society and share information with others. From then on, it's time **(6)**............... the computer, whether the Internet or the vast number of family histories stored on a CD-ROM.

Genealogy can be a frustrating hobby, full of dead ends and misleading trails, but, although no amount of software is a substitute for patience and an enquiring mind, with the Internet it has never been easier to pursue.

**A** to look through photo albums
**B** to produce a family tree
**C** to write everything down
**D** to find out the basic facts
**E** to get into what
**F** to look for useful documents
**G** to decide on what
**H** to take them back
**I** to make good use of

**Task analysis**

**3** Look again at questions 1 and 2. Did you rule out each of the other options because they don't fit the meaning? because they don't fit grammatically?

**Discussion**

**4** Would you think of taking up genealogy as a hobby? Why?/Why not?

# Language development 2

▶ Grammar reference page 182

## Verb + -ing or infinitive?

**1 a** Some verbs can only be followed by an -ing form or an infinitive with to. Mark the correct form of the verb in each pair.

1 Many people have contemplated *to find / finding* out more about their past.
2 Sometimes family members volunteer *to help / helping*.
3 Some organisations guarantee *to find / finding* the information for you.
4 I had hoped *to trace / tracing* my family back 500 years.
5 The research involves *to spend / spending* hours on the Internet.
6 I agreed *to share / sharing* the information I found with the whole family.
7 I fancied *to draw / drawing* up a huge family tree.
8 I yearned *to discover / discovering* a famous ancestor.

**b** Complete the questions using a verb in the correct form. Then take turns asking and answering with a partner.

1 Have you ever contemplated … ?
2 Could you imagine … ?
3 Have you ever been forced … ?
4 Would you consider … ?
5 Have you ever pretended … ?
6 Would you refuse … ?

## Verb + object + infinitive/ing

**2** Five of the following sentences contain mistakes. Find and correct them.

1 We chose Alice representing us at the investigation.
2 I never expected to find out so much information.
3 I arranged the library to send me all the information.
4 Strangely, I sometimes miss Amanda's moaning about the company.
5 I didn't expect they to discover anything very exciting.
6 Can I recommend you visiting the industrial museum in town?
7 I was made go first because I was known to have experience.
8 I didn't like their suggesting that we were unprepared.

## Verb + -ing form/infinitive with a change in meaning

**3 a** Put the verbs in brackets into the appropriate form. Be prepared to explain the difference in meaning.

I remember **(1)**.................. (*visit*) Greece many years ago. My friend and I meant **(2)**.................. (*spend*) the summer island hopping. On Crete, we stopped **(3)**.................. (*learn*) a little about its history. I'll never forget **(4)**.................. (*see*) the palace at Knossos for the first time. However, the next day we missed our ferry because we had forgotten **(5)**.................. (*set*) the alarm clock the night before. The delay meant **(6)**.................. (*wait*) a week for the next one. We tried **(7)**.................. (*find*) other ways off the island, and even tried **(8)**.................. (*hitch*) a ride on a cargo ship, but then we stopped **(9)**.................. (*worry*) and went on **(10)**.................. (*have*) the best week ever. We returned to Knossos and went on **(11)**.................. (*explore*) the ruins for the whole week. We had such a good time, we never regretted **(12)**.................. (*miss*) that ferry.

**b** Think of a time when you discovered something or saw something for the first time and complete the sentences with your own ideas.

1 I won't forget …
2 I remember …
3 I tried …
4 I stopped …
5 I'll always regret …

**4** Match the halves to complete the sentences and discuss the difference in usage in each pair.

1 a I like to pay    i less than other people for things.
    b I like paying    ii my bills at the start of the month.
2 a I prefer reading    i about an exhibition before I see it.
    b I'd prefer to read    ii about the exhibition before I see it.
3 a I saw the driver drop    i his ticket before he went into the museum.
    b I saw the driver dropping    ii people off outside the museum all afternoon.
4 a I can't bear to go    i to museums when I'm on holiday.
    b I can't bear going    ii to a museum today.
5 a I watched him painting    i a portrait; it only took 30 minutes.
    b I watched him paint    ii a portrait; he only did the nose while I was there.
6 a I left Duncan waiting    i for the gallery to open while I bought us some coffee.
    b I left Duncan to wait    ii for the gallery to open and went home.
7 a I don't want you to go    i there every night.
    b I don't want you going    ii there tonight.

## Writing 2   Guidebook entry (Paper 2 Part 2)

**Lead-in**

1 Discuss these questions.
1 Do you take a guidebook with you if you travel? Why do people use them?
2 What would you expect to find in a good guidebook?

**Understand the task**

▶ Writing reference page 194

2 Read the task and answer these questions.
1 What is the PURPOSE of the chapter you've been asked to contribute to? Who is the target reader?
2 How many PARTS are there to the question? Mark them.
3 Will you give FACTS or OPINIONS or BOTH?
4 What STYLE will you use?
5 Will you try and 'sell' the places to the reader?
6 What will make the reader think it is a USEFUL entry?

> A guidebook in English is to be produced for visitors to **your** country. You have been asked to contribute to a chapter called *Special attractions*. You have been sent these guidelines.
>
>> The chapter on *Special attractions* will be aimed at tourists who like to see something unique, unusual or very interesting. You should briefly describe **two** attractions in your area, such as places of historical interest, interesting museums, etc. They can be similar or different. You should cover the following points:
>> - why the places are interesting
>> - in what way they are similar/different.
>> - what visitors can see there
>
> Write your entry for the guidebook in approximately 250 words.

**Plan your entry**

3 a Think of two places of special interest in your area and make some notes for each point in the task.

b Make a plan for your contribution. Will you need headings? How many paragraphs will you have?

c Choose from your notes in Exercise 3a what you will include in each paragraph.

**Language and content**

4 a Read the guidebook extracts. How is their approach similar or different? Mark any words, phrases and stylistic devices that are used to make each place sound interesting.

A

### Attractions and Museums

Billed as a museum with a difference, the London Dungeon is now one of the capital's top tourist attractions. It may be described as a museum of simulated horror from history, recalling atrocities from the past, a place where you can journey back to the darker side of European history.

The museum has a wide variety of attractions, including up-to-date multimedia displays. You can experience walking down a Victorian street to unravel the terrible truth about Jack the Ripper or see how terrible punishments were carried out, such as beheading, boiling or drowning.

With over 40 exhibits, it is not recommended for those of a nervous disposition or unaccompanied children.

B

# From the past to the present ...

In the heart of the city between Abbey Church Yard and Stall Street is the amazing complex of Roman Baths, built around natural hot springs. The water is likely to have fallen as rain about 10,000 years ago, and yet the King's Spring still produces over 250,000 gallons of water each day at a constant temperature of 46° Centigrade.

The Temple and Baths flourished between the first and fifth centuries AD. The remains, including sculpture and jewellery, are undoubtedly the finest in the country and are brought to life by personal audio guides.

C

Idiosyncratic, fascinating and eclectic, the Horniman Museum is worth the trip.

Frederick Horniman was a Victorian tea trader, and he collected all sorts of interesting things from around the world. After a while, this had built up to such an extent that he opened his house to the public, and people would visit and marvel at the extraordinary exhibits.

Then in 1901, he had a museum built and presented it to the council on the understanding that it would be free for the public to visit.

In the Horniman Museum, you can see all sorts of fascinating cultural artefacts from some very diverse cultures around the world, including Egyptian mummies, stuffed animals and musical instruments. There's an Aquarium Gallery, where strange and wonderful fish still think they are living in their natural habitat. And in the darker parts of the ancient collection, some really spooky and unnerving things.

b Choose and complete suitable expressions from this list for your paragraphs.

| | |
|---|---|
| **Drawing in the reader** | *If there's one place that really … , it is …*<br>*This is not just another … , but a …*<br>*If you want a different kind of experience, …*<br>*If you have a few hours to spare, … is well worth seeing.* |
| **Describing location** | *Located/Situated (just a few miles away from/outside …) is …*<br>*Built (by the side of/just next to …) is …*<br>*Just beyond (the …) is …*<br>*Some (…) minutes from … stands …* |
| **Giving background information** | *Throughout its history, …*<br>*… is by far the oldest …/was the first …/is the best-known …*<br>*Originally a … , but now …*<br>*In recent years, …*<br>*Known locally as … , …* |
| **Describing attractions** | *What is particularly (spectacular) is …*<br>*Recent additions/changes include …* |
| **Making qualifying comments** | *Naturally, children will absolutely adore … , but …*<br>*… whereas … (is really intended for younger people)*<br>*… , however, will require much more time to take in.*<br>*In fact, (both) are best avoided if …* |

## Write your guidebook contribution

5 Now write your contribution for the guidebook, using some of the ideas and the language on these pages. Write your answer in approximately 250 words.

## Check your answer

6 Edit your entry using the checklist on page 188.

▶ Writing reference page 188

▶SRB p69

# Module 6: Review

**1 Decide which word or phrase best fits each space.**

1 Robert Scott was ........ the best explorer of his times.
   **A** looked upon   **B** respected for   **C** honoured
   **D** regarded as

2 I'm sceptical ........ claims that virtual health care on the Internet will replace doctors.
   **A** that   **B** of   **C** seeing   **D** concerning

3 The painting was restored with ........ attention to detail.
   **A** meticulous   **B** undivided   **C** exact   **D** finicky

4 The children ........ behind, tired and fed-up.
   **A** strode up   **B** wandered around
   **C** trudged along   **D** strolled through

5 The economy is expected to ........ over the coming year.
   **A** go down   **B** deteriorate   **C** slip   **D** depreciate

6 I didn't like the exhibition; I was bored ........ .
   **A** in my mind   **B** to my mind   **C** on my mind
   **D** out of my mind

7 You have to ........ the pros and cons of DNA research.
   **A** weigh up   **B** pump up   **C** burn up   **D** think up

8 We need to ........ the trend towards centralised power.
   **A** repeal   **B** reverse   **C** overturn   **D** undo

9 Mobile phones have been ........ for a long time now.
   **A** about   **B** round   **C** around   **D** along

10 There's no ........ evidence to support your thesis.
   **A** ample   **B** considerable   **C** certain   **D** firm

**2 Correct the mistakes with the choice of word or word form in each sentence.**

1 There has been a startling raise in the number of anti-ageing products on the market.

2 Do you believe the world will be troubleless in the future?

3 I'm a pessimist. I don't hold out much hope to a better world.

4 First published in the 1930s, the data remains an absolutely undispensable resource.

5 Most health-food companies have online guidebooks of their products.

6 He has a very selected memory – he only remembers what he wants!

7 Can you pointpin the site on the map?

8 The government's refusal to hand back the relics caused a major diplomatic accident.

9 What is the price of admitting to the exhibition?

10 We need many alternate forms of fuel.

11 We need to insure there are fewer nasty weapons about.

12 He runs a very solitary life.

**3 Rewrite each sentence using the word in brackets so it has a similar meaning. Do not change the word in any way.**

1 I'm really sorry I couldn't come to the museum with you. (*regret*)

..................................................................................

2 We anticipate that the space shuttle will reach its destination by next Tuesday. (*expected*)

..................................................................................

3 They think it's the most daring space mission yet. (*considered*)

..................................................................................

4 They made us work 12 hours a day. (*What*)

..................................................................................

5 The archaeologist doesn't talk to his assistant any more. (*stopped*)

..................................................................................

6 Could I possibly share your programme? (*sharing*)

..................................................................................

7 The director decides who goes on the mission. (*It*)

..................................................................................

8 They are no longer making any effort to find life on Mercury. (*given*)

..................................................................................

**4 Complete the text by putting one word in each gap.**

Sir James Clark Ross (1800–1862) was a remarkable explorer. The places **(1)**............ he carried out his explorations **(2)**............ treacherous polar regions where no man had ever been before. **(3)**............ enabled him to mount some of the most successful expeditions in history **(4)**............ his scientific approach to exploration. This included **(5)**............ sure that his crew had a balanced diet. Another **(6)**............ why his trips didn't end in failure was **(7)**............ his ships had unusually thick hulls. **(8)**............ was Ross **(9)**............, in 1831, first located the magnetic North Pole. One of the other **(10)**............ he is remembered for **(11)**............ that he was the first explorer to use sounding weights. This enabled him **(12)**............ explore the bottom of the sea and examine the minute living organisms to **(13)**............ found there. What he **(14)**............ was drop the weights and collect samples of sediment. **(15)**............ the limitations of these explorations, scientists acknowledge their importance.

# MODULE 7

# Breaking the mould

## Overview

- **Reading:** multiple-choice questions (Paper 1 Part 3)
- **Vocabulary:** words related to motivation; rephrasing; idiomatic phrases and collocations
- **Listening 1:** sentence completion (Paper 4 Part 1)
- **Language development 1:** spelling rules
- **English in Use 1:** error correction (spelling and punctuation) (Paper 3 Part 3)
- **Writing 1:** using your own words
- **Listening 2:** multiple matching (Paper 4 Part 4)
- **Speaking:** describing emotions; talking about change; long turn (Paper 5 Part 2)
- **English in Use 2:** word formation (Paper 3 Part 4)
- **Language development 2:** past tenses for hypothetical meanings; *wish/if only*; other expressions (*It's time, I'd rather*, etc.)
- **Writing 2:** letter of complaint and note (Paper 2 Part 1)

## Lead-in

- In what ways are the people in the photos 'breaking the mould'?
- What do you think makes these people do things like this?
- Do you take part in any sport or other activity that is potentially dangerous? If so, why do you do it?
- Which activities in the average person's daily life do you think have an element of risk?

## Reading (Paper 1 Part 3)

**Before you read**

1 Look at the headline and subheading of the newspaper article, and the photo. Discuss these questions.
   1 Why do you think a person might be motivated to row alone across an ocean?
   2 What personal qualities do you think are needed to do this?

**Skimming**

2 Skim the article quickly. How does the writer answer the questions in Exercise 1? Do you agree with him?

**Multiple-choice questions**

▶ Task strategies page 168

3 Read the article and answer questions 1–6. Mark the letter A, B, C or D. Give only one answer to each question.

   a Before you start the task, think about the strategy you will follow.

   b Look at question 1 and read the first paragraph. Try to decide what the answer is.

   c Now look at the options and think about these questions to help you decide which is correct.
      A: If you break a record, you are the first to do or the best at doing something. Is Andrew Halsey the first or the best?
      B: Does the writer actually say that Andrew wasn't expecting it to be difficult?
      C: Does the writer give a reason why he is doing it?
      D: Is it actually stated that he will win money?

   d Continue in the same way and complete the task.

# DEMONS THAT DRIVE US TO ROW IT ALONE

**Jonathan Gornall, who tried to row across the Atlantic in 2001, explains what motivates solo oarsmen**

When I heard that the solo rower Andrew Halsey was struggling against contrary winds and tides in his second bid to cross the Pacific ocean, I saw in my mind the seascape threatening hourly to engulf a
5 small boat; a boat held true to its course by a man driven by demons. My colleagues smiled at the idea of this eccentric man splashing about in a small boat in huge seas, risking his life, his slender funds and the happiness of his family – in pursuit of what? Nobody
10 yet has ever got rich rowing across an ocean. And there's no chance of Andrew scoring a first; the route he is rowing was ticked off 30 years ago.

In 2001, I set off with a friend to row across the Atlantic in a race. My partner left the boat after ten
15 days, and I plugged on alone. In all, I spent 48 days and 1,100 miles at sea before succumbing to mental and physical pressures I had never experienced before and accepting a lift from a passing yacht. My 24-foot boat – the boat I had spent months and a small
20 fortune building myself – was declared a hazard to shipping and burnt before my eyes. It was, I told myself, the right decision at the time. I regretted it within hours.

The determination to go back and prove I can do it informs nearly every aspect of my life, which is why I understand what Andrew means when he says he will do or die. This is no great quest for riches or cures or peace. The desire to succeed against the odds is a shallow, selfish and, I believe, ultimately destructive force which most people fail to understand. Quite why it grips some individuals and spares the fortunate contented majority is beside the point. We all have strange compulsions and we all choose to prove ourselves in different ways. Some pursue academic or artistic excellence, others wealth. Some seek primitive physical dominance over others in sport, or even by bullying people.

What is missing in modern life that drives people – especially the middle-aged – to tempt fate like this? My grandfather, like so many of his generation, would not have understood the compulsion to bungee jump or white-water raft. But then at 15, he had already 'proved himself' in war, which I haven't. So perhaps it comes down to a primitive urge to keep faith with the past, with people for whom adventure was not a diversion but survival. We might live longer and enjoy better health, but perhaps we need to be free of our comfortable lives at times; to push ourselves and see how far we can go.

It is a mistake to dismiss this urge as macho posturing; it is far from being a male preserve. Debra Veal was in the same race as me and made front-page news when her husband declared he had had enough and left her to it, one week into a 3,000-mile trip. Although she had never contemplated doing a solo trip, she finished the competition, unlike me. But what drove this recently married, successful businesswoman to risk everything at sea? 'When you smash those thresholds, particularly when you are alone, it makes you realise what you are capable of, and I thrive on that. Ocean voyages also put things in so much better perspective when you're on dry land.'

The real danger is that one can also discover what one is not capable of. Beaten once by the Pacific, dry land had no allure for Andrew Halsey. From his perspective, he would be incomplete until the crossing was his. So, as you shudder at the thought of your nightmare journey to and from work today, spare a thought for a man haunted by his sense of self-worth and wish him well. As my granny used to say, worse things happen at sea.

1 What does the writer suggest about Andrew Halsey in the first paragraph?
A He is motivated by the desire to break a record.
B He has miscalculated the difficulty of his trip.
C He has no obvious reason for making the trip.
D He is determined to try and win a cash prize.

2 Why was the writer unsuccessful in his bid to row across the Atlantic?
A He couldn't tolerate being on his own for so long.
B He lost interest when he realised he wouldn't succeed.
C He felt that conditions on the boat were no longer tolerable.
D He was persuaded by others to abandon the attempt.

3 What does the writer say about Andrew's determination to row the Atlantic?
A It would be better applied to a more worthwhile cause.
B It is a symptom of something Andrew is unable to control.
C It is a strong desire which many people can relate to.
D It has always been encouraged by those around him.

4 In the fourth paragraph, the writer suggests that
A modern lifestyles lead to increased recreational risk-taking.
B human beings have a basic need to set themselves challenges.
C risk-taking sports are part of a wider desire for health and fitness.
D people look to past generations for a model of courageous behaviour.

5 What do we learn about Debra Veal from the article?
A She became famous when she managed to win a rowing competition.
B She was the first woman to row one particular Atlantic route on her own.
C She was able to focus her mind on her business interests whilst at sea.
D She succeeded in rowing the Atlantic despite an unexpected setback.

6 What does the writer imply about Andrew in the final paragraph?
A He is unlikely to succeed in his attempt to row the Pacific.
B He deserves our sympathy rather than our admiration.
C He is unable to come to terms with his limitations.
D He will return from the Pacific a better man.

Task analysis 4 Compare and justify your answers with reference to the text. To identify the correct options, did you need to:
a find specific details in a paragraph?
b understand the overall message of a paragraph?

Discussion 5 Discuss these questions.
1 According to the writer of the article, 'The desire to succeed against the odds is a shallow, selfish and, I believe, ultimately destructive force.' How far do you agree? Think of other examples to support your arguments.
2 Give examples of behaviour that you would consider:
• eccentric • macho • reckless
3 If you decided to set yourself a personal challenge, what would it be?

# Vocabulary

## Motivation

**1 a** Match the expressions in column A to the ones with a similar meaning in column B, which come from the text on pages 104–105.

| A | B |
|---|---|
| 1 manage (to + *inf.*) | a push (sb./oneself) |
| 2 show one's ability | b compulsion (for/to + *inf.*) |
| 3 interest/affect strongly | |
| 4 force (sb./oneself) to work hard | c quest (for) |
| | d prove oneself |
| 5 able (to + *inf.*) | e succeed (in -ing) |
| 6 highly motivated | f grip (sb.) |
| 7 strong desire/urge (to + *inf.*) | g driven (by/to + *inf.*) |
| 8 search (for) | h capable (of -ing) |

**b** Read text A about Erik Weihenmayer, the first blind man to climb Everest. Then use expressions from column B in Exercise 1a to complete text B below, so that the information is the same.

**A**

Despite great difficulties, Erik Weihenmayer managed to reach the summit of Everest in May 2001. For him, it wasn't a search for fame; he was motivated by the need to demonstrate to himself that he could do it. Erik has been extremely interested in climbing since he was a teenager and refused to give up his burning desire to climb, despite the problem of losing his sight at the age of 13. He has never given in to his blindness and works himself hard to show that blind people are able to live exciting lives.

**B**

Against the odds, Erik Weihenmayer (**1**)............................ reaching the summit of Everest in May 2001. For him, it wasn't a (**2**)............................ for fame; he was (**3**)............................ by the need to (**4**)............................ . Erik has been (**5**)............................ by climbing since he was a teenager and refused to abandon his (**6**)............................ to climb, despite the setback of losing his sight at the age of 13. He has refused to be defeated by his blindness and (**7**)............................ to prove that blind people are (**8**)............................ living exciting lives.

**c** Read texts A and B again and mark other expressions with similar meanings.

## Rephrasing

**2** Rewrite these sentences starting with the words given and using the phrases in brackets from the text on pages 104–105. Make any changes necessary.

1 This record will never be beaten. (*no chance of*)
There ............................................................................
................................................................................ .

2 It's not important that someone else has already climbed Everest. (*beside the point*)
The fact that ....................................................................
................................................................................ .

3 It is not only men who feel compelled to succeed against the odds. (*far from*)
The compulsion to ..............................................................
................................................................................ .

4 The explanation for this compulsion to take risks may lie in a basic human need for challenges. (*come down to*)
This compulsion ..................................................................
................................................................................ .

5 People who crave risk are not attracted by the routines of everyday life. (*no allure*)
The routines ......................................................................
................................................................................ .

## Idiomatic phrases and collocations

**3 a** Look at these examples of useful expressions with the word *risk* from the *Longman Dictionary of Contemporary English*.

> a calculated risk    an element of risk    worth the risk
> take a risk    at risk    run a risk    at your own risk
> health/fire/security risk    a good/bad/poor risk
> risk life and limb    a risky business

**b** Use expressions from Exercise 3a to complete these sentences.
1 Tourists should avoid the area because of the ............................ risk.
2 Some people are prepared to risk ............................ taking part in adventure sports.
3 There is an ............................ in any venture.
4 Crossing the Atlantic in a rowing boat is a ............................ .
5 If you leave your car here, it's ............................ risk.
6 Without a vaccination, you ............................ the risk of catching measles.

**c** Choose one or two of the following words and find useful collocations and expressions in your dictionary for those words. Add them to your vocabulary notebook.
- competition
- doubt
- success

*David Blunkett, politician*

*British Open Athletics Championships*

## Listening 1 (Paper 4 Part 1)

**Before you listen**

1 Each of the people in the photos has a disability. What difficulties do you think they may have encountered during their careers?

**Sentence completion**

▶ Task strategies pages 170 and 171

2 🎧 Do the task below. Read the task strategies and use the Help clues if necessary. Listen to the recording twice.

You will hear part of a radio programme about the famous musician Evelyn Glennie. For questions **1–8**, complete the sentences.

### Evelyn Glennie

When the speaker first heard Evelyn play, he was most impressed by the [ 1 ] of her music.

Evelyn is unusual in being able to play both [ 2 ] and forcefully during the same performance.

On stage, Evelyn's unconventional choice of [ 3 ] as well as instruments reflects her individuality.

Everyday objects which Evelyn uses as musical instruments include [ *and* 4 ]

On her concert tours, Evelyn travels with as many as [ 5 ] different kinds of instruments.

Because Evelyn was deaf, she was at first rejected by a number of [ 6 ]

Evelyn runs a [ 7 ] which aims to educate people about music.

The speaker uses the term [ 8 ] to describe the influence that Evelyn has had on him.

**HELP**

➤ **Question 2**
Listen out for when the speaker begins to talk about Evelyn's style of playing. The answer comes soon afterwards.

➤ **Question 4**
You are listening for two plural nouns. Be careful: there are several sets of nouns in this piece of text, but only one of them includes everyday objects.

➤ **Question 8**
In what way is Evelyn important to the speaker? Listen for a term (two words) which is often used in this context.

**Discussion**

3 Do you think a disability of some kind makes a person more determined to succeed? Can you think of other examples of people who have made it to the top of their chosen career in spite of a disability?

# Language development 1

▶ Writing reference page 202

## Spelling rules

**1** **a** **Correct the underlined spelling mistakes in these extracts from students' work. Then check the rules in the Writing reference.**

1 I've got <u>boxs</u> of photos of all my <u>heros</u>.
2 February is a <u>wonderfull</u> month for <u>visitting</u> my country.
3 I stopped <u>swiming</u> regularly when I <u>enterred</u> university.
4 As a <u>beginer</u>, his <u>sucess</u> in the competition was <u>surpriseing</u>.
5 She's a <u>beautifull</u> girl; a lot <u>prettyer</u> than her sister.
6 Ramón really <u>regreted</u> <u>canceling</u> his course.
7 I <u>paniced</u> when I heard they were <u>arriveing</u> that night.
8 I bought a gift for my <u>neice</u>, but she hasn't un<u>wraped</u> it yet.
9 To tell <u>humourous</u> stories well, you have to <u>practice</u> a lot.

**b** **Find and correct the words that are spelt incorrectly.**

1 Although we live in diferent citys, our familys often have holidays together.
2 I was relieved to discover that I hadn't lost the reciept for my shopping.
3 We won't be moveing in the foreseeable future.
4 Should I sign this letter 'Yours truely' or 'Yours sincerely'?
5 My nieghbour is openning a restaurant in the town centre.
6 I need your advise about what to wear.

**2** **Mark any words in these sentences that look wrong. Try rewriting them in different ways until they look right.**

1 If you need somewhere to stay, speak to the acomodation officer.
2 It's really not necesary to bring a present.
3 We can't wait any longer; we need to start imediately.
4 Laser surgery is a remarkable achievement of modern medecine.
5 Could we have seperate bills for the meal, please?
6 I must try to improve my pronounciation.
7 My brother is a profesional footballer and he's very skillful.
8 It would be impossible to finish the job without assistence.

## Words that are easily confused

**3** **a** **Choose the correct word from each pair.**

1 *lose / loose*
  a You shouldn't let your dog ............. on the road.
  b In a crisis, try not to ............. your head.
2 *stationary / stationery*
  a You can buy paper, pens, etc. in the ............. department.
  b Our car was ............. when the truck ran into it.
3 *complementary / complimentary*
  a Acupuncture and other ............. medicines are becoming more common.
  b John was very ............. about my new outfit.
4 *affect / effect*
  a My parents' divorce had a big ............. on me.
  b How will the changes ............. you?

**b** **Now make sentences to show the difference in meaning between these pairs. Use your dictionary to help.**

1 there / their      4 idol / idle
2 hear / here      5 miner / minor
3 heel / heal      6 through / thorough

## Hyphens

**4** **Add hyphens where necessary in these sentences.**
**EXAMPLE:** We went for a ten kilometre walk.
*We went for a ten-kilometre walk.*

1 The BBC offers a 24 hour up to the minute news service.
2 The band split up in 1998, but reformed after a three year break.
3 She still sees her exboyfriend quite regularly.
4 His costar in the film was a very down to earth person.
5 The economy has enjoyed a consumer based recovery.
6 There have been several break ins in our neighbourhood recently.

## Improving your spelling

**5** **Do you use any of these techniques to help you to remember spellings? Which ones work best?**

- Rules, e.g. *-y* changes to *-ie* when adding *-s* or *-d* (*cry-cries-cried*)
- Grouping words with similar patterns, e.g. *pay-paid, say-said, lay-laid*
- Mnemonics, e.g. '*i*' before '*e*' except after '*c*'
- Breaking the word into parts, e.g. *in-de-pend-ent*
- Associating words with pictures
- Writing out a word many times
- Using a dictionary to check words
- Keeping a record of words you find a problem

# English in Use 1 (Paper 3 Part 3)

## Lead-in

1 **Discuss these questions.**
 1 Look at the photo. Why do you think Cathy Freeman is carrying both the Australian and the Aboriginal flag?
 2 What difficulties do you think she had to overcome to become an Olympic champion?

*Cathy Freeman, gold-medal winner, Sydney Olympics 2000*

## Error correction

▶ Task strategies page 169

2 a **Read the title and the text and answer these questions. (Ignore the mistakes at this stage.)**
 1 In what way has Cathy Freeman created history?
 2 Why is her present life another big challenge?

 b **Read the instructions and look at the examples (00) and (000). What kind of errors are shown?**

 c **Do the task. Check the task strategies if necessary.**

 In **most** lines of the following text, there is **either** a spelling **or** a punctuation error. For each numbered line, write the correctly spelt word or show the correct punctuation. **Some lines are correct**. Indicate these lines with a tick (✓). The exercise begins with three examples (**0**), (**00**) and (**000**).

### CATHY FREEMAN – AN AUSTRALIAN LEGEND

|  | | |
|---|---|---|
| Cathy Freeman had to triumph over prejudice to become the | **0** | ✓ |
| first Aboriginal to be selected for the Australian athletic's team. | **00** | athletics |
| Then, in 2000, on one incredibley emotional night at the Olympic | **000** | incredibly |
| Games in Sydney she went on to fulfil her lifelong ambition of | **1** | |
| wining a gold medal. When she wrapped herself in both the Australian | **2** | |
| and Aboriginal flags after the race, millions of Australians wanted | **3** | |
| to believe that, reconciliation between the Australian settlers and | **4** | |
| Aboriginals was finally possible. Cathy has always accepted her | **5** | |
| position as a role model to other Aboriginal children telling them | **6** | |
| that, 'like me, you can do whatever you want if you set your | **7** | |
| heart on it. After her great triumph in 2000, Cathy took a 15-month | **8** | |
| rest from competing. she spent the time in the United States with | **9** | |
| her husband, learning italian and working as a volunteer for a | **10** | |
| newspaper that supported homeless people. Afterwards getting | **11** | |
| back to serious training was difficult. She was wieghed down | **12** | |
| by injuries and personal problems, and was'nt giving it the effort | **13** | |
| needed. As a result, in races she did not have the succes she had | **14** | |
| grown used to. Eventually, Cathy conceeded that the challenge | **15** | |
| was too great and, in 2003, anounced her decision to retire. | **16** | |

## Task analysis

3 **Answer these questions about the task.**
 1 What kind of spelling errors were tested?
 2 What kind of punctuation errors were tested?

## Discussion

4 Why do you think Cathy took a break after her Olympic triumph?
 Why do you think she was unable to repeat her success?

*Orkney Islands*

SCOTLAND

# Writing 1 Using your own words

## Writing strategy

In Paper 2 Part 1, you need to re-express the relevant information in the input texts in your own words in a suitable way for the text you are writing. Make sure you:
- build on key words in the input, but avoid using whole phrases
- use the correct register.

1 You recently went on an exchange trip to one of the Orkney Islands, near Scotland, and stayed with a family for four weeks. The editor of the English-language newspaper at your college has asked you to write an article for the newspaper, describing what you enjoyed about the visit.

   a Read the extracts from the original advertisement, on which you have made notes, and an extract from a letter from your exchange student.

   b Decide what information you can use in your article, and mark it.

*That's true! Loved it.*

### STUDENT EXCHANGE PROGRAMMES WITH A DIFFERENCE

We give you the opportunity to improve your English the natural way in unusual and often remote parts of the English-speaking world.

We offer four-week exchange programmes, in which we match you with someone the same age as yourself and you live as part of their family. In return, you agree to host the student in your family at a mutually convenient time next year.

*Character-forming. Realised I could be independent if I had to be.*

*Great way to get to know people from a different culture.*

*Very hospitable! Not there long, but they really made me feel at home.*

I hope you weren't too lonely. I know you were very scared at the beginning because it was the first time you'd ever been away from home, let alone your country. It was very brave of you! Also, you were the first person we'd ever met from your country, so we were a bit nervous, too! My parents really appreciated it when you said that it made you realise that it doesn't matter where people come from, they have the same aspirations: to lead a happy life in safety!

Look forward to visiting you next year.

2 Read two extracts from a student's answer to the task. Match the information included in the extracts to the information in Exercise 1. How has the writer paraphrased the key points?

**A**

I have just returned home after the best four weeks of my life. For 30 days, I lived on one of the Orkney Islands, just off the coast of Scotland, as part of a student exchange programme. The organisers partnered me up with a boy my own age and, although I was there only a short time, I became one of the family. Next year, I will be welcoming their boy, Tom, into my own home at a time which suits both of us.

**B**

What I also enjoyed was learning about how people in other countries live. I began to understand that no matter who we are or where we live, we all want the same thing: to live happily and safely.

3 a Write your own answer to the task.

   b Exchange your work with a partner and compare how you re-expressed the relevant information.

# 7B Kicking the habit

## Listening 2 (Paper 4 Part 4)

**Before you listen**

1  a  Read the instructions for the task below and look at the list A–H.

   1  Why do you think people become obsessive about everyday activities like these?

   2  In what ways could these activities be bad for you if you did them to excess?

   b  Make a list of words and expressions connected to each of the activities listed.

   EXAMPLES: *mobile phone, keep in touch, annoying other people*

## Multiple matching

▶ Task strategies pages 170 and 171

2  🎧 Listen and do the task below. Read the task strategies and use the Help clues if necessary. You will hear the recording twice.

You will hear five short extracts in which different people are talking about habits that they are unable to control.

---

**TASK ONE**

For questions **1–5**, choose from the list **A–H** the habit which each speaker mentions having a problem with.

A  making unnecessary calls

B  attempting to lose weight

C  playing computer games

D  watching soap operas

E  consuming unsuitable food

F  making needless purchases

G  taking excessive exercise

H  surfing the Internet

| 1 |
| 2 |
| 3 |
| 4 |
| 5 |

---

**TASK TWO**

For questions **6–10**, choose from the list **A–H** what each person says has happened as a result of their habit.

A  I have unpredictable moods.

B  My friends have deserted me.

C  My work is suffering.

D  I have spent a fortune.

E  My health has deteriorated.

F  It has made me deceitful.

G  A close relationship has been affected.

H  My family has complained about it.

| 6 |
| 7 |
| 8 |
| 9 |
| 10 |

---

**HELP**

➤ Question 1

The speaker mentions eating, playing computer games and going to the gym, but which has *taken over* his life?

**HELP**

➤ Question 6

Listen to the end of the text. Who *never calls* anymore? Which option does this match?

## Discussion

3  Work in pairs.

STUDENT A: Think of a habit you have that you can't break (e.g. eating chocolate, drinking coffee, smoking). Explain the problem to your partner and ask for advice.

STUDENT B: Give your partner advice on how to break his/her habit. Use expressions like these.

*Have you tried …?  If you …, you might …  Would you consider … instead?*

▶SRB  p77

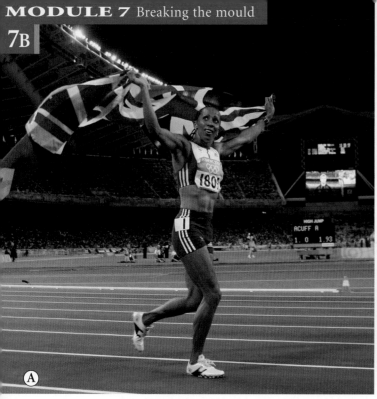

(A)

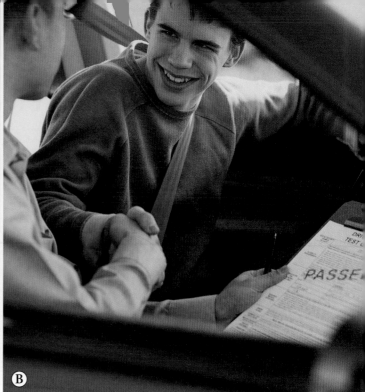

(B)

## Speaking (Paper 5 Part 2)

Vocabulary:
describing emotions

**1 a** Which of the words and expressions in the box are related in meaning to the words in capitals below?

| | | | | |
|---|---|---|---|---|
| *astonished* | *regretful* | *anxious* | *thankful* | *thrilled* |
| *apprehensive* | *grateful* | *stunned* | *elated* | *dejected* |

1 PLEASED    2 RELIEVED    3 WORRIED    4 SURPRISED    5 SAD

**b** Rewrite the sentences using expressions from the box, making any changes necessary.

| | | |
|---|---|---|
| *have no regrets* | *prey on your mind* | *come as a huge surprise* |
| *be a weight off your mind* | *be over the moon* | |

1 Now the exams are over, I feel very relieved.
2 We were astonished when we heard the news.
3 My parents were thrilled when they heard I was getting married.
4 The thought of losing my job has been worrying me for months.
5 Even though I didn't win, I'm not sorry I took part.

**c** Look at the photos. Describe the situation in each photo and say how you think the people are feeling. Use some of the expressions above and others that you know.
EXAMPLE: *The man in this photo has passed his driving test. He must be feeling really thrilled about it.*

Talking about change

**2 a** How do you think a person's life might change as a result of the situations in the photos? Match the sentence halves.

1 If you won lots of money,
2 As the winner of a big competition,
3 One consequence of passing your driving test would be that
4 With a new baby,
5 After retiring,

a you'd have to adapt your lifestyle completely.
b you'd have a lot more independence.
c you'd be treated like a celebrity and invited onto TV chat shows and such like.
d it might be hard to get used to not having a structure to your day.
e you'd be able to give up working.

**b** What other changes can you think of for each situation?

ⒸⒹⒺ

**Sample answer**

▶ Task strategies pages 171 and 172

**3 a** 🎧 Look at the photos again and listen to the examiner's instructions. What are the two parts of the task?

**b** 🎧 Listen to someone doing the task. Which photos did she talk about? Do you agree with the points she made about them?

**c** How successfully did the speaker complete the task? Did she follow the task strategies?

**Useful language**

**4** Listen again and identify expressions the speaker uses for
1 organising and structuring (e.g. *Right, well, …*)
2 comparing and contrasting (e.g. *both … and … are*)
3 speculating/giving views (e.g. *I suppose …*)

**Long turn**

**5** Work in pairs.

**a** Take turns to do the task in Exercise 3. Each of you should use a different combination of photos. The person who is not doing the task should time the other one. (About one minute each)

**b** Look at all the photos again and decide together whose life is likely to change most. (About one minute)

**Task analysis**

**6** In the sample answer, the speaker used specific language to organise and structure what she said. What did you use to do this?

**Discussion**

**7** Discuss these questions.
1 Have you ever been in a similar situation to those in the photos? How did you feel? If something like this happened to you, how would you feel?
2 Think of other crucial milestones in your life, in the past and future. Describe how you felt/might feel.

## English in Use 2 (Paper 3 Part 4)

### Word formation

▶ Task strategies pages 169 and 170

1 a Read through each text quickly, without looking at the words on the right. What is each text about? What link can you think of between the two topics?

b Do the task. Check the task strategies on pages 169 and 170 if necessary.

For questions **1–15**, read the texts below. Use the words in the boxes to the right of the texts to form **one** word that fits in the same numbered space in the text. The exercise begins with an example (**0**).

ENCYCLOPAEDIA ENTRY

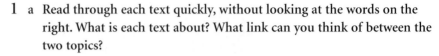

# The History of Chocolate

It was in 1519 that the Spanish conquerors of Mexico first tasted *cacahuatl*, a drink which the Aztec Indians made from cacao beans. These beans were considered to be **(0)** p̲r̲i̲c̲e̲l̲e̲s̲s̲ treasures by the Aztecs, and some were taken back to Spain. But *cacahuatl* was very bitter, and the Spaniards found it **(1)**............. until they sweetened it with sugar and served it hot. After **(2)**............. experiments, the rich, milky drink that gives **(3)**............. to so many people today developed its **(4)**............. taste, and cocoa production became a **(5)**............. industry. **(6)**............., its secrets were kept from the rest of Europe for nearly a hundred years. Spanish monks finally let the secret out, and the drink became acclaimed throughout Europe as not only delicious but also **(7)**............. to health. It was not until the 19th century that solid chocolate was introduced.

| | |
|---|---|
| **(0)** | **PRICE** |
| **(1)** | DRINK |
| **(2)** | COUNT |
| **(3)** | PLEASE |
| **(4)** | DISTINCT |
| **(5)** | PROFIT |
| **(6)** | BELIEF |
| **(7)** | BENEFIT |

BOOK REVIEW

## THE POWER OF HYPNOSIS

Do you wish you could change some anti-social aspect of your **(8)**.............? Have you ever tried to curb an unpleasant, self-destructive habit, only to find your methods totally **(9)**.............? If so, then perhaps it's time you looked to the **(10)**............. power of self-hypnosis for help. This new book will be essential reading. In conventional hypnosis, the hypnotist brings the client into a deeply **(11)**............. state in order to access **(12)**............. parts of the mind and deal with whatever it is that is causing the problem. In self-hypnosis, you go through a similar **(13)**............., but without the **(14)**............. of a hypnotist. Of course, in order to get into an hypnotic trance you'll need as few **(15)**............. as possible, but the authors claim the method is not dangerous, as at no time are you fully asleep.

| | |
|---|---|
| **(8)** | BEHAVE |
| **(9)** | EFFECT |
| **(10)** | MIRACLE |
| **(11)** | RELAX |
| **(12)** | KNOW |
| **(13)** | PROCEED |
| **(14)** | ASSIST |
| **(15)** | DISTRACT |

### Task analysis

2 Answer these questions about the task.
1 Which questions required more than two changes to the stem?
2 Which questions required a plural form to fit the meaning?

### Dictionary work

3 Choose two or three useful words from the task and use a dictionary to help you list all the derived forms in your vocabulary notebook.

# Language development 2

▶ Grammar reference page 183

## Past tenses for hypothetical meanings

**1** Mark the option in the second sentence that best reflects the meaning of the first sentence.

1  She wishes she had more energy.
   She *is / was* often tired.

2  If only I was at home watching TV.
   I want to *be alone / watch TV*.

3  I wish it would stop raining.
   I'm *optimistic / not optimistic* that it will stop.

4  If only I'd known where he was last night.
   I didn't *keep it a secret / know*.

5  He acts as though he lived there.
   He *might / doesn't* live there.

6  Come on, it's time we were leaving.
   We *should leave now / have already left*.

7  I'd sooner you didn't smoke in my house.
   You *shouldn't smoke / smoked* in my house.

8  Supposing I said something to her, would it help?
   I *might / won't* say something.

## *wish/if only*

**2 a** For each sentence, mark the options which are possible. If more than one is possible, discuss any difference in meaning.

1  I *wish / hope / want* I can pass my exams.

2  I wish I *can / could / will* see Graham more often.

3  If only I *was / am / will be* going away with you tomorrow.

4  My brother *wish / wishes / wished* he could drive.

5  I wish James *wasn't / didn't / hadn't* cut his hair so short.

6  I wish they *have to / must / had to* come this way more often.

7  If only I *could / would / should* break this spending habit.

8  I wish *I / you / he* wouldn't smoke in here.

9  If *you / you only / only you* knew how happy I was to get home.

10 I wish I *paid / had paid / had been paying* more attention to my finances recently.

**b** Complete the second sentence so it means the same as the first.

1  What I need is a personal trainer, but I don't have one.
   I wish I ........................................................... .

2  I ate far too much last night, and now I feel terrible.
   I wish I ........................................................... .

3  He keeps sending me text messages, and it annoys me.
   I wish ........................................................... .

4  I would really like to get into these clothes I had five years ago.
   If ........................................................... .

5  I wasn't paying my girlfriend enough attention, so she left me.
   I wish ........................................................... .

## Other expressions

**3 a** For each sentence, mark the options which are possible. If more than one is possible, discuss any difference in meaning.

1  It's time *I stop / to stop / I stopped* smoking.

2  It's high time *for changing / you change / you changed* your diet.

3  I'd prefer it if you *stopped / would stop / will stop* offering me biscuits.

4  My doctor talks to me as if I *am / was / were* stupid.

5  Suppose I *get / got / had got* a self-help book. Do you think I'd read it?

6  What if your diet *doesn't / didn't / won't* work?

7  They looked as though they *know / knew / had known* the secret of looking good.

**b** Rewrite the sentences using expressions from the box.

| I'd rather    It's time    I'd sooner    as if    supposing |

1  I really should go back to work now.

2  It's unlikely I'll join the gym, but how much would it cost me per month?

3  I don't like you spending all your time watching TV.

4  He looked like someone who'd been sitting in front of a computer all night.

5  Why did you tell me what the film was about before I'd seen it?

**4** Read the text and put the verbs in brackets into the correct form.

It's time I **(1)**.............. (*do*) something about my lifestyle. Yesterday, I ran upstairs and it felt as if I **(2)**.............. (*not do*) any exercise for ages! I wish I **(3)**.............. (*go*) to the sports centre a bit more often recently. My friend Roger is very fit and he certainly looks as though he **(4)**.............. (*exercise*) regularly. Sometimes I wish I **(5)**.............. (*be*) like him, but I'd rather he **(6)**.............. (*not try*) to give me fitness advice all the time. To be honest, I prefer watching sport on TV than doing it. If only I **(7)**.............. (*get*) fit sitting at home!

**5** Think about your lifestyle and any changes you would like to make. Complete the following sentences so they are true for you.

1  I wish I could …

2  If only I didn't have to …

3  It's high time …

4  Supposing …

# Writing 2   Letter of complaint and note (Paper 2 Part 1)

### Lead-in

**1  Discuss these questions.**

1  In your country, are people allowed to smoke in public places?
2  Should there be any restrictions on where people smoke?

### Understand the task

▶ Writing reference pages 193 and 195

**2  Read the task and answer the questions.**

1  WHO are you and WHAT is the situation?
2  WHAT are you going to write and what is the PURPOSE of each piece of writing?
3  What is the CONTEXT and AIM of each piece of input?
4  WHAT INFORMATION in each piece of input is relevant to the task?
5  What do you hope or expect to achieve by writing your letter? How will the STYLE and REGISTER differ from your note? Do you want to be aggressive, friendly or diplomatic but firm? Do you want to please, antagonise or persuade the reader?

You are studying in an English-speaking country, and to support yourself, you work part time at a café popular with tourists. The City Council has just announced plans to introduce a ban on smoking in public places. You are concerned about the effect this will have on the café's business and your job.

Read the extract from the information leaflet sent out to local businesses by the City Council, on which you have made some notes, an email you have received from a local journalist friend, and a letter you wrote to a foreign student you met while travelling to the country. Then, using the information appropriately, write a letter to the Council complaining about the proposed ban, and a note to your journalist friend saying what you plan to do.

The City Council has held discussions with local medical experts and concluded that the health risks associated with 'passive smoking' in the city's public places are unacceptably high. We believe that smokers are putting the lives of non-smokers, especially children, at risk. We have therefore decided that, as from the beginning of next month (1 November), smoking will be prohibited at all times in the following places

- all workplaces, including entertainment centres, cafés, bars and restaurants
- outdoor bars and restaurants where seating is provided
- outdoor sports venues where seating is provided
- public transport

Any trader flouting the law will face the possibility of a heavy fine and/or imprisonment.

*Why such short notice – and no discussion? No time for people to get used to the idea!*

*Why not encourage them to provide non-smoking areas instead?*

*Ridiculous! Totally unenforceable.*

You never responded to my last email. The Council seems to be serious – and very determined. Since it affects you, why don't you write and complain? Tell them what happened in your country when your Government tried to ban smoking.
I'm also planning a series of articles. I'll probably get back to you some time and ask you for a contribution. No need to say yes or no now.

*Worrying news. In the city where I'm working, they want to ban smoking in public places. I remember back home we tried that a few years ago. It failed, and the politicians had to change their minds. For a start, hardly anyone took any notice of the law. Of course, most businesses were against it. There were a few restaurants that tried to stop people smoking – half their customers disappeared overnight. If that happens here, I could lose my job. I'm going to write and complain, although it probably won't make much difference. I'm also thinking of writing an article for a newspaper, which I'm more hopeful about.*

Now write:

a)  a letter to the City Council complaining about the proposed ban (about 200 words)
b)  a note to your journalist friend, saying what you are going to do (about 50 words)

## Plan your letter and note

**3**  **a**  Look back at the input and decide:

1  which of the following points you will include in your letter and in your note. Tick them. Which are irrelevant? Cross them out.
- a reference to your job
- an apology
- public transport
- the effect of the smoking ban on business
- a promise to write an article
- the punishment for breaking the law
- what happened in your country

2  what other points you will include.

**b**  Make a paragraph plan for your letter, and write notes for each paragraph. How many paragraphs will you need?

**c**  Write down the points you will include in your note.

## Language and content

**4**  **a**  Mark the correct alternative in these phrases. Which phrases could you use in a) your letter? b) your note?

1  *pull / drop* (someone) a line (to tell them something)
2  *take / give* (their) custom elsewhere (if they're unhappy)
3  *introduce / start* a ban (on smoking)
4  (a ban could) *injure / damage* business
5  go *round / through* checking to make sure people are not breaking the law
6  the *greater part / majority* of people
7  *wider / higher* (public) debate (is needed)
8  (many people) *oppose / object* the ban
9  business will *hurt / suffer*
10  to have to back *down / along* (when you are wrong)
11  have (much) *affect / effect*
12  (some people feel they have) the *right / entitlement* to smoke

**b**  Which of these sentence openings would be better and why?

A  The letter
1  I am writing to express my extreme concern about …
2  I am writing because I am very angry that …

B  The note
1  I would like to apologise for not …
2  Sorry not to have …

**c**  Decide which of these expressions you could use in your letter. Match them to the paragraphs in your plan in Exercise 3. How can you complete them in a way which is appropriate?

| | |
|---|---|
| *I appreciate the reasons for … , but …* | *In my view, (the scheme) simply won't …* |
| *At present I am working …* | *First,/For a start, … Secondly, … In the end, …* |
| *I fear that …* | *This strikes me as …* |
| *On top of that (I think the amount of notice) …* | *I urge you to …* |
| *To support my argument, (I would like to tell you) …* | |

**d**  Decide what is wrong with this extract from a note written by a student in answer to the task.

> I never responded to your last email because I've been so busy, I apologise. I'm going to write and complain to the City Council, although it probably won't make much difference. I'm also thinking of writing an article for your newspaper, which I'm hopeful about. I can say yes now.

## Write your letter and note

**5**  Now write your letter and note using the ideas and some of the language above. Remember to avoid copying whole phrases from the input.

## Check your letter and note

**6**  Edit your work using the checklist on page 188.

▶ Writing reference page 188

# Module 7: Review

**1 Decide which word or phrase best fits each space.**

1 In my job, there's a considerable ........ of risk.
   **A** calculation **B** piece **C** factor **D** element

2 He's a very nice person, but that's ........ .
   **A** not made an issue of **B** no matter
   **C** beside the point **D** insignificant

3 I give a different answer ........ who I am talking to.
   **A** depending on **B** in case of **C** subject to
   **D** determined by

4 Her achievements speak ........ themselves.
   **A** by **B** for **C** to **D** with

5 When he set off in his boat, he was deeply ........ .
   **A** nervous **B** tense **C** apprehensive **D** scared

6 He exposes himself to so many ........ risks.
   **A** hopeless **B** worthless **C** useless **D** needless

7 When it ........ it, can you really afford to smoke?
   **A** comes down to **B** goes in for **C** carries on with
   **D** makes up for

8 He ........ to temptation and had a large piece of
   chocolate cake.
   **A** submitted **B** surmounted **C** succumbed
   **D** conceded

9 Don't ........ your money on computer games – save it!
   **A** lose **B** run out of **C** tie up **D** throw away

10 I still ........ at the memory of the accident I had
   when climbing the mountain.
   **A** shake **B** spin **C** shudder **D** wobble

11 ........ for me tomorrow, when you're on the beach
   and I'm still here.
   **A** Turn your thoughts **B** Collect your thoughts
   **C** Give a thought **D** Spare a thought

12 They agreed to meet at a ........ convenient time.
   **A** commonly **B** mutually **C** doubly **D** both

**2 Rewrite each sentence using the word in brackets so it has a similar meaning. Do not change the word in any way.**

1 Let's share the cost and get her a great leaving
   present. (*club*)
   If we ................................................................ .

2 When I was ill in bed recently, I became really
   interested in TV soap operas. (*hooked*)
   I ................................................................ when
   I was ill in bed recently.

3 He spends money for no particular reason. (*sake*)
   He ................................................................ it.

4 I'm sorry I didn't ring you. (*apologise*)
   I ................................................................ you.

5 She's got a lot of money. (*short*)
   She ................................................................ money.

6 It's pointless making him work too hard. (*pushing*)
   There's ................................................................
   too hard.

7 I never say I'm going to win in case I lose! (*fate*)
   I ................................................................
   I'm going to win in case I lose!

8 When I heard her speak, it affected me profoundly.
   (*impact*)
   Her speech ................................................................ .

9 He really wants to succeed. (*drives*)
   What ................................................................
   the desire for ................................................................ .

10 I'll never give up eating chocolates! (*chance*)
   There's ................................................................ .

**3 Correct the spelling, vocabulary and punctuation mistakes.**

1 He's very complementary about the amount of
   skiing practise I do.

2 You didn't follow the correct process when you
   enterred my country.

3 Do you realize the treasures in this collection are
   absolutely pricey?

4 Unbelievibly, I think we might loose this match.

5 I've had a two year break from swiming.

6 Unknowing to most people, he's actually a very
   idol person.

7 The heals have come off these new shoes, but
   unfortunately I haven't got a reciept for them.

8 Their are many unprofittable industries.

9 She's very beautifull, but her behaving is awful.

10 I can truely say he's a very unaffective manager.

**4 Complete the text by putting one word in each gap.**

This is a great surfing beach. You should see me lying
next to my board, all cool and suntanned, just
(**1**)............ if I (**2**)............ a real surfer. All the same, I
wish you (**3**)............ be here with me – I'd feel a lot
more confident. I'm determined to get up and have a
go, but I do wish the wind (**4**)............ calm down a bit
and the waves (**5**)............ a bit smaller. Also, it's a bit
cold. If (**6**)............ I (**7**)............ brought along a wetsuit
of some kind! And I'd (**8**)............ there (**9**)............ fewer
people around – the waves are a bit crowded right
now with some really good surfers. I keep asking
myself: (**10**)............ if I make a mess of it and get
thrown onto some stones? To be honest, I (**11**)............
now I (**12**)............ had a few lessons!

# MODULE 8
# Making life better?

## Overview

- **Reading:** gapped text (Paper 1 Part 2)
- **Vocabulary:** verb phrases; word formation
- **Listening 1:** multiple-choice questions (Paper 4 Part 4)
- **English in Use 1:** register transfer (Paper 3 Part 5)
- **Language development 1:** emphasis: inversion and fronting
- **Writing 1:** attitude clauses and phrases
- **Listening 2:** sentence completion (Paper 4 Part 3)
- **Speaking:** fighting crime; collaborative task (Paper 5 Parts 3 and 4)
- **English in Use 2:** open cloze (Paper 3 Part 2)
- **Language development 2:** comparison
- **Writing 2:** report (Paper 2 Part 2)

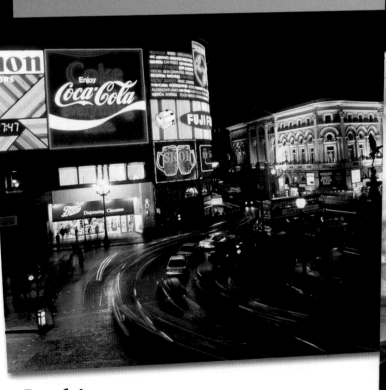

## Lead-in

- Look at the photos. What different types of advertising do they show?
- Which methods do you think reach the most people and are most effective?
- How far do you think you are influenced by advertising?
- Which of the things advertised here would you find it hardest to live without?

# 8A  A changing society

## Reading (Paper 1 Part 2)

**Before you read** 1 Look at the title and subheading of the article below. What do you think the effects of introducing television might have been?

**Reading** 2 Read the main text to check your ideas in Exercise 1. (Ignore the missing paragraphs for the moment.) Does the article mention any effects that you didn't think of?

**Gapped text** 3 For questions 1–6, you must choose which of the paragraphs A–G on page 121 fit into the numbered gaps in the article. There is one extra paragraph which does not fit in any of the gaps. Use the Help clues if necessary.
▶ Task strategies page 168

# How television changed a Himalayan kingdom

**In 1999, Bhutan was the only country on earth with no television. Then the King bowed to popular pressure and allowed it to be introduced. We went to investigate the effect it has had on the country.**

The 700,000 inhabitants of Bhutan, an isolated Buddhist kingdom perched high in the Himalayas, are not accustomed
5 to serious law-breaking; or at least they weren't until recently, because the tiny state has been experiencing a sudden crime wave. At one time, the only
10 social vice there seemed to be was over-indulgence in rice wine. Why, then, does it appear to be falling victim to the kind of crime associated with urban life
15 in the West?

| 1 | |

Only a few years later, it stands accused of threatening to destroy an idyll where time has stood still for half a
20 millennium. This tiny country was created by a monk from Tibet in 1616, as a Buddhist refuge from the ills of the world.

So successful were his descendants at isolating themselves that,
25 by the 1930s, virtually all that was known of Bhutan in the West was through the novel *Lost Horizon*, in which it was recreated as the secret Himalayan paradise of Shangri-La.

| 2 | |

When his son came to power, he announced a new policy goal: maximising the nation's spiritual contentment. But this proved to be
30 an elusive concept, and a delegation was sent abroad to investigate whether happiness could be measured. They were disappointed to learn that, for most people in the world, it equalled

around $5,000 a year – the minimum on which one could
35 live comfortably. It was an irrelevant answer to the Bhutanese, whose average annual salary was barely $1,000, and whose outlook was
40 not quite so materialistic.

| 3 | |

Later that same year, though, the King announced he would cede power to the National Assembly, completing
45 Bhutan's transition into a modern democracy. Television, it was decided, could play a crucial role in this transformation, teaching people
50 how democracies work in other parts of the world. So it was that, in June 1999, the Dragon King stood before his people to announce – to deafening cheers
55 – that they could now watch TV whenever they wanted. 'But not everything you see will be good,' he warned. 'It is my sincere hope that the introduction of television will be good for our country.'

| 4 | |

It was to try and limit the impact of foreign influences such as this
60 that the government launched a national broadcasting service. But years later, its programmes can still only be received in the capital, which means the cable companies have had no trouble capturing the market. The sudden deluge of foreign culture has, according to a study by Bhutanese academics, brought dramatic changes to this

<sup>65</sup> hermit nation: crime, corruption and changing attitudes to relationships. More than 35 per cent of parents say that they prefer to watch TV than talk to their children. Almost 50 per cent of children watch for up to 12 hours a day.

messages from sponsors come every five minutes. Cable TV has created, with acute speed, a nation of hungry consumers from a kingdom that once acted collectively and spiritually.

---

**5** [                                                        ]

They are even abandoning their traditional robes for jeans and T-<sup>70</sup> shirts. We saw their parents loitering for hours in the Welcome Guest House, in the spiritual capital of Punakha, transfixed by footballer David Beckham on TV. In one village, so many farmers were watching TV that an entire crop failed. Meanwhile, their wives ogle adverts for a Mercedes that would cost more than a lifetime's wages. Furniture <sup>75</sup> 'you've always desired', accessories 'you've always wanted' – the

---

**6** [                                                        ]

Everyone is too polite to say it, but, like all of us, the Dragon King <sup>80</sup> underestimated the power of TV, perceiving it as a benign and controllable force, believing that his country's culture was strong enough to resist its messages. But television is a portal, and in Bhutan it is systematically replacing one culture with another, skewing the notion of happiness, persuading a nation of novice <sup>85</sup> consumers to become preoccupied with themselves rather than searching for their selves.

---

A  Beneficial or not, it is certainly omnipresent, as we found on our recent visit to this crowded country, where the entire population shares fewer than two dozen names. As we passed medieval fortresses and pressed-mud towers, a brand new screen flickered within every candle-lit house. And outside the headquarters of the biggest cable operator, Sigma, a wriggling crowd of children pressed their faces against the window, screeching with glee at a violent Australian programme, *BeastMaster*.

B  In the real Bhutan, however, there were no public hospitals or schools until the 1950s, and no paper currency, roads or electricity for years after that. And when the current Dragon King's father eventually initiated a careful attempt to try to bring Bhutan into the 20th century, he was wary of the effect of foreign influences on Bhutanese culture, and attempted to inhibit conspicuous consumption: no Coca-Cola; no advertising hoardings; and definitely no television.

C  The minister for health and education is one of the few government ministers to voice concerns about the effect of this new materialism. For the first time, he says, children are confiding in their teachers that they feel envious and stressed. Boys have been caught mugging for cash. Another unwelcome side effect is that the Bhutanese are in danger of becoming a nation of couch potatoes. 'We used to think nothing of walking three days to see our in-laws,' he said. 'Now we can't even be bothered to walk to the end of the street.'

D  The explanation for the change seems to lie with five large satellite dishes planted in a vegetable patch and ringed by sugar-pink flowers on the outskirts of the capital, Thimpu. When Dragon King Jigme lifted a ban on television in 1999, as part of a radical plan to modernise the country, the Bhutanese signed up in their thousands to a cable service that provided 46 channels of round-the-clock entertainment.

E  Schoolteachers do their best to prepare their pupils for this onslaught of foreign images on television. The class of 15-year-olds we meet are inquisitive and smart. 'How many of you have television?' we ask. Laughter fills the room. 'We all have TV, sir and madam,' a girl at the front pipes up. 'What do you like about TV?' we ask. They reel off a list of American comedy programmes and pop stars. None of the children saw the documentary on Buddhist festivals last night.

F  It wasn't completely spiritual, either, though. In 1998, the football-mad kingdom was driven into a frenzy of envy of those who were able to watch the World Cup on television. Public pressure was so overwhelming that the government relented, and a giant screen was erected in the Thimpu's Changlimithang Stadium – on the understanding that it would only be temporary.

G  The last people to learn of the lifting of the television ban were those charged with the job of setting up a national broadcasting service. They were given three months to make it work, which was rather ambitious given that they had little experience and even less funding.

---

**HELP**

➤ **Question 1**
Which paragraph in the box provides an answer to the question before the gap?

➤ **Question 2**
- *Shangri-La* was a fictional place, not a real one. Which extract starts with a contrasting idea?
- The paragraph after the gap refers to *his son*. So the missing paragraph must refer to a *father*.

➤ **Question 3**
Look for an extract that introduces a contrast to *materialistic*.

➤ **Question 4**
Look for a synonym for *good*.

---

**Discussion**  4  Read through the article again, and mark the parts of the complete article that refer to life in Bhutan a) **before**, and b) **since** TV was introduced. Discuss these questions.

1  Do you think the King was right to allow his people to have television? Why?/Why not?

2  Why do you think the effects have been so extreme?

3  What do you think will happen to Bhutan in the future?

# Vocabulary

## Verb phrases

**1** **a** Match the halves of the extracts from the text on pages 120–121 and mark the verb phrases.

1 The Dragon King bowed
2 Television could play
3 Cable companies have had no trouble capturing
4 We used to think
5 Now we can't be
6 Dragon King Jigme lifted
7 Children reel off
8 Television stands

a nothing of walking three days.
b a list of comedy programmes.
c a ban on the small screen.
d a crucial role in the transformation of the country.
e to popular pressure.
f accused of threatening to destroy the country.
g the market for TV viewers.
h bothered to walk to the end of the street.

**b** Read this text and replace the phrases in italics with phrases from Exercise 1a. Make any changes necessary.

In some countries, computer games are becoming more popular than TV. Although there are a number of systems, Sony and Microsoft have **(1)** *a large percentage of the sales.* Many teenagers can **(2)** *quickly tell you* the names of lots of popular games. It's ironic that some people **(3)** *believe it's perfectly normal to play* a computer football game for hours, and yet they **(4)** *are too lazy* to go into the garden to actually kick a football. It has been said that these games can **(5)** *be important* in developing co-ordination. As I don't want **(6)** *people to say I am* resisting progress, I have decided, this year, **(7)** *to give in to the family's demands.* I'm going to **(8)** *remove the prohibition* on computer games in my house.

**2** **a** Complete the leaflet with the following verbs in a suitable form.

> maximise   initiate   relent   confide in
> transform   consume   inhibit   erect

**b** Discuss these questions.

1 Which of the changes do you agree with?
2 What changes would you like to see in society?

## Word formation

**3** **a** Complete the table with the appropriate word used in the text on pages 120–121.

| Adjective | Noun |
|---|---|
| 1 ............................ | materialism |
| influential | 2 ............................. |
| 3 ............................ | preoccupation |
| content | 4 ............................. |
| 5 ............................ | popularity |
| 6 ............................ | control |
| 7 ............................ | spirituality |
| idyllic | 8 ............................ |
| 9 ............................ | benefit |

**b** 🎧 Mark the stressed syllable in each word in Exercise 3a. What patterns do you notice? For which words does the stress change according to the word class? Listen and check.

**c** Use the appropriate word from Exercise 3a to complete the text below.

More and more people in the West are rejecting the **(1)**............................ values of the consumer society and turning to Eastern philosophies. Yoga, for example, is becoming increasingly common as more people discover its **(2)**............................ effects. B.K.S. Iyengar has been one of the most **(3)**............................ yoga teachers, responsible for much of its growing **(4)**............................ here. He understood that not everyone is **(5)**............................ with money and success.

   Some people are drawn to the **(6)**............................ aspect and the deep **(7)**............................ gained from a period of meditation. Others are drawn to the physical side, learning about their posture and **(8)**............................ of their breathing. And you don't need to go off to some **(9)**............................ location to learn. You can even practise at home.

# The People's Party

We would like to **(1)**............. a debate about what fundamental changes you would like to see in our society. So far we plan to:

- punish companies that **(2)**............. too much energy.
- **(3)**............. the tax system so most people pay less.
- **(4)**............. the amount of money spent on community projects.
- **(5)**............. more public sports halls and facilities for people to use.
- outlaw anything that **(6)**............. people's freedom.
- get the government to **(7)**............. on its safety laws, such as the compulsory wearing of seatbelts and crash helmets.

It's time for you, the silent majority, to tell us what you really want. Talk to us, the party you can **(8)**............. .

▶SRB   p83

# Listening 1 (Paper 4 Part 4)

**Lead-in** 1 What kinds of things would you like to be able to do at any time of the day or night? Think of shopping, leisure activities, entertainment facilities, etc. What are the advantages and disadvantages of 24-hour access to places like this?

## Multiple-choice questions

▶ Task strategies pages 170 and 171

2 🎧 Listen and do the task below. Check the task strategies if necessary. Listen to the recording twice.

You will hear five short extracts in which different people are talking about the 24-hour society. For questions **1–10**, choose the correct answer **A**, **B** or **C**.

**Speaker 1**

1 The first speaker is talking about
   A the expansion of 24-hour opening.
   B the disadvantages of 24-hour working.
   C the opportunities offered by 24-hour shopping.

2 How does she feel about the 24-hour society?
   A She accepts the need for it in the modern age.
   B She's unable to understand the attraction of it.
   C She doubts whether it will really become the norm.

**Speaker 2**

3 The second speaker predicts that the 24-hour society will result in
   A increased levels of unemployment.
   B further changes in shopping habits.
   C people working more flexible hours.

4 What concerns him about the 24-hour society?
   A the attitudes of employers towards it
   B the pressures it may put on employees
   C the way that changes may be introduced

**Speaker 3**

5 What worries the third speaker most about the 24-hour society?
   A the effects on those closest to her
   B the effects on those with family commitments
   C the effects on people who choose not to work unsocial hours

6 What is her opinion about the 24-hour society?
   A It is something which doesn't suit her personal circumstances.
   B It is something which should have been foreseen.
   C It is something which is here to stay.

**Speaker 4**

7 The fourth speaker sees the 24-hour society as
   A a solution to urban congestion.
   B an extension of daytime problems into the night.
   C an opportunity to do things you wouldn't otherwise do.

8 What does he warn against?
   A the temptation to do everything by night
   B the risk of paying more for things at night
   C the fact that services may be inferior at night

**Speaker 5**

9 The fifth speaker regards night-time working as
   A unnatural for all people.
   B unwise for the majority of people.
   C unsuitable in the case of unhealthy people.

10 What does she suggest about people who enjoy living their lives at night?
   A They may come to wish that they hadn't done it.
   B They could find it hard to resume a daytime lifestyle.
   C They will soon find themselves getting fed up with it.

**Discussion** 3 Which of the speakers do you agree/disagree with?

# English in Use 1 (Paper 3 Part 5)

**Lead-in**

**1 a** What type of products do you think these slogans are advertising?

**A** MAYBE. JUST MAYBE.

**B** *SNAP! CRACKLE! POP!*

**C** Let your fingers do the walking

Check your answers on page 207.

**b** What is the purpose of a slogan?

**Register transfer**

▶ Task strategies pages 169 and 170

**2 a** Read both texts quickly.
1 What is the purpose of the first text?
2 How is the style of the second text different from the first?

**b** Do the task. Look at the task strategies and use the Help clues if necessary.

Read the following publicity leaflet. Use the information to complete the gaps in the memorandum. The words you need **do not occur** in the leaflet. **Use no more than two words for each gap**. The exercise begins with an example (**0**).

**PUBLICITY LEAFLET**

## WIN A NEW DVD CAMCORDER!

You can't buy better DVD camcorders anywhere, and we're giving you the chance to win one. Simply invent a new slogan for our ads. (Why not first ask for a shop demonstration of our latest models?)

If you'd like to enter our competition, just follow these rules.

### RULES
1 Entrants must be at least 18 years of age and should never have been company employees.
2 Any entry will be accepted, as long as it's original.
3 Slogans must be sent together with any artwork you want included.
4 Entries must get to us by 12th December.

### FORMAT
1 The slogan must be a maximum of ten words.
2 Handwritten entries will not be accepted.

### PRIZE
• A panel of five judges will select the best entry.
• The winner will be contacted within a fortnight of the closing date.
• The judges' decision will be final.

**MEMORANDUM**

**To:** All sales staff
**From:** Tom Bell (Marketing Director)
**Subject:** Slogan Writing Competition

We all know our DVD camcorders are the best on (**0**) the market, and we have decided to give potential customers a unique (**1**)............... to win one. All they have to do is (**2**)............... with a short, catchy phrase we can use in our advertisements. Anyone wishing to (**3**)............... in the competition should observe (**4**)............... rules.
They must be 18 or (**5**)..............., and at no time should they have been employed by the company. All entries will be accepted, (**6**)............... they do not appear in other advertisements elsewhere. They must be (**7**)............... any artwork that goes with the slogan, and (**8**)............... the company's offices by 12th December. In terms of format, the slogan must be (**9**)............... than ten words, and entries which are not typed will be (**10**)............... .
The winning slogan will (**11**)............... by a jury of five managers, and I will get (**12**)............... with the winner within two weeks of the closing date. Of course, no one will be allowed to (**13**)............... against the judges' decision!
A publicity leaflet is at the printer's. In the meantime, start letting people know.

**HELP**
➤ Question 2
What phrasal verb fits here?
➤ Question 6
What is a slightly more formal phrase for *as long as*?

**Task analysis**

**3** Answer these questions about the task.
1 Which questions require two-word answers?
2 Which questions require a synonym for an equivalent word in the first text?
3 Which phrases in the second text are used to emphasise part of a sentence?

**Discussion**

**4** Work in pairs and think of your own slogan for the DVD camcorder. Each pair should then read out their slogan and the class should choose the best.

# Language development 1

▶ Grammar reference page 183

## Emphasis using negative introductory expressions

**1 a** Compare the sentences and answer the questions below.

1 a They should not have been employed by the company at any time.

   b At no time should they have been employed by the company.

2 a I didn't know how dangerous the expedition would be.

   b Little did I know how dangerous the expedition would be.

3 a He arrived late and forgot to bring the tickets.

   b Not only did he arrive late, (but) he also forgot to bring the tickets.

1 Which sentence in each pair is more emphatic?

2 How has this been achieved?

3 What changes have been made to the position of subject and verb?

4 What verb form has been inserted in sentence 3b?

**b** Rewrite these sentences to make them more emphatic, starting with the expressions in brackets. Make any changes necessary.

1 We will not enter into correspondence with competitors under any circumstances. (*Under no circumstances*)

2 The judges will not discuss their decision on any account. (*On no account*)

3 This slogan is witty and it is also original. (*Not only ... also*)

4 I haven't been so excited since winning the school poetry prize. (*Not since*)

5 You don't often get the opportunity to visit such a remote place. (*Rarely*)

6 We had only just arrived, when we were besieged by reporters. (*Hardly*)

7 They are only now beginning to realise what a mistake they made. (*Only now*)

8 He didn't say a word all evening. (*Not a*)

9 I had just dropped off to sleep, when there was a knock at the door. (*No sooner ... than*)

10 I refuse to go to the party wearing that! (*No way*)

**2** Complete the text by putting one word in each space.

Recently, I took up my bank's offer of a 24-hour telephone banking service. I thought this would save me time. Not (1).......... could I check my balances, (2).......... I could also pay my bills with a single phone call. Little (3).......... I know how hard it would turn out to be. I rang the number the other day, but barely (4).......... I started talking (5).......... the line went dead. I redialled, but no (6).......... had I managed to get through (7).......... I was put on hold. Only after five minutes (8).......... I able to speak to a real person. By that time, I had forgotten my password! (9).......... have I been so embarrassed in all my life. Finally, I managed to remember it, only to be told that I didn't have enough in my account to pay the bill. Never (10).......... it taken so long not to pay a bill!

## Emphasis through fronting parts of the sentence

**3** It is possible to move parts of a sentence or clause in front of the subject

- for emphasis
- to provide a clear link with what came before.

**a** Look at these sentences and decide which part has been emphasised. Re-express them without the emphasis, making any necessary changes.

EXAMPLE: The door opened and out they came.
   *The door opened and they came out.*

1 'He's going to resign.' 'That I find hard to believe.'

2 We arrived at the base of the mountain. Then began the long trek to the summit.

3 Hours I spent thinking of a slogan for the competition!

4 Difficult it may be, but impossible it isn't.

5 The restaurant serves excellent food. Best of all are their starters.

6 Such has been the response to our offer that the deadline has been extended.

7 The King is very worried about the situation, as is his government.

8 Try as we might, we will never surpass their achievements.

**b** Rewrite these sentences, using an appropriate structure from Exercise 3a. Make any changes necessary.

1 The competition was so tense that tempers flared.

2 However hard they tried, they weren't able to overtake the leaders.

3 Shakespeare wrote many plays, but his best-known work is *Hamlet*.

4 We stayed in a hotel in the old part of town. There was a statue of the city's founder opposite the hotel.

5 His work is so good that he deserves the Nobel prize for literature.

6 I'm anxious for news, and the other team members are, too.

7 It took us weeks to finish the project.

8 'It's a beautiful place and very cheap.' 'It may be beautiful, but it isn't cheap.'

# Writing 1   Attitude clauses and phrases

▶ Writing reference page 203

## Writing strategy

In some types of writing that require you to give facts, opinions and recommendations, using 'attitude phrases' to indicate your attitude to the information or comment on its truth will make your writing sound natural and fluent.

**1 a** Compare the two extracts from a report. In extract B,
   1 which expression introduces a statement that is true in most cases but not always?
   2 which structure is used to emphasise the importance of a point?

**A**

> Many of the young people we interviewed said they were interested in technology, but, unless they had had a scientific education, less than 15 per cent felt they were very well-informed.

**B**

> Generally speaking, the young people we interviewed said they were interested in technology. What was particularly noticeable was that, unless they had had a scientific education, less than 15 per cent felt they were very well-informed.

**b** Read these two further extracts and add the expressions in italics to the categories below.

**C**

*Understandably*, perhaps, the general level of interest in technology was higher among older teenagers than younger ones. What became clear, moreover, was that, *generally speaking*, boys were much more interested in technology than girls. *Indeed*, when we spoke to foreign students as part of our research, we established that the same difference in male/female attitudes was also true in other countries.

**D**

*As we shall see*, most young people believe that technology will improve their daily lives. *Surprisingly*, the majority of those we interviewed felt the growth of technology was a less important issue than health care, law and order or education. *Evidently*, they see no link between technological developments and improvements in these other areas, although *admittedly*, we gave no specific examples in our interviews, such as being able to consult a doctor online.

> **Generalising:** *all things considered,* .............................................................................................
> **Giving your opinion about/reaction to some event:** *annoyingly, naturally, strangely,* ...............................................................................................................................
> **Commenting on the truth or likelihood of some event:** *arguably, in fact,*
> .......................................................................................................................................................
> **Emphasising what you have just said:** *in fact,* .........................................................................
> **Admitting that something is true:** *granted,* ...............................................................................

**2** Read the text and mark the most appropriate expression in each pair.
(**1**) *Generally speaking, / Rightly,* the people we interviewed were positive about the growth of technology. (**2**) *As we shall see, / For example,* they enjoy being able to communicate easily with friends and family on their mobile phones or by email. (**3**) *In fact, / Clearly,* many of them commented on how frustrating it used to be when they had to rely on 'snail mail' and land lines. (**4**) *On the other hand, / Not only that,* all the people we spoke to were positive about how advances in communication technology can benefit education. (**5**) *Judging by what they said, / Presumably,* the more ways educational institutions can think of to deliver knowledge and training the better!

**3 a** Interview other students, friends and family about the benefits or otherwise of technology in these areas:
   • education (e.g. calculators, computers, video, teleconferencing)
   • shopping (e.g. supermarkets, Internet, credit cards)
   • housework (e.g. washing machines, microwaves, robots)

▶ Writing reference page 191

**b** Plan and write a report of your findings.

▶SRB  p86

## Listening 2 (Paper 4 Part 3)

**Before you listen**

1 Discuss these questions.
1 What kind of offences are typically associated with young people under 18 (e.g. joy riding, arson)?
2 Why do you think children commit these sorts of offences (e.g. peer pressure, social problems)?
3 What do you think can be done to prevent them?

**Sentence completion**

▶ Task strategies pages 170 and 171

2 🎧 Do the task below. Follow the task strategies on pages 170 and 171 and use the Help clues if necessary. Listen to the recording twice. Remember that in Part 3, most of the sentences will be telling us about the attitude, opinion and feelings of the main speaker.

You will hear part of an interview with Martin Taylor, who helped to initiate a new project which aims to prevent young children turning to crime, and Mary Johnson, whose son, Glenn, has benefitted from the project. For questions **1–9**, complete the sentences.

### A New Project to Prevent the Crimes of Tomorrow

Martin has helped to set up a project with the name [＿＿＿＿ 1 ]

Martin's project operates in an area where crime and [＿＿＿＿ 2 ] are common.

Mary describes Glenn's behaviour at four years old as [＿＿＿＿ 3 ] and aggressive.

Mary feels that the use of the policy known as [＿＿＿＿ 4 ] at Glenn's school was unsuccessful.

Mary says she has observed local children committing offences such as [＿＿＿ *and* ＿ 5 ]

Mary got information about the project from a [＿＿＿＿ 6 ] she found at the library.

Glenn's parents enrolled on something called a [＿＿＿＿ 7 ] offered by the project.

Mary says she learned to reward Glenn's good behaviour with the [＿＿＿＿ 8 ] he needed.

Mary says that Glenn is now giving her [＿＿＿＿ 9 ] for the first time.

**HELP**
➤ Question 1
You are listening for two words, and *project* isn't one of them!
➤ Question 7
What sort of things do you enrol on?
➤ Question 9
You are listening for a noun – what sort of things could a son give his mother? Think of abstract nouns as well as concrete nouns.

**Discussion**

3 Discuss the questions.
1 According to the recording, what are the key risk factors that make it likely a child may become involved in crime and anti-social behaviour?
2 What help and support does the project offer to families with problem children?
3 Such schemes are controversial. What do you think are the pros and cons?

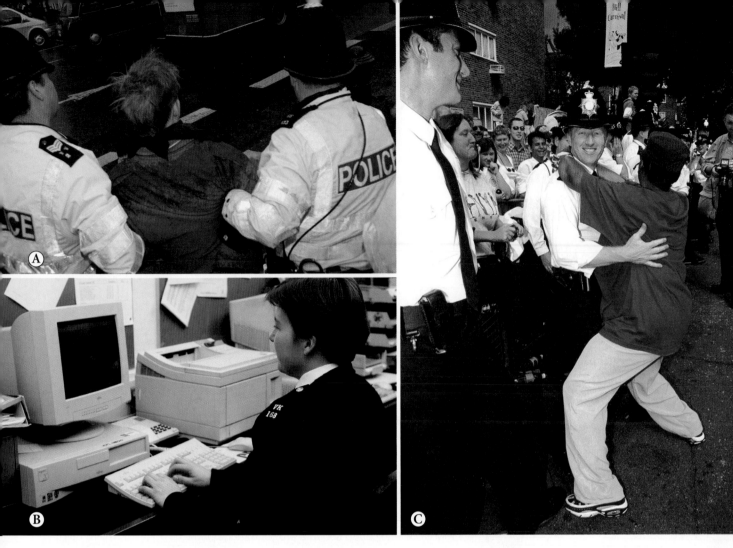

# Speaking  (Paper 5 Parts 3 and 4)

**Vocabulary:** fighting crime

1 a Look at the photos, which show some of the roles of the police in the fight against crime. Say what is happening in each photo, using some of the expressions in the box.

> catch speeding motorists     crowd barrier     carry out desk work
> patrol the streets     appear in court     seal off the area
> attend the scene of a crime     carry out protection duties
> use a speed gun     carry out crowd control duties     chase a suspect
> arrest somebody (for being drunk and disorderly/disturbing the peace)

b What other functions do the police carry out to maintain law and order?

c A National Crime Survey in the UK asked the public what they considered to be the best methods of tackling crime. Which of the following would **you** give most support for?
   • Increasing police numbers and resources
   • Liaising with schools and colleges to educate young people about crime
   • Regular amnesties for weapons
   • Increasing penalties for offenders
   • Greater cooperation between the police and the public
   • Clamping down on street gangs
   • Reporting information to help the police detect crime and catch criminals
   • Carrying out more frequent 'stop and search' checks

d Compare your ideas with the results of the survey on page 207.

e What other approaches can you suggest? What has proved effective in your country/town?

2 a Read about Crimestoppers. Mark the correct option in each set.

# CRIMESTOPPERS' SUCCESS STORY

**Crimestoppers** is a registered charity which works with local communities and helps to harness public support in the fight against crime. By providing its 0800 555 111 number, **Crimestoppers** allows the **(1)** *general / common / ordinary* public to alert the police to criminal activities that affect their community, such as drug-**(2)** *bargaining / dealing / trading*, armed robbery, burglary or murder.

The key to the success of the **(3)** *scheme / plan / action* is that the callers always retain their **(4)** *secrecy / anonymity / identity*. No names are asked for, calls are not recorded, and no written **(5)** *statement / assertion / declaration* or court appearance is required. For people who might possess vital information, **Crimestoppers** creates an opportunity for them to **(6)** *come forward /*

*volunteer / show willing* without fearing **(7)** *vengeance / revenge / reprisals*. The caller is given a unique code, which **(8)** *permits / enables / entitles* them to a reward if the information secures a conviction. Only four per cent of callers actually take **(9)** *on / up / over* this offer.

Since it was set **(10)** *up / on / off* in 1988, **Crimestoppers** has received over 480,000 calls with useful information, resulting in the **(11)** *custody / arrest / incarceration* of over 44,000 suspected offenders. Over £55 million worth of property has been **(12)** *redeemed / recuperated / recovered*, as well as drugs to the value of over £60 million. Every five days, someone is **(13)** *accused / charged / arraigned* with murder or attempted murder, following calls to **Crimestoppers**.

b Is there a similar scheme in your country?

3 What penalties do you think are appropriate for the crimes listed below? What factors would influence your decision?

- a prison sentence (*say how long*)
- life imprisonment
- a fine (*say how much*)
- an anti-social behaviour order
- community service (*say how many hours*)

- forging the signature on a credit card
- hacking into computer programs
- shoplifting
- armed robbery
- joy riding
- libel or slander

- damaging public property
- arson, in order to make an insurance claim
- stealing and using credit or debit card PIN numbers
- assault on an elderly person
- drunk driving

### Collaborative task

▶ Task strategies pages 171 and 172

**4 a** 🎧 Look at the photos on pages 128–129 again and listen to the examiner's instructions. What do you have to do?

**b** Work in pairs and do the task. Time yourselves.

**c** Tell the class briefly which photos you have chosen and why.

### Sample answer (Part 4)

▶ Task strategy page 172

**5 a** Read the following Part 4 questions, which develop the topic in Part 3. Think about what answers you would give.

1 Do you think there is more crime now than in the past, or are people just more afraid of crime?

2 Is crime worse in big cities than in small towns and villages?

3 How can ordinary people protect themselves against crime?

4 Do you think sending criminals to prison is the best way to stop them re-offending?

5 Do you think violent films and computer games encourage people to commit crimes?

**b** 🎧 Listen to two people answering two of the questions above.

1 Which questions did the examiner ask?

2 Did the speakers follow the advice in the task strategy when answering the questions?

3 What expression did the male speaker use to 'buy time'?

### Useful language: unreal tenses

**6 a** Listen to the sample answer again and complete the following sentences. What does the choice of tense form indicate?

1 The newspapers send out panic signals, as if muggers ........................................ around every corner.

2 I wish people ........................................ that crime is really quite low.

3 It's time the police ........................................ into preventing people dying on the roads.

4 I'd really rather they ........................................ violent films on TV when children are likely to see them.

5 Suppose someone with violent tendencies ........................................ a film like this … they might get ideas.

**b** Which statements in Exercise 6a do you agree/disagree with?

**c** Rewrite these sentences beginning with the words in brackets.

1 We don't need more prisons – crime isn't any higher than it used to be. (*It's not as if*)

2 They should really find an alternative to prison. (*It's time*)

3 I think it would be better if the courts passed more Community Service Orders. (*I'd rather*)

4 I'd like the government to ban violent computer games. (*I wish*)

### Developing the discussion

**7 a** Work in pairs. Take turns to ask and answer the questions in Exercise 5a.

**b** Compare some of your ideas with the rest of the class.

# English in Use 2 (Paper 3 Part 2)

**Lead-in** 1 Look at the photo and the title of the text below. Have you heard of Butch Cassidy? Why do you think he became 'a legend'?

**Open cloze** 2 a Read the title and the text below quickly. (Ignore the spaces at this stage.) What information do you find out about Butch Cassidy?

▶ Task strategies page 169

b Do the task. Follow the task strategies.

For questions **1–15**, complete the following article by writing each missing word in the space. **Use only one word for each space**. The exercise begins with an example (**0**).

# Butch Cassidy – a legend of the American West

*Butch Cassidy 1866–1908*

Robert Leroy Parker, or Butch Cassidy (**0**) as he was popularly known, was one of the most prolific bank and train robbers of the American West. However, (**1**)......... most other notorious criminals of the time, for (**2**)......... killing was routine, Cassidy was far (**3**)......... being a violent man, claiming he had never murdered another human being.

On the contrary, during his robberies he did his best to be the model (**4**)......... politeness, seeing (**5**)......... as a 'Gentleman's Outlaw'. On (**6**)......... occasion, when he broke (**7**)......... a tailor's shop, he even left contact details, saying he would pay for the clothes on his next visit. Unfortunately for Cassidy, the shopkeeper was less (**8**)......... impressed and informed the authorities, although all charges (**9**)......... eventually dropped.

After a term in prison (**10**)......... stealing horses, Cassidy organised the 'Wild Bunch', and from 1886 to 1901, robbed well (**11**)......... a dozen banks and trains throughout the West. Unfortunately, during a Montana train robbery, in which they stole $65,000 – the (**12**)......... they'd ever managed to get away with in one go – a railway employee was killed. As a result, Cassidy and his right-hand man 'The Sundance Kid' fled to Argentina, and (**13**)......... looks as if for a few years they managed to live peacefully as ranchers. No one knows (**14**)........., but the pair finally resumed (**15**)......... criminal ways and were killed in a gun battle with soldiers in Bolivia.

**Task analysis** 3 Answer these questions about the task.
  1 Which questions test
    • pronouns?
    • prepositions?
    • comparative structures?
  2 How many other comparative structures can you find in the text?

**Discussion** 4 The story of Butch Cassidy and the Sundance Kid was made into a Hollywood movie in 1969 and starred Paul Newman and Robert Redford. What other films can you think of that have romanticised criminals in a similar way?

# Language development 2

▶ Grammar reference page 184

## Comparatives and superlatives

**1** **a** Read the text. Seven of the sentences contain either one or two mistakes. Find and correct them.

New York was once notorious as one of the world's most dangerous city. Nowadays, however, it is far more safe. There are considerably few crimes, and people are not as much afraid to walk around the streets. The crime rate is now much the same than in other comparable cities and nothing like it was. A key reason for the improvements was the introduction of new laws that were great deal stricter. Penalties are now by far tougher the city has ever seen. There are some people who say life is not as much fun these days and that they feel less restricted. However, for most residents it is, without doubt, the best of times to live in the city.

*Bank clerk learns to fire pistol (New York, 1922)*

**b** Match words from columns A and B to make comparative expressions. There may be more than one possibility.

EXAMPLE: *It is easily the safest …*

| | A | B |
|---|---|---|
| It is | ~~easily~~ | like as safe |
| | far/considerably | less safe |
| | nowhere | ~~the safest~~ |
| | nothing | about the safest |
| | by | same (as) |
| | just | safer |
| | one | far the safest |
| | somewhat/slightly | deal safer |
| | (not) nearly as | safe (as) |
| | a great | near as safe |
| | much the | of the safest |

**c** Use the structures in Exercise 1b to compare your town/city/neighbourhood with the way it was ten, 20 or more years ago. You could talk about safety, size, graffiti, cleanliness, nightlife or anything else of interest. Give possible reasons for any changes.

EXAMPLE: *My neighbourhood is far livelier than it was ten years ago. It's because …*

## Other ways of making comparisons

**2** **a** Mark the correct option in each pair.

1 I'd sooner take a taxi *than / as* walk home.
2 Rather than just worry about crime, I'd *want / prefer* to do something about it.
3 It was such *a terrible / terrible a* crime that people could hardly believe it.
4 He was working *like / as* a security guard, but acted more *like / as* the Chief of Police.
5 I thought his behaviour was *stranger / more strange* than suspicious.
6 *More / The more* people understand crime, *less / the less* they worry about it.
7 The fight against crime is getting *more and more / the more* sophisticated.
8 This was as bad a crime *as / than* we'd ever seen.

**b** Rewrite the follow sentences using the expressions in brackets.

1 As people read more about crime, they become increasingly afraid. (*the more*)
2 I am more relieved than happy that he has been caught. (*not so much*)
3 He's not as reliable a witness as Jim. (*such*)
4 Crimes using weapons are happening increasingly frequently. (*more and more*)
5 Some people no longer go out because of their fear of crime. (*too afraid*)
6 I think it would be better to have more police officers on the street than more CCTV cameras. (*sooner*)
7 The new regulations are so complicated I can't understand them. (*too*)

**3** Complete the texts by putting a suitable word in each space.

**A**

In my view, **(1)**............. the best way to deal with crime is by dealing with its causes. The **(2)**............. effective course of action is to give criminals long prison sentences. Strange as it may seem, **(3)**............. fewer people they put in prison, **(4)**............. better. The idea of rehabilitating criminals in the community may seem **(5)**............. alarming to appeal to voters, but it isn't **(6)**............. a bad idea when you consider the alternatives.

**B**

**(1)**............. the fear of crime increases, so **(2)**............. and more people are taking self-defence classes. Although such classes are somewhat **(3)**............. popular with women, they are **(4)**............. useful for men. On one recent course, I learnt that women are not nearly **(5)**............. likely as young men to be the victim of street violence. There was **(6)**............. near enough time to cover everything, but I learnt useful tips such as how to use a hairbrush or umbrella **(7)**............. a weapon, and that in some situations it's a great **(8)**............. better to shout 'Fire' than 'Help'.

▶ SRB p89

# Writing 2 Report (Paper 2 Part 2)

**Lead-in**

1 Why do you think many students enjoy living in a hall of residence such as the one in the photo? What security measures are sometimes necessary to make such a place safe for students?

**Understand the task**

▶ Writing reference page 191

2 Read and analyse the task below. What are the main questions you need to ask yourself about the task? What are the answers?

> You are studying at a residential summer school in an English-speaking country. There have been reports of intruders on the premises, and many students do not feel safe. As you are the Student Representative, you have discussed the situation with the students. They have asked you to write a report to the School Administrator describing the general security situation, giving examples of security issues that concern them, and outlining their suggestions for improvement.
>
> Write your **report** in approximately 250 words.

**Plan your report**

3 a Decide how many paragraphs you will need in your report and write a heading for each paragraph. Will you include a paragraph about how you obtained the information?

 b Think of ideas and make notes under each heading.

**Language and content**

4 a Choose and complete an opening sentence for each section of your report from the following.

> *This report outlines/looks at …*
> *The aim of this report is to …*
>
> *In recent days …/Recently …*
> *At present …*
> *On the whole …*
>
> *This report is based on/draws on …*
> *I conducted …*
> *According to some students, …*
>
> *It might well be that … but …*
> *In light of the above, we believe the following measures …*
> *In the short/long term, we suggest you should consider …*
> *To improve the situation, we recommend …*

 b Rewrite these student suggestions so that they would be suitable for inclusion in your report. You might need to think of a verb like *install*, *introduce*, etc.

1 'I think they should lock the front door during the day.'

2 'Why not get an unarmed security guard to patrol the premises?'

3 'I don't like the idea much, but I guess eventually we should have security cameras, security lighting. That sort of thing.'

4 'Maybe individual safes for all students to put our valuables in – to be kept in the main office.'

5 'ID cards might be the way forward – of course, the security guard would have to check them.'

**Write your report**

5 Now write your report in about 250 words, using some of the language above.

**Check your report**

▶ Writing reference page 188

6 What questions should you ask yourself when editing your report? Edit your work using the questions as a checklist.

# Module 8: Review

**1** **Decide which word or phrase best fits each space.**

1 German firms have ........ 70% of the market.
   **A** caught more than **B** take over from
   **C** captured over **D** clutched at
2 The law requires equal treatment for all, ........ race, religion or sex.
   **A** regardless of **B** in spite of **C** despite
   **D** with regard to
3 The government bowed ........ popular pressure.
   **A** from **B** with **C** over **D** to
4 This digital music player suits me ........ .
   **A** down to the ground **B** down to earth
   **C** off the ground **D** down and out
5 Parents play a ........ role in a child's upbringing.
   **A** title **B** supporting **C** starring **D** crucial
6 The man was ........ armed robbery.
   **A** charged with **B** arraigned on **C** accused by
   **D** arrested on
7 All our efforts will be worth it ........ .
   **A** before long **B** to cut a long story short
   **C** in the long run **D** a long way away
8 The government has published some highly ........ new proposals for educational reform.
   **A** arguable **B** controversial **C** potential
   **D** available
9 Some people can't even ........ to lock their car.
   **A** get into trouble **B** be worth the hassle
   **C** be bothered **D** care less
10 We don't want to ........ people from expressing their views.
   **A** inhabit **B** inherit **C** inhibit **D** hibernate

**2** **Rewrite each sentence using the word in brackets so it has a similar meaning. Do not change the word in any way.**

1 The company changed the rules to allow people to work nights. (*lifted*)
   ................................................................................
2 Only one witness has offered to help. (*forward*)
   ................................................................................
3 The newspapers only seem to write about young people. (*preoccupied*)
   ................................................................................
4 Someone robbed him last night. (*victim*)
   ................................................................................
5 We need to cut back on the amount of traffic on our roads. (*congestion*)
   ................................................................................
6 He didn't realise he'd done something wrong. (*offence*)
   ................................................................................

7 It's time we got the public talking about terrorism. (*initiated*)
   ................................................................................
8 Suddenly there was a lot of crime. (*wave*)
   ................................................................................

**3** **Correct the mistakes in negative expressions, inversion and comparatives.**

1 I'd sooner to have more police officers on the beat as more CCTV cameras.
2 Little I realise that there were such many serious crimes in so small place.
3 The hackers' attacks are nowhere near intense like last week's.
4 No way I will work like a community officer in my spare time!
5 Sometimes, less we know, better is it.
6 He acted more as a criminal as a police officer!
7 On no account you should feel too scared report the crime.
8 Not once anyone broke into the house!

**4** **Complete the second sentence so that it has a similar meaning to the first.**

1 I'm more disheartened than desperate at the slow progress we're making.
   I'm not so much ................................................
2 There hasn't been so much interest in a piece of new technology since the first PC.
   Not since ................................................
3 The device isn't as simple as I thought.
   It isn't such ................................................
4 It's almost impossible to get one anywhere.
   To get ................................................
5 It doesn't make as much noise as the other one.
   It's somewhat ................................................
6 It had only just appeared on the market, when a major flaw came to light.
   Hardly ................................................
7 The bug was so complicated that they couldn't fix it immediately.
   The bug was too ................................................
8 As I think about the problem more, I become more worried about it.
   The more ................................................
9 He solved the problem and he discovered a way of making the device work better.
   Not only ................................................

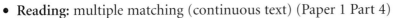

# Communication

## Overview

- **Reading:** multiple matching (continuous text) (Paper 1 Part 4)
- **Vocabulary:** words with similar meanings; sound words; animal idioms
- **Listening 1:** multiple-choice questions (Paper 4 Part 3)
- **English in Use 1:** error correction (extra word) (Paper 3 Part 3)
- **Language development:** reported speech; patterns after reporting verbs
- **Writing 1:** sentence accuracy
- **Listening 2:** sentence completion (Paper 4 Part 2)
- **Speaking:** complete Paper 5
- **English in Use 2:** word formation (Paper 3 Part 4)
- **Writing 2:** proposal (Paper 2 Part 1)

## Lead-in

- Who or what does each of the photos show?
- What 'message' are they trying to communicate in each case?
- 'It's not what you say, it's how you say it.' How far do you agree? Give examples from your experience that support your views.

# Something to say

## Reading (Paper 1 Part 4)

**Before you read**

1 Read the title and subheading of the magazine article opposite. How much do you know about how animals communicate with each other?

**Scanning and skimming**

2 Look at the list of animals in the multiple-matching task. Scan the article to find where they are mentioned and write the letters A–H next to them. Now quickly read the text about each animal to find out how they communicate.

**Multiple matching**

▶ Task strategies page 168

3 For questions 1–17, choose your answers from the animals A–H. You may choose any of the animals more than once. Take no more than 25 minutes for this task.

| A Stink bug | C King penguin | E Ring-tailed lemur | G Chimpanzee |
| B Elephant | D Tiger | F Vervet monkey | H Prairie dog |

According to the article, which animal uses a form of communication that

helps family members to find each other again after a long separation?   **1** ...........

is designed to help individuals feel a part of the social group?   **2** ...........

varies according to the gender of the individual?   **3** ...........

is designed to deter those threatening the species?   **4** ...........

is designed to mark out a particular locality for a number of individuals?   **5** ...........

was originally intended to help members of another species?   **6** ...........

helps a species in areas where visibility may be poor?   **7** ...........

allows one individual to attract or repel another?   **8** ...........

shows that it can identify which members of another species may be dangerous?   **9** ...........

is designed for use in confrontations between members of the species?   **10** ...........

enables a group of individuals to maintain contact over large distances?   **11** ...........

identifies which other species may be posing a threat at any one time?   **12** ........... **13** ...........

makes use of a plant to transmit a message between individuals?   **14** ........... **15** ...........

allows individuals to be identified within a group?   **16** ........... **17** ...........

**Task analysis**

4 Were you able to complete the task within the time limit?

**Discussion**

5 Discuss these questions.

1 What are the main purposes of animal communication according to the text?

2 How do you think these compare with humans? How do human behaviours differ from animal behaviours in similar situations?

3 Did you learn anything about animal communication from the text that you didn't know before? Did anything surprise you particularly?

# Calls of the Wild

**The television presenter and zoologist, Dr Charlotte Uhlenbroek has been exploring the secrets of animal communication.**

Although we share the same physical world with many other creatures, we often see, hear and smell that world in quite different ways. But as technology advances, we are beginning to get unprecedented insights into the sensory world of animals. Charlotte Uhlenbroek tells of how one day she studied some tiny **stink bugs** crawling up a vine leaf. Wearing headphones wired up to a computer, she eavesdropped on the tiny green insects' conversation — an exchange conducted by infinitesimally small vibrations along a network of branches. She heard the rhythm of five scratchy pulses punctuated by a pause, sent out by the female of the species, and a reply from a male; pure-toned pulses followed by noisy bursts of sound. If a rival male comes in on the conversation, however, the female can tap out a different rhythm to make him go away. Listening in on their conversation, the insects' equivalent to a first date, Uhlenbroek gained an astounding insight into the hidden world of animal communication, a secret code that scientists are only now beginning to crack.

Sound is one of the most pervasive and persuasive forms of communication. As Uhlenbroek explains, 'Patterns of sound are almost infinite, and calls can include a huge variety of information.' In using sound to find a mate, look after offspring, locate food or warn of danger, individual animals and groups can convey messages far more detailed and subtle than scientists had previously realised. **Elephants**, for example, use very low-pitched sounds to communicate over distances of several miles, whereas trumpeting is a sound of excitement, an expression of surprise or alarm, or a cry for help. If an old female elephant, the herd's leader, senses danger, she raises her trunk and roars in fury, flapping her ears as she emits a loud trumpeting sound. If this doesn't scare away a predator, she charges, hurling her body at her enemy at speeds of up to 25 miles per hour. In peaceful times, a call which is frequently used is the contact rumble, which allows feeding elephants to keep in touch in areas where dense vegetation prevents them from keeping an eye on one another. Yet we only hear part of their calls. Elephants can produce a sound as low as 8Hz, known as 'infrasound'. This may account for the seemingly telepathic way widely dispersed elephants move in relation to one another. Elephants recognise the calls of about 100 other herd members, while they can identify each other's rumbles at a range of over a mile; the human equivalent of hearing the voice of a friend on the other side of a small town.

One clue to how animals might encode identity has been found after studying the **king penguins** of the Crozet Islands in the Indian Ocean. When chicks are a month old, both parents have to venture out to sea, sometimes 300 miles away, if they are to find sufficient food for their offspring. On their return, parents and chicks relocate each other by calling. Research carried out in France has shown that there are clues buried within the calls which help penguins to discriminate between one chick and another. To find out where these may lie, researchers modified various parts of the parents' calls and played back recordings to the chicks, who responded to the bass frequencies of the calls but not to the high treble frequencies. This reflects the fact that bass sounds travel further and more efficiently than treble frequencies. The first quarter of a second of the call was enough for the chicks to correctly identify the parents.

*A tiger leaves its mark.*

*Ring-tailed lemurs*

Animals also use chemicals to communicate. **Tigers** leave traces for each other by marking trees in the forest — by digging its claws deep into the bark and spraying it with scent, each individual tiger impregnates the chosen trunk with a great deal of information about itself. By acting as relay stations, the trunks play a vital role in animal communication. Male **ring-tailed lemurs** maintain their group's territory with scent-marking and a plaintive call that can be heard up to half a mile away. To intimidate rivals, a male secretes a pungent substance from its arms and rubs its tail against these glands. The other male responds in kind, and sooner or later the smellier tail wins, and the overwhelmed contender backs off.

*Vervet monkey*

Animals from species facing common dangers may effectively communicate with one another by making use of each other's alarm calls. In Ambroseli National Park, **vervet monkeys** look to the starling for signs of danger. If these birds emit a harsh cry, a sign of a predator approaching on the ground, the monkey will take to the trees, while a clear whistle, a response to hawks or eagles, will make them look up to the sky.

In future, it looks as though science will help us understand more about the language of animals. 'Communication involves much more than just the exchange of information,' says Uhlenbroek. If you watch **chimpanzees** grooming each other for hours, you realise this is a vital part of communicating, the purpose of which is to create an impression, to persuade, to bond them to the family or tribal unit.

The **prairie dogs** of Arizona exhibit very sophisticated behaviour. Small rodents living in burrows, they are hunted by a great number of predators, from hawks, foxes, dogs and cats to humans. As a defence, they have evolved a special alarm call for each one. Latest findings have shown that the animals have a word for *human* in their vocabulary and can describe individual people in detail, down to their size, or whether they are carrying a gun. Uhlenbroek concludes, 'If small rodents show such extraordinary sophistication, what might we find animals saying to each other in future?'

*Prairie dogs*

# Vocabulary

## Similar meanings

**1** a Find words and expressions in the text on page 137 that could be replaced in this context by the following. Add the noun phrase from the text where there is one.

EXAMPLE: learn things we've never known before about (sth.)

***get unprecedented insights into*** *the sensory world of animals*

**Paragraph 1**
1 extremely tiny
2 interrupts
3 solve

**Paragraph 2**
4 common
5 communicate
6 makes
7 frighten off
8 explain

**Paragraph 3**
9 put into a code
10 identify the difference
11 The reason for this is that

**Paragraph 4**
12 small signs
13 sad
14 frighten
15 strong smelling
16 does the same
17 moves away

**Paragraph 5**
18 depend on
19 climb

**Paragraph 7**
20 show
21 developed
22 including

b Look back through the text and find more expressions in the text that you would like to add to your vocabulary notebook. Check their meaning in your dictionary.

## Sounds

**2** a The following words, some of which are used in the text on page 137, describe animal sounds. Match the sound to an animal, then decide if each sound is loud/quiet, high/low, long/short, musical/not musical.

1 trumpet    a snake
2 roar    b frog
3 rumble    c elephant
4 whistle    d mouse
5 squeak    e lion
6 hiss    f dog
7 growl    g starling
8 croak

b Which of the verbs in Exercise 2a would you associate with the following?

1 an engine
2 thunder
3 an audience (in a theatre, etc.)
4 the wind
5 an old door
6 a burst tyre
7 a sporting event
8 someone boasting
9 nervousness
10 anger
11 getting attention

c Complete the sentences using verbs from Exercise 2a in the correct form. Use each verb once only.

1 'Get out of my way,' .............. the old man as he pushed past me.
2 The company is proudly .............. the fact that it has won the contract.
3 The audience, which hated the speaker, booed and .............. throughout his talk.
4 The rubber soles of my shoes .............. on the shiny floor.
5 'Help,' she ............., her throat dry with fear.
6 Fans yelled and .............. with excitement when the band came on stage.
7 Everyone .............. with laughter when he told the joke.
8 James was so hungry that his stomach .............. all through the meeting.

## Animal idioms

**3** a Choose a suitable animal from the box to complete the idioms 1–7. Then match the idioms to their meanings a–g.

| donkey  goose  cat  parrot  rat  horse  rabbit |
|---|

1 to smell a ..............
2 to let the .............. out of the bag
3 to hear something (straight) from the ..............'s mouth
4 to talk the hind leg off a ..............
5 to .............. on about something
6 wouldn't say boo to a ..............
7 to say something .............. fashion

a to be quiet or shy
b to be told something directly from the source
c to be suspicious about what you hear or see
d to talk for a long time in an annoying way
e to speak at length about unimportant things
f to give away a secret
g to repeat something without understanding it

b Use the idioms in Exercise 3a to complete the following sentences.

1 I know this information is true – I heard it ................................................... .
2 My aunt Sally never stops chatting; she could ................................................... .
3 It was supposed to be a surprise party, but someone must have ................................................... .
4 I am surprised Jen stood up to her boss like that; normally she ................................................... .
5 Gary said he was going to work, but he's obviously somewhere else. I ...................................................!
6 I'm not surprised Kathy's phone bill is so high the way she ................................................... .
7 At school we had to learn poems and then repeat them ................................................... .

▶SRB  p94

# Listening 1 (Paper 4 Part 3)

**Before you listen**

1 To make a good impression at a job interview, how should you
 a) dress?  b) greet people?  c) sit?  d) speak?

**Multiple-choice questions**

▶ Task strategies pages 170 and 171

2 🎧 Listen and do the task below. Listen to the recording twice.

You will hear part of a radio programme in which two recruitment experts, Jodie Bradwell and Gary Smart, are talking about how candidates should behave at job interviews. For questions **1–7**, choose the best option **A**, **B**, **C** or **D**.

1 What is Jodie's opinion of the research she mentions?
 A She's sceptical about it.
 B She's very impressed by it.
 C She regards it as unrealistic.
 D She doubts how influential it will be.

2 Gary fears that the research they are discussing could lead to
 A over-complicated recruitment procedures.
 B inappropriate behaviour at job interviews.
 C people taking job interviews too seriously.
 D the wrong people being selected at interviews.

3 Jodie reminds Gary that the research deals with
 A attitudes that interviewers are unaware of.
 B issues that interviewers discuss after the interview.
 C impressions that may be adjusted during an interview.
 D behaviour that may help identify the weaker candidates.

4 What advice does Gary give about how to dress for an interview?
 A Wear the same clothes as you would in the job.
 B Find out what other interviewees will be wearing.
 C Wear the clothes that you feel most comfortable in.
 D Make it clear that you've thought about your appearance.

5 According to Jodie, how do interviewers respond to candidates' body language?
 A They notice when people are behaving unnaturally.
 B They are looking for signs of positive character traits.
 C They are suspicious when it doesn't match what they hear.
 D They make allowances for the fact that people are nervous.

6 Gary describes a role-play that demonstrates how body language can
 A make candidates speak more confidently.
 B influence how candidates feel about the interview.
 C help candidates to think more clearly in an interview.
 D alter candidates' perception of the questions they are asked.

7 In conclusion, what advice does Jodie give candidates about body language?
 A It's a good idea to practise sending out the right signals.
 B It should be adjusted to match that of the interviewers.
 C It shouldn't be something you worry about too much.
 D It's better not to think about it during the interview.

**Discussion**

3 a After listening to the programme, would you change any of your ideas in Exercise 1?

 b Prepare a list of Dos and Don'ts for candidates based on the information you have heard in the programme.

"I'm sorry, I always fall to pieces at interviews."

# English in Use 1 (Paper 3 Part 3)

Lead-in

**1 Discuss these questions.**

1 Do you know what your first words were when you were a baby?
2 How much do you know about how babies learn to speak?
3 Look at the title of the text below and the photo, from the film *L'Enfant Sauvage* by the French director Truffaut. What do you know about this 'wild boy'?

Error correction

▶ Task strategies page 169

**2 a Read the text, ignoring the mistakes at this stage. What do you find out about the boy in the photo?**

**b Complete the task. Follow the task strategies.**

In **most** lines of the following text, there is **one** unnecessary word. It is either grammatically incorrect or does not fit in with the sense of the text. For each numbered line (**1–16**), find this word and write it in the box. **Some lines are correct.** Indicate these lines with a tick (✓) in the box. The exercise begins with two examples (**0**) and (**00**).

## WILD BOY OF AVEYRON

| | | |
|---|---|---|
| 'Victor' was the name given to a boy who was first seen in 1797 | **0** | ✓ |
| was wandering wild and naked in the woods near Toulouse in | **00** | was |
| France. On two occasions, he was captured himself by villagers, | **1** | |
| but on each time he managed to escape. However, a few years later, | **2** | |
| 'Victor' emerged from the forest on his own, making people | **3** | |
| wonder if that he had grown used to human company during | **4** | |
| his capture. 'Victor', who assumed by the locals to be about | **5** | |
| 12 years old, couldn't speak any really language because | **6** | |
| he had lived in the wild all his life. Indeed, some people | **7** | |
| thought of he had probably grown up among wild animals. As | **8** | |
| 'Victor' was an extremely unusual boy, he was examined | **9** | |
| by these experts, including a hearing specialist who tried | **10** | |
| with teaching him to speak. He managed to learn to understand | **11** | |
| some language and read simple words, but his progress was quite | **12** | |
| so slow that it was decided to abandon the experiment. To the | **13** | |
| disappointment of those and who had hoped he could be | **14** | |
| taught a language, the only words Victor ever learnt to speak | **15** | |
| which were the French words for *milk* and *Oh, God*. | **16** | |

Discussion

**3 What does this story tell us about the way we learn our first language?**

# Language development

▶ Grammar reference page 185

## Patterns after reporting verbs

**1** Cross out the option that does not fit the sentence. Then rewrite the sentence using the option you have crossed out.

1 She ........................ him about the problem.
   **A** complained   **B** reminded   **C** warned   **D** told

2 Mike ........................ having eaten all the ice cream in the fridge.
   **A** admitted   **B** denied   **C** confessed   **D** regretted

3 The lawyer ........................ that I should contact him immediately.
   **A** insisted   **B** requested   **C** recommended   **D** advised

4 Jackie ........................ to write the letter for her.
   **A** agreed   **B** offered   **C** requested   **D** refused

5 Peter suggested ........................ you.
   **A** emailing   **B** that I email   **C** to email   **D** I emailed

6 A number of people ........................ on how easy she was to talk to.
   **A** commented   **B** noticed   **C** remarked   **D** agreed

7 The report ........................ people to spend more time together as a family.
   **A** suggests   **B** urges   **C** advises   **D** persuades

8 They objected to ........................ the phone.
   **A** our using   **B** us using   **C** using   **D** use

**2** **a** Match the verbs in the box to the quotations below. Then report each statement, using patterns from Exercise 1.

> *announce   remind   apologise   regret   advise*
> *explain   admit   blame*

1 'I'm sorry I forgot to record the programme.' Emily …

2 'Listen everyone, the programme I made is on TV tomorrow.' Mike …

3 'If I were you, I'd get rid of the TV.' Kevin …

4 'I reckon it was Laura who broke the TV.' Claudio …

5 'Don't forget to switch the TV off before you go to bed.' Stella …

6 'I shouldn't have stayed up late to watch that film.' Richard …

7 'It's true, I have been watching a lot of TV recently.' Doug …

8 'The reason why I always have the TV on is that I don't like being on my own.' Susanna …

**b** Ask a partner questions about their TV habits.
EXAMPLES:
* Do you watch too much TV?
* What type of programme do you never watch?
* What programmes do you recommend?

**c** Report your partner's answers to someone else.
EXAMPLE: *Georgia claims that she never watches TV. She says the reason is because …*

## Impersonal report structures

**3** **a** Look at these examples and mark the impersonal report structures.
EXAMPLE: Dolphins are said to be highly intelligent.

1 It is claimed that gorillas are as intelligent as humans.

2 It is known that Penny Patterson taught a gorilla, Koko, to communicate.

3 Koko is reputed to have acquired 645 words.

4 It's been suggested that Koko understands grammar.

5 It is hoped that more research can be done in future.

**b** Report these comments using an impersonal form. In some cases, two structures are possible.

1 People say that Koko has an IQ of 85–95.

2 Koko's trainers report that she can make logical sentences.

3 Some people have hinted that Koko's trainers imagine she is cleverer than she is.

4 Some people argue that Koko knows only words and not grammar.

5 They suggest that the word order she uses is either memorised or random.

6 Some people believe that human language is outside the capacity of other species.

7 Many people accept that human language is a unique phenomenon without significant similarity in the animal world.

**c** Discuss these questions.

1 It has been claimed that the ability to use language sets human beings apart from other animals. Do you agree?

2 Is there anything else that you think makes humans unique?

"HE'S NICE ENOUGH, BUT IT'S HARD TO GET AN INTELLIGENT CONVERSATION OUT OF HIM."

# Writing 1    Sentence skills: accuracy

▶ Writing reference pages 201 and 204

## Writing strategy

In Paper 2 of the exam, you are assessed on your ability to write clearly and accurately, with a minimum of errors. Mistakes that impede comprehension are penalised. Be aware of the typical errors you make and try to avoid them. Reread what you have written at least three times and check
• sentence structure and punctuation
• grammatical accuracy
• choice of words and spelling.

1   Identify and correct the errors in each group of extracts from students' work.

a   Sentence structure and punctuation
1   This autumn starts a new series of wildlife programmes on TV.
2   Language is complex and subtle, however most children are able to learn their mother tongue very rapidly.
3   I really enjoy being able to speak a foreign language. Because this enables me to find out more about the country's culture and customs.
4   If students do summer work abroad, they should not expect to earn a lot of money, the pay is usually quite low.
5   The leisure centre has several tennis courts. A great opportunity for anyone who enjoys knocking a ball about.
6   Trainees need not have any previous experience, it is much more important their willingness to learn.
7   Children listen carefully to their parents learning from their mistakes.

b   Grammatical accuracy
1   There is a lot of things to do in my town.
2   A hamburger with French fries are my favourite meal.
3   At the sports centre, you can take up a sport most of you have never hear of: curling.
4   Why not taking up jogging?
5   If I didn't throw away the receipt, I could have get my money refunded.
6   All what concerns him is how much he earns.
7   Both hotels offer full board; however, not only the Swan Hotel has a more extensive menu, but also take care of clients' special diets.

c   Choice of words and spelling

1   I beleive you should include a film review to attract more readers. A competition of some kind would also rise the sales of the magazine.

2   After the tour of the factory, there will be a presantation which will give you farther inform about the company, and suggest ways of cooperation. I really wish you will enjoy your visit to my company.

3   'Hey, let's go bungee jumping!' a friend of mine sugested. Everyone accepted to try it out exept from me, as I was scared to death. But then, as I am too shy to say my fear, I agreed. I am so pleased that I did. Bungee jumping is a fantastic sport. Everyone should practice it and feel the adrenaline bump.

2   Plan and write your answer to this task.

An English-language newspaper in your country has asked you to contribute to a series of short articles on people's experiences of learning English. Write about your experiences, covering the following points:
• what you found easy/difficult about learning English
• whether or not you have enjoyed the experience
• what helped you make most progress.

Write your **article** in approximately 250 words.

3   Exchange your work with a partner. Edit each other's work for accuracy.

# 9B Making a statement

## Listening 2 (Paper 4 Part 2)

**Before you listen**

1 Discuss these questions.
   1 Why do you think T-shirts are so popular? Describe your own favourite T-shirt.
   2 How much do you know about the origins of the T-shirt?

**Sentence completion**

▶ Task strategies pages 170 and 171

2 🎧 Do the task below. Read the task strategies before you start and use the Help clues if necessary.

You will hear part of a talk by the fashion historian Tina Bedell about the history of the T-shirt. For questions **1–8**, complete the sentences. **Listen very carefully, as you will hear the recording ONCE only.**

---

### The history of the T-shirt

Cotton undershirts were first worn by [____ 1 ] sailors during the First World War.

In the 1930s, the [____ 2 ] of cotton cloth led to the popularity of cheap cotton underwear.

The original T-shirts had longer [____ 3 ] than modern ones.

Only people like soldiers, [____ 4 ] and workmen wore T-shirts in public before the 1950s.

Tina uses the term [____ 5 ] to describe the T-shirt which Marlon Brando wore on stage in 1950.

The T-shirt became a symbol of [____ 6 ] amongst 1950s teenagers.

From the 1960s, T-shirts began to be used for [____ 7 ] purposes.

In the 1970s, ordinary people often used T-shirts to express their [____ 8 ] opinions.

---

**HELP**
➤ Question 1
  We hear about both French and US sailors, but which wore the cotton undershirts first?
➤ Question 4
  Who, apart from soldiers and workmen, might have found T-shirts comfortable?
➤ Question 5
  You are listening for the actual word(s) that Tina uses.
➤ Question 6
  You are listening for an abstract noun – and the idea is repeated as a simple noun in the name of a film. Which word do you write?

## Task analysis

3 Compare and discuss your answers. What clues in the recording helped you to identify the information you needed?

## Discussion

4 Discuss these questions.
   1 The recording describes the evolving role of the T-shirt from the 1950s to the 1970s. How would you describe its role today?
   2 Can you think of examples of other popular garments that were originally intended for a different purpose?
   3 What other examples can you give of clothing and accessories being used to make a statement?

 ▶SRB p99

143

# Speaking (complete Paper 5)

### Paper 5 Quiz
▶ Task strategies pages 171–172

1 a Can you answer these questions about the Speaking paper?
   1 How long does the test take altogether?
   2 How many candidates normally take the Speaking test together?
   3 How many examiners are there? What are their roles?
   4 How many parts are there, and how long does each one take?
   5 What do you have to do in each part?
   6 What criteria are you assessed on?
   7 What strategies should you follow in each part?

   b Check your answers on pages 171 and 172. How much did you know?

### Part 1: social interaction

2 a Work in groups of four and choose a role.
   INTERLOCUTOR: Ask *some* of the questions on page 207. Stop the discussion after three minutes.
   CANDIDATES A AND B: Respond to the interlocutor.
   ASSESSOR: Listen and evaluate the candidates' performance.

   b Change roles so that everyone has a turn at answering the questions.

### Part 2: long turn

3 Work in the same group as Exercise 2 and change roles, or form different groups. Look at the photos on page 145.
   INTERLOCUTOR: Give Candidate A the instructions on page 207.
   CANDIDATE A: Follow the interlocutor's instructions (about one minute).
   INTERLOCUTOR: Give Candidate B the instructions on page 207.
   CANDIDATE B: Follow the interlocutor's instructions (about one minute).
   INTERLOCUTOR: Give Candidates A and B the instructions on page 207.
   CANDIDATES A AND B: Follow the interlocutor's instructions (about one minute).
   ASSESSOR: Listen and evaluate the candidates' performance.

### Part 3: collaborative task

4 Work in the same group as Exercise 3 and change roles, or form different groups. Look at the photos on page 146.
   INTERLOCUTOR: Give Candidates A and B the instructions on page 207.
   CANDIDATES A AND B: Follow the interlocutor's instructions (about four minutes).
   ASSESSOR: Listen and evaluate the candidates' performance.

### Part 4: extending the discussion

5 Work in the same group as Exercise 4 and change roles.
   INTERLOCUTOR: Ask Candidates A and B the questions on page 207.
   CANDIDATES A AND B: Answer the interlocutor's questions (about four minutes).
   ASSESSOR: Listen and evaluate the candidates' performance.

### Task analysis

6 Discuss your performance in the test.
   1 Which part do you feel most/least confident about?
   2 In which areas do you feel you would like to improve?

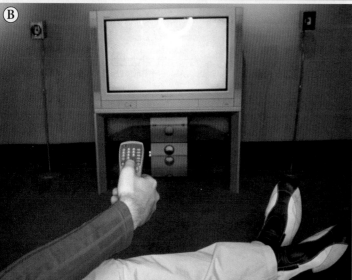

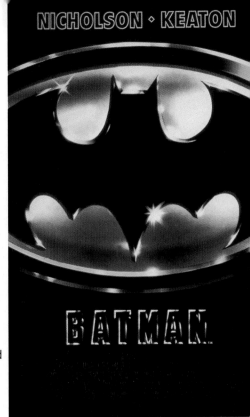

NICHOLSON • KEATON

BATMAN

## English in Use 2 (Paper 3 Part 4)

**Lead-in**

1 Read the titles of the two texts below. What do you think is the connection between the topic of each text?

**Word formation**

▶ Task strategies pages 169 and 170

2 a Read through each text quickly and summarise what each one is about.

b Do the task. Check the task strategies if necessary.

For questions **1–15**, read the texts below. Use the words in the boxes to the right of the texts to form **one** word that fits in the same numbered space in the text. The exercise begins with an example (**0**).

**EXTRACT FROM COLLEGE TEXTBOOK**

# What is 'hype'?

Hype is (**0**) continuous publicity designed to persuade us that something is good, and a perfect example of it is the build-up to the Batman films. (**1**)............., Batman was a cartoon hero who made his first (**2**)............. in a comic book in 1939 and was later turned into a rather silly but, for most people, (**3**)............. character in a 1960s television show. Before the latest darkly (**4**)............. Batman series first came to the screen in 1989, the world was subjected to an extraordinary amount of hype. The first film itself cost $40 million – a (**5**)............. sum of money at the time – and a further $10 million was spent on (**6**)............. . Even more money than that went on producing everything from Batman clothes to Batman stationery. Many people thought the hype was (**7**)............. , but it was nevertheless effective, as the films were very popular.

| | |
|---|---|
| (**0**) | CONTINUE |
| (**1**) | ORIGIN |
| (**2**) | APPEAR |
| (**3**) | FORGET |
| (**4**) | ATMOSPHERE |
| (**5**) | SUBSTANCE |
| (**6**) | MARKET |
| (**7**) | EXCEED |

**MAGAZINE ARTICLE**

# Our car is the message – or is it?

According to some (**8**)............. , cars make a clear statement about their (**9**)............. . The drivers of flashy, soft-top sports cars are either living out a childhood dream of romance or wanting to show how (**10**)............. they are to the opposite sex. Equally, some town dwellers are saying how (**11**)............. independent they are, while wanting to give the impression of (**12**)............. and calm by going around in large, heavy vehicles designed for the countryside. However, the Road Safety Institute complains that, in (**13**)............. , such huge vehicles can give their drivers an excessive sense of (**14**)............. , so that even normally sensitive souls can become (**15**)............. aggressive behind the wheel. Which goes to show that judging people by the cars they drive may be a more complex matter than it seems!

| | |
|---|---|
| (**8**) | PSYCHOLOGY |
| (**9**) | OWN |
| (**10**) | DESIRE |
| (**11**) | FIERCE |
| (**12**) | RELAX |
| (**13**) | REAL |
| (**14**) | SECURE |
| (**15**) | CHARACTER |

**Task analysis**

3 Which stem words have more than one form with the same word class as the gap? What is the difference in meaning? How did you decide which one fitted the gap?

**Dictionary work**

4 Give more examples of 'hype' surrounding a film, concert, etc. How effective was it?

# Writing 2 Proposal (Paper 2 Part 1)

**Lead-in**   1 What activities would you expect to find in an outdoor Adventure Centre? If you were the director of a new centre, how would you try to attract customers?

**Understand the task**   2 Read the task and answer these questions.

▶ Writing reference page 198

   1 WHO are you, and WHAT are you going to write?
   2 What is the PURPOSE of your piece of writing?
   3 WHAT INFORMATION does each piece of input contain?
   4 In what way is a proposal SIMILAR to and DIFFERENT from a report?
   5 What STYLE will you use for your proposal?

You are employed as a Senior Administrator in the Bookings Department of an outdoor adventure centre in England. The Managing Director has asked you to write a proposal suggesting ways of promoting the centre and increasing bookings.

Read the memo from the Director, some feedback from past customers, on which you have written some notes, and an email from one of your colleagues. Then, using the information carefully, write a proposal making the suggestions requested.

MEMO
From:   Douglas Banks, Managing Director
Subject: Improving the performance of the centre

Unfortunately, bookings for the centre have shown no increase over the last year. Can you examine customer feedback, get the views of colleagues in your department and decide what the problem is? I'd like to persuade the Board of Directors to allocate more money in next year's budget for promotion and, if necessary, new facilities. Could you write a proposal that I can send to them, suggesting how we could best raise the profile of the centre, and saying whether or not we should extend our facilities.

*I'd never heard of the centre until a friend told me about it.* — Could have regular open days and invite journalists as well (press, radio, TV?)

*The centre's great. It's got everything I want.* — That seems to be the general view.

*Have you got a website? My search engine couldn't find one.* — We must do something about that!!

*I was surprised how empty the centre was. Why no school groups? It would be ideal for them.* — Offer special deals for school groups?

Hi!
Re your email, yes, I agree our profile needs raising. I was looking at the website this morning – it's not at all user-friendly – very slow, very hard to find what you want. It needs redesigning by specialists!
Also, a better brochure would be a good idea with more useful information, and some attractive, exciting posters that could be put up in Tourist Information Centres.
My other suggestions would be to invite a journalist from the local paper to visit the centre and run a feature.
If we could offer reduced prices for low-season dates, that would really help, I think.

Now write your **proposal** for the Director as outlined above (approximately 250 words). You should use your own words as far as possible.

**Plan your proposal**

3 a Look back at the input and mark the content points you will use in your proposal. Note that related points appear in different parts of the input. Which points can be grouped together? What will be the main focus of your proposal?

b Which of the following could be main headings and which subheadings?

**Introduction   The website   Facilities   Pricing policy   Conclusion
Publicity material   Special events   Suggestions and recommendations**

c Choose from the headings in Exercise 3b for the different sections of your proposal or think of your own. Make notes under each heading, using the information from the input. Remember to use your own words in your notes.

**Language and content**

4 a Choose and complete an opening sentence for each section of your proposal from the following.

> *It is clear from customer feedback that …*
> *The last year's results have been …*
> *With regard to … , the general view seems to be …*
> *To raise the profile of the centre, …*
> *The aim of this proposal …*
> *Perhaps the most effective way of …*
> *If the centre is to attract more customers, it is vital …*
> *A programme of … could …*

b Reword these suggestions using some of the phrases below.
   1 Get a specialist web-design company to redesign the website.
   2 Invite journalists to visit the centre.
   3 Contact Tourist Information Centres and ask them to display posters of the centre.
   4 Increase the promotional budget for next year.

> *We recommend that … should …*
> *It would be a good idea to …*
> *We suggest/propose that …/-ing …*
> *We urge … to …*

**Write your proposal**

5 Now write your proposal in about 250 words using some of the ideas and language above. Remember to avoid copying whole phrases from the input.

**Check your proposal**

6 Edit your work using the checklist on page 188.

▶ Writing reference page 188

▶SRB  p104

# Module 9: Review

**1** Decide which word or phrase best fits each space.

1 The level of hype surrounding the launch of this car is ......... .
   **A** unprecedented   **B** unqualified
   **C** unaccustomed   **D** unrivalled

2 Let's hope that everything goes ......... plan.
   **A** accordingly   **B** in accordance   **C** according to
   **D** in accord with

3 Peter could talk the hind leg off a ......... .
   **A** rabbit   **B** horse   **C** parrot   **D** donkey

4 Genetically modified crops could pose a ......... to wildlife.
   **A** menace   **B** threat   **C** hazard   **D** trap

5 Many kids can't discriminate ......... one brand and another.
   **A** between   **B** against   **C** in favour of   **D** from

6 She ......... a peculiar screech which startled the audience.
   **A** emanated   **B** emitted   **C** omitted   **D** admitted

7 They swore at me, so I answered ......... .
   **A** in kind   **B** of its kind   **C** one of a kind
   **D** nothing of the kind

8 I'm sometimes ......... by the sheer amount of junk mail I receive.
   **A** flooded   **B** conquered   **C** outdone
   **D** overwhelmed

9 Some people ......... to crimes they haven't committed.
   **A** object   **B** insist   **C** confess   **D** deny

10 Back ......... , will you! We'll tell you when we're ready.
   **A** out   **B** off   **C** down   **D** up

**2** Complete the second sentence so that it has a similar meaning to the first.

1 He persuaded everyone with his arguments.
   His arguments were ..................................... .

2 The need for extra publicity was gradually accepted.
   There was ..................................... of the need for extra publicity.

3 It seems to be impossible to get them to speak clearly.
   Getting them to speak clearly is a ..................................... task.

4 The dress she wore was very much in fashion.
   She wore a ..................................... .

5 His quietness today was out of character.
   He was ..................................... today.

6 I'd like a job somewhere locally.
   I'd like a job somewhere in ..................................... .

7 They could tell she was nervous from her voice.
   ..................................... showed in her voice.

8 The people who owned the house previously had left the place in a mess.
   The previous ..................................... had left the place in a mess.

**3** Report the sentences in the past using the words in brackets.

1 'Don't forget to bring your laptop, Tom!' (*I/remind*)

2 'I don't want to say anything about the report.' (*he/comment*)

3 'They want to sack the advertisers!' (*it/suggest*)

4 'Can you all work out what the message means?' (*we/urge*)

5 'Europe's very expensive to visit.' (*she/complain/high cost*)

6 'I don't want to see him again.' (*she/refuse/anything more*)

7 'I hate it every time Carl speaks to Anna – I'm jealous.' (*I/admit/feel*)

8 'They think the economy could improve soon.' (*it/hope*)

**4** Correct the ten mistakes with noun clauses, sentence structure and vocabulary.

There has been known for some time that learning languages can stimulate intellectual development in young children, now research in Canada has suggested that to speak more than one language
5 also helps us to stay mentally alert in old age. Indeed, researchers there have noticed about how much more quick-thinking older bilinguals are than non-bilinguals. They claim that not only bilinguals are more mentally efficient at all the ages they tested,
10 but their memories decline less rapidly in old age.
   They admit that, as yet, they manage to find no evidence to show that learning a language below bilingual level made a difference to adults. However, they hope making further research in this area
15 shortly and have promised they will publish the results at the earliest opportunity. All the same, they remind us on the growing body of evidence suggesting that *any* intellectual activities may have a beneficial effect on the health of our brain.

# MODULE 10
## The world of entertainment

## Overview

- **Reading:** multiple-choice questions (Paper 1 Part 3)
- **Vocabulary:** similar words; noun + preposition + noun phrases; prefixes
- **Listening 1:** sentence completion (Paper 4 Part 2)
- **Language development 1:** participle and *to*-infinitive clauses
- **English in Use 1:** error correction (spelling and punctuation) (Paper 3 Part 3)
- **Writing 1:** sentence variety
- **Listening 2:** multiple-choice questions (Paper 4 Part 3)
- **Speaking:** music; collaborative task (Paper 5 Part 3)
- **English in Use 2:** gapped text (Paper 3 Part 6)
- **Language development 2:** nouns, adjectives, verbs + prepositions; preposition + *-ing* form; confusing pairs
- **Writing 2:** review (comparative) (Paper 2 Part 2)

## Lead-in

- Look at the photos. Which activities best illustrate your idea of having a good time?
- What other forms of entertainment do you enjoy?
- Which do you prefer: being entertained or taking part?
- Discuss this quotation by Walt Disney. How far do you agree?

*'I would rather entertain and hope that people learned something than educate people and hope they were entertained.'*

## Reading (Paper 1 Part 3)

**Before you read**

1 Look at the title and subheading of the article and the photo. Discuss these questions.

   1 Have you ever seen any of Rowan Atkinson's comedy programmes or films? From the photo, what kind of humour would you associate him with (e.g. slapstick, mime, satire)?

   2 From the title and subheading, what aspects of Atkinson's career do you think you are going to read about in this article?

**Skimming**

2 Skim the article quickly. Then try to explain the references in the title to:
   • the rubber-faced joker   • the burden of comedy   • the joy of fixing a plug

**Multiple-choice questions**

▶ Task strategies page 168

3 Read the magazine article and answer questions 1–6. Mark the letter A, B, C or D. Give only one answer to each question.

# Fears of a clown

## He's the rubber-faced joker with millions in the bank, yet Rowan Atkinson would still swap the burden of comedy for the joy of fixing a plug.

The well-known comedy film writer Richard Curtis remembers a day in 1976 when he and a group of fellow students at a university drama club got together to discuss sketch material for their summer review. 'Suddenly, Rowan,
5 this rather odd electrical engineering student who had come to all the meetings but never uttered a word, stood up and started to mime and talk at the same time. I'd never seen anything like it. It was pure genius!' It was as a result of this that Rowan Atkinson stumbled across his future
10 vocation, going on to gain valuable performing experience and forging a professional relationship with Curtis that would underpin his career. He'd done some acting at school, but says there is nothing in his 'old-fashioned and establishment' farming background which indicates the
15 path he would later follow, unless it was perhaps the desire to break out and rebel.

Less than three years after leaving university, Rowan Atkinson was a star, albeit a most unlikely one. True, the disjunction between an intensely private, shy, serious man
20 and a compellingly watchable performer such as he is is not unusual among comedians. But in Atkinson, the division goes deeper, for his comic persona exists in a parallel world dominated by his lifelong passion for cars and machinery. Friends say he is a 'motor mechanic
25 dreaming he is an actor', and his passion for collecting and driving cars seems to be all-consuming. While on tour, theatre riggers were astonished to witness the star performer unplugging the cables, unbolting the scenery and lifting crates. It was almost as if he was pursuing a
30 separate existence as the electrical engineer he had originally planned to be.

Despite being acknowledged all over Europe as the heir to the mime greats of the past, Atkinson insists that he is an actor rather than a comic, and says he hasn't been funny off-stage or screen since adolescent self-consciousness set in at the age of 11. He may have natural gifts – his trademark pliable 'rubber face', the ability to turn nondescript words like 'bag' into lumps of volatile comic explosive, an instinctive knack for mime – but he claims that he needs an audience and the formality of staging or a camera before he can be somebody else. 'I must have a good script to disappear into,' he says. 'Any apparent spontaneity is deceptive. It is all entirely contrived.'

Successful as Atkinson is, he still works hard to extract maximum leverage from his talents, paying incredible attention to detail, always terrified of the risk of failure. 'I constantly believe that there is a better performance just out of reach. That is quite a debilitating and negative experience,' he says. So why doesn't he stop? 'The prospect of doing a role is fun. Looking back on having done it is fine. But the reality of rehearsals and performance!' he shudders visibly. 'Show business is a sandwich with a vicious filling. But even though I hate the filling, I still like the sandwich.'

Whether or not you find its silent slapstick funny, Mr Bean is one of the most successful international exports in British comedy; the highest-rating comedy show on commercial TV in the 90s, it has been sold to more than 245 countries. Atkinson's character communicates through an impressive arsenal of facial expressions and contorted body parts. But Atkinson is adamant that 'the most embarrassing man on the planet' was not based on anybody. 'He was a rehearsal-room creation, emerging spontaneously from visual jokes. As soon as words were denied me, I became Bean, and I find I can turn him on and off like a tap.' Asked to explain the phenomenal success of Bean, he adds, 'The lack of words can't be the key to his appeal. And he's a thoroughly unpleasant man. I think it's the child in a man's body which is the common factor of most visual comedians. As such, he must represent to adults from many nations the child within them, who behaves as we would like to behave, but feel we can't.'

Although impressed by what he has seen of the low-key reality-based comedy that has emerged in the last few years, Atkinson has found himself better suited to exaggerated, visual comedy. And while he is interested in what his family and friends think about his work, he doesn't feel as though he needs their approval. He is aware that Mr Bean is the target of disdain in certain quarters, particularly the more educated critics, but seems to relish Bean's intellectual shallowness. 'It's myself and the audience out there who I'm interested in,' he says. 'My tastes are pretty simple, and I have an inner confidence that what I find funny finds a wide audience. I'm not particularly intellectual or clever or minority-focused in my creative instincts or ambitions.'

1 In the first paragraph, we learn that Rowan Atkinson's desire to be an actor may have resulted from
   A a reaction against his conventional background.
   B a desire to follow up on his university studies.
   C a chance meeting with a well-known writer.
   D a lifelong ambition to perform in public.

2 What is suggested about Rowan Atkinson in the second paragraph?
   A He is an unusually shy man to be a comedian.
   B He shows no signs of enjoying the celebrity lifestyle.
   C His colleagues fear that he regrets his choice of career.
   D His true interests lie outside the world of entertainment.

3 What does Rowan Atkinson suggest about his comic skills?
   A He needs to be in character to make people laugh.
   B His success is largely due to the scripts he has written.
   C He is uneasy when required to speak rather than mime.
   D His particular brand of humour depends on improvisation.

4 What aspect of being an actor does Rowan Atkinson particularly dislike?
   A being compared to fellow performers
   B feeling dissatisfied with his own performance
   C receiving negative feedback after a performance
   D realising that he was insufficiently prepared for a performance

5 To what does Rowan Atkinson attribute the universal success of the character he created, called Mr Bean?
   A the accident-prone nature of the character
   B the fact that people identify with this character
   C the spontaneous way the character was created
   D the fact that the character's comedy is purely visual

6 Which of the following is implied about Rowan Atkinson in the last paragraph?
   A He aims to gain the respect of an intellectual minority.
   B He is embarrassed by the superficial nature of Mr Bean.
   C He doesn't take a great deal of notice of what the critics say.
   D His success is a result of research into what people find amusing.

## Discussion

4 Discuss these questions.
   1 What kind of comedy makes you laugh? Do you prefer visual comedy or comedy based on verbal wit? Give examples.
   2 What are the most popular comedy television programmes or films in your country? Who are the most popular comedians?
   3 Do you think other nationalities would find them funny, or does humour depend on a cultural context?

# Vocabulary

## Similar meanings

**1 a** Find words and expressions in the text on pages 152–153 that could be replaced in this context by the words in italics.

**Paragraph 1**
1 never *said anything*
2 *discovered* his future vocation *by chance*
3 *developing* a strong relationship
4 *provide a solid basis for* his career

**Paragraph 2**
5 a passion *that is so strong that he thinks of little else*

**Paragraph 3**
6 *easily recognised and widely known* face
7 *very ordinary* words
8 apparent spontaneity *that is in fact carefully planned*

**Paragraph 4**
9 a *harmful* experience
10 he *shakes (because he thinks of something unpleasant)*
11 a *nasty and unpleasant* filling

**Paragraph 5**
12 *insists that*
13 an *unusual and impressive* success

**Paragraph 6**
14 *enjoy*

**b** Complete the following collocations with the correct form of words from Exercise 1a.
1 a/an ............... achievement/increase
2 a/an ............... satire/headache
3 a/an ............... suburban house/grey suit
4 a/an ............... story/comedy
5 a/an ............... interest/preoccupation
6 ............... an agreement/alliance
7 ............... a sound/name
8 ............... at the thought/with embarrassment

**c** Look back through the text and note down any more useful expressions you would like to remember. Check their meaning in your dictionary.

## Noun + preposition + noun phrases

**2 a** Add the missing prepositions to these phrases from the text.
1 his passion ......... collecting
2 a knack ......... mime
3 the risk ......... failure
4 attention ......... detail
5 the prospect ......... doing a role
6 the key ......... his appeal
7 a target ......... disdain

**b** Complete the gaps in the text with a noun and preposition combination from Exercise 2a.

Impressionists are people with a **(1)**............ copying the voices and expressions of others. Politicians are often a **(2)**............ this type of comedy, and few relish the **(3)**............ being caricatured. When an impressionist copies a well-known personality, **(4)**............ detail is very important. The **(5)**............ success is to exaggerate the person's outstanding features and to pick up on anything that they have a **(6)**............ , such as food, football or music. It's a difficult form of comedy, and there is always a huge **(7)**............ failure.

**c** Complete the questions with the correct preposition, then ask a partner.
1 Is there anything you have a special knack ......... ?
2 Would the prospect ......... becoming an actor appeal to you? Why?/Why not?
3 Do you have a passion ......... something? And what things do you do as a result of that passion?

## Prefixes

**3 a** What meaning do the prefixes add in these adjectives from the text?
1 The well-known comedy film writer ...
2 He hasn't been funny off-stage or screen since adolescent self-consciousness set in ...
3 What he has seen of the low-key reality-based comedy ...

**b** Which of the prefixes in Exercise 3a can be used with the following words/adjectives?

assured  confident  duty  established  guard
important  level  line  paid  profile  respecting
road  risk  satisfied  tech  track  travelled  worn

**c** Add two more words to each group.

**d** Complete the sentences using a compound from Exercise 3b.
1 Atkinson is now a ............... comedy actor.
2 However, he is very modest and not at all ............... .
3 An actor's career can easily go ............... if they choose the wrong part.
4 No ............... actor would appear in a shampoo commercial.
5 Acting tends to be a ............... job, so actors often need to find other work.
6 Photo-journalists try to catch celebrities ............... to get more natural pictures.
7 Atkinson seldom gives interviews and prefers a ............... lifestyle.

**e** Which of the adjectives beginning with *self-* describe you?

▶SRB p105

"I'M A VERY FUNNY GUY. ALL MY EMPLOYEES SAY SO."

## Listening 1 (Paper 4 Part 2)

**Before you listen** 1 **Discuss the following questions, giving reasons for your answers.**

1 Why and in which situations do people usually laugh?
2 What kind of humour is illustrated in the cartoons? Which kind do you prefer?
3 How important is a sense of humour in everyday life?
4 Does laughing have an effect on your health? In what ways?

**Sentence completion** 2 🎧 **Do the task below. Follow the task strategies.**

▶ Task strategies pages 170 and 171

You will hear part of a radio programme in which a psychologist, Anna Marston, is talking about the social and psychological benefits of laughter. For questions **1–8**, complete the sentences. **Listen very carefully as you will hear the programme ONCE only.**

### LAUGHTER

Anna explains that laughter is often a way of releasing emotional [          1    ]

Anna feels that a good sense of humour can make someone into a [        2    ] person.

Anna says that no more than [          3    ] of laughter is a response to humour.

Anna has found that people use laughter to make [        4    ] easier.

The physical effect of laughter is to increase both [        5    ] and blood pressure.

Laughter can help in the prevention of illnesses such as [      *and*       6    ]

According to recent research, laughter may help people to cope with [        7    ]

Psychologists see laughter as a sign of the [        8    ] needed to face life's difficulties.

**Discussion** 3 **Discuss these questions.**

1 Do you agree with the points made by the speaker? Can you give examples from your personal experience to support them?
2 Are you good at telling jokes? Have you got a favourite joke? Tell the class.

# Language development 1

▶ Grammar reference page 186, Writing reference page 203

## Participle and *to*-infinitive clauses

**1 a** Read these extracts from the text on pages 152–153. Then look at the Grammar reference on page 186 and match the highlighted participle clauses to the uses described there.

1 Less than three years after leaving university, Rowan Atkinson was a star …

2 Despite being acknowledged all over Europe as the heir to the mime greats of the past, Atkinson insists that he is an actor rather than a comic …

3 Atkinson … works hard to extract maximum leverage from his talents, paying incredible attention to detail, always terrified of the risk of failure.

4 Although impressed by what he has seen of the low-key reality-based comedy that has emerged in the last few years, …

**b** How could you re-express the participle clauses using finite verbs (i.e. verbs with a tense)?

**2** Rewrite these sentences, replacing the parts in italics with a suitable participle clause. Make any changes necessary.

1 John became a household name *after he appeared* in a popular sitcom.

2 *I glanced at the TV page* and saw that my favourite comedy was on later.

3 *Sam is very witty*, so he's a great performer.

4 Sarah *spent five years working* in the theatre, so she has lots of stories to tell.

5 *I was bored* with the normal TV channels, so I decided to get cable TV.

6 *As a generalisation, I'd say* few young people like opera.

**3 a** Combine these sentences using a suitable participle clause. Make any changes necessary. You may need to change the order of the sentences.

1 I'd seen the film already. Therefore I didn't go to the cinema with the others.

2 I was amazed by the special effects. I went to see the film three times.

3 I thought I'd get a better view if I sat in the front row.

4 I had hoped the concert would be better. I'd had such a lot of trouble getting tickets.

5 Finally Pavarotti walked off stage. He blew kisses to the audience as he went.

6 I've bought my sister tickets to see *Carmen* at the Opera House. I know how much she likes it.

**b** Combine these sentences using a *to*-infinitive clause.

1 You should see her perform live. You'd think she's been doing it for years.

2 My grandmother saw *The Sound of Music* many times. As a result, she knew all the songs off by heart.

3 I rushed home to watch *Friends*. I was disappointed when I discovered it was a repeat.

4 Phil has directed a lot of plays. He knows what he's talking about.

5 I like opera, but I can never understand the story. I have to read the programme notes.

6 The show is not for everyone. Or in other words, it's pretty unusual.

**4** Read the text and use participle and *to*-infinitive clauses to rewrite the underlined parts more economically.

One day, <u>when I was feeling generous,</u> I volunteered to take my five-year-old niece Amy to a musical. <u>I thought</u> *Chitty Chitty Bang Bang* would be good for children, <u>so</u> I booked two tickets.

<u>If I planned the outing well,</u> I was sure it would all go smoothly and we would have a great time. <u>We had stopped</u> a few times on the way to the theatre, <u>so</u> we arrived just as the show was starting. We found our seats, <u>but we discovered</u> that we were sitting behind a very tall family. <u>Because she wasn't able to see,</u> Amy had to sit on my lap for the full three hours!

At first, she was spellbound. <u>If you saw her face,</u> you'd think that she believed she was really in the car. <u>But she found the Child Catcher frightening, so she</u> started howling.

<u>Because I wanted to distract her,</u> I offered to buy her an ice cream. <u>We crept</u> through the darkness and found somewhere <u>where we could buy one,</u> then returned to our seats.

<u>She had apparently got over her fear, so</u> she sat back in my lap and enjoyed the rest of the show. At the end, <u>she stood and clapped</u> until the curtain came down for the final time.

I don't know how the actors felt at the end of the evening, but <u>after I had seen</u> the show with Amy I was exhausted! Nevertheless, <u>if I consider the evening as a whole</u>, it was a great success.

'ONE OF THE MOST ENJOYABLY EYE-POPPING SPECTACLES LONDON HAS EVER SEEN'

'CHITTY CHITTY BANG BANG IS A SURE-FIRE HIT
OH WHAT A CAR!'

'FANTASTIC' 'SENSATIONAL' 'A SMASH HIT'

'AN AGELESS PLEASURE AND A PLEASURE FOR ALL AGES
SHEER THEATRICAL MAGIC'

▶ SRB   p106

# English in Use 1 (Paper 3 Part 3)

**Lead-in**

**1** Discuss these questions.

1 How popular is shopping as a leisure activity in your country?
2 What have shops and stores done in recent years to attract customers and make shopping more pleasant?

**Error correction**

▶ Task strategies page 169

**2 a** Read the title and text below and find answers to question 2 in Exercise 1. (Ignore the mistakes at this stage.)

**b** Do the task. Remember to follow the task strategies.

In **most** lines of the following text, there is **either** a spelling **or** a punctuation error. For each numbered line, write the correctly spelt word or show the correct punctuation. **Some lines are correct**. Indicate these lines with a tick (✓). The exercise begins with three examples (**0**), (**00**) and (**000**).

## Putting the fun into shopping

| | |
|---|---|
| These days, throughout the length and breadth of Britain shopping | **0**   Britain, |
| centres not only provide customers with a formidable array of | **00**   ✓ |
| products to chose from, but employ a range of subtle entertainment | **000**   choose |
| tecniques to make you want to buy them. Sometimes it is a simple | **1** |
| idea, such as a bookshop providing a café where customers' can sit and | **2** |
| read in comfort, or a fashion show put on by a department store. | **3** |
| Sometimes the concept is more hi-tech, like, the electronic games and huge | **4** |
| video screens showing cartoons in a childrens' toy shop. Whatever | **5** |
| the method, retailers realise that offering some kind of plesurable | **6** |
| experience is good for bussiness, particularly nowadays with so many | **7** |
| people buying their goods online. Strolling throught a town centre on | **8** |
| a saturday, the country's busiest shopping day, you might come across | **9** |
| such things as drama workshops a fairground ride or even a brass band | **10** |
| raising money for charity, all of which are part of a campaign | **11** |
| to encourage people into town Some ideas are becoming increasingly | **12** |
| inovative, with one coffee-bar chain considering offering music | **13** |
| downloads in it's stores. Customers can listen to the latest tracks | **14** |
| while they drink coffee order the ones they like and have | **15** |
| them copied onto a CD, which they then buy when they leave. | **16** |

**Task analysis**

**3** Find an example of a participle clause in the text. How could you rephrase it?

**Discussion**

**4** Can you think of more ideas for in-store entertainment that shops and stores could consider?

# Writing 1   Sentence variety

▶ Writing reference page 204

**1** a  Look at the main sentence patterns of English on page 204, then do Exercise 1b.

 b  Combine these sentences into one sentence, using a combination of patterns, making any changes necessary. Try to avoid *and*, *but* or *so*. Make sure your punctuation is correct. There is more than one right answer.

1  I love various forms of entertainment, like the cinema and the theatre. I am also someone who relishes a challenge. I like to learn something new in my spare time.

2  Mark works hard all day. In the evenings, he needs to relax. He plays computer games. This is unusual for someone who enjoys the company of others so much.

3  Our ancestors had more leisure time than we do. The reason is that they were not slaves to the work ethic. This is despite the fact they had fewer labour-saving devices.

4  Some people think board games are very old-fashioned. However, they are still very popular. They are a great way of families having fun together.

5  I like relaxing in a hot bath in the evenings. It helps me to get a good night's sleep. I need to be wide-awake and ready for work the next morning.

**2** a  Read this task and mark the points you have to include in your answer.

> You see this announcement in an English language magazine.
>
> **COMPETITION**
> Think about **one** modern form of entertainment technology (e.g. TV, cinema, computer games). Is this really the best way of enjoying ourselves? Write and tell us
> • if you think this form of entertainment is a good thing
> • the reason it is so popular
> • whether or not there are better ways of spending our leisure time.

 b  Now edit part of one student's answer by combining some of the sentences so that there is a greater variety of sentence patterns. Make sure you link the ideas clearly using appropriate linking expressions.

> **(1)** The problem is that these days many people lead very busy lives. **(2)** They don't have so much time on their hands. **(3)** This is particularly true when they start work. **(4)** They have a long, hard day at the office. **(5)** After that, the last thing they feel like doing is making much of an effort to go out. **(6)** Many hard-working people don't go to the theatre or the cinema. **(7)** They prefer to slump in the armchair in the evening and watch TV.

**3** a  Complete the sample answer in Exercise 2b or plan and write your own answer to the task.

 b  Exchange your work with a partner. Edit each other's work for range of sentence structures.

# 10B Taking part

*Paul Daniel with Denise Leigh and Jane Gilchrist, the joint winners of the* Operatunity *competition*

## Listening 2 (Paper 4 Part 3)

**Before you listen**

1 Read the introduction to the exam task below.

1 How popular do you think a competition like this would be in your country? What kind of people would it appeal to?

2 Do you like listening to opera? Do you ever go and watch it? Why?/Why not?

## Multiple-choice questions

▶ Task strategies pages 170 and 171

2 🎧 Do the task below. Read the task strategies before you start if necessary. Listen to the recording twice.

The English National Opera Company organised a singing competition called 'Operatunity', which was filmed as part of a television documentary series. You will hear an interview with Paul Daniel, one of the judges from the opera company, and Jane Gilchrist, one of the contestants. For questions **1–7**, choose the correct answer **A**, **B**, **C** or **D**.

1 Paul says that the opera company's main reason for holding the competition was to
   A encourage a broader range of people to enjoy opera.
   B emulate the success of other television talent shows.
   C recruit a group of singers to perform a particular opera.
   D help unknown singers who wanted to fulfil their potential.

2 Jane feels she doesn't fit the popular idea of an opera singer because
   A she doesn't come from a musical family.
   B she has a rather unglamorous occupation.
   C she has no experience of singing in public.
   D she hasn't had the benefit of voice training.

3 How does Jane feel now about not having gone to music college when she was younger?
   A She wishes that she hadn't put her family first.
   B She accepts that it would have been a bad idea.
   C She realises that she missed an opportunity in life.
   D She resents the fact that she was given poor advice.

4 How did Jane feel when she first heard about the competition?
   A determined to prove something to her friend
   B put off by the complicated application process
   C under a certain amount of pressure to apply
   D unconvinced about her chances of success

5 Paul says that, in the auditions, the judges mainly focused on assessing
   A the quality of the contestants' voices.
   B the range of the contestants' musical skills.
   C the nature of the contestants' temperament and character.
   D the strength of the contestants' performance in certain roles.

6 Paul says that, compared to young professional singers, the finalists in the competition were often
   A less able to respond quickly to feedback.
   B unhelpfully defensive in the face of criticism.
   C surprisingly competent on a technical level.
   D much more enthusiastic in their approach.

7 How did Jane react to being filmed during the training sessions?
   A She did feel slightly vulnerable at times.
   B She forced herself to ignore the cameras.
   C She realised how unprepared she was for it.
   D She found it more intrusive than she'd expected.

**Discussion**

3 Do you have any special talents, e.g. singing, playing a musical instrument? What have you done to develop them?

# Speaking (Paper 5 Part 3)

## Vocabulary: music

*Ravi Shankar, the 'godfather of world music'*

**1 a** Look at the types of music listed. Which types do you prefer? Can you give examples of a piece of music, a composer, singer, orchestra or band?

| | | | | |
|---|---|---|---|---|
| classical music | jazz | folk music | opera | rock music |
| pop music | | heavy metal | soul | Latin music |
| rhythm and blues | | country and western | | musicals |
| rap/hip hop | | world music | Caribbean music | |

**b** Divide the following instruments into categories. Then say which instruments are typically associated with the musical genres above.

| | | | | |
|---|---|---|---|---|
| acoustic guitar | banjo | bodhran | cello | clarinet | double bass | drums |
| electric guitar | flute | French horn | harp | maracas | marimba | organ |
| panpipes | piano | saxophone | sitar | synthesiser | trumpet | violin |

| Strings | Woodwind | Brass | Percussion | Keyboard |
|---------|----------|-------|------------|----------|
|         |          |       |            |          |

**2** Work individually and make notes.

**a** Which kinds of music
- cheer you up?
- help you relax?
- evoke particular memories?
- would you find it hard to live without?

**b** Which kinds of music
- bore you?
- get on your nerves?
- do you find too highbrow?
- do you find too trashy?

**c** Which instruments
- would you like to learn?
- can you play?
- have the most beautiful sound?

**d** Choose three pieces of music that are especially important to you and note down why.

**3** Work in groups and discuss your musical preferences. Find out:
- which type of music is the most/least popular and why
- who plays a musical instrument
- what the group's favourite pieces of music are and why.

**4 a** Read this description of a concert and choose the best option in each pair.

Damon Albarn and his band Blur came to define the short-lived but intense musical movement of the mid-90s known as 'Britpop'. Last month, they could be seen **(1)** *performing / showing* again in front of a **(2)** *live / living* audience, but this time ten years older: reinvented. The **(3)** *location / venue* was the grandiose Brixton Academy, a concert hall that **(4)** *holds / contains* over 3,000 people, and three concerts were to take place over three days. Could they pull it **(5)** *off / through*?

The last ten years have **(6)** *resulted in / meant* changes for Blur, but they still remain a band, **(7)** *despite / although* having lost their guitarist, who left the band during the **(8)** *recording / filming* of their last album. With a line-up **(9)** *consisting / comprising* both old hits and new material, Blur showed **(10)** *how / what* great entertainers they are. When Damon Albarn belted out the lyrics of the song *Universal*, 'It really, really, really can happen,' you couldn't help **(11)** *but / and* believe him. Aiming at a different target audience now, the older established fans rather than the young, aware music connoisseurs, Blur really did make it happen.

**b** Describe a memorable live performance you have seen.

►SRB p110

## Collaborative task

▶ Task strategies pages 171 and 172

5 a Look at the photos and work in pairs to do this task. Time yourselves. You should take about four minutes.

'Here are some photos that illustrate ways in which music is part of our lives. Talk to each other about the pleasure people derive from these different musical experiences, and then decide which ones you think are the most satisfying for young people.'

b Tell the class briefly which photos you have chosen and why.

## Developing the discussion

▶ Task strategies pages 171 and 172

6 Work in pairs. Take turns to ask and answer the questions.
1 Does music play an important part in your culture and traditions?
2 How do you think musical tastes have changed over the last 50 years?
3 To what extent do you think music trends are manipulated by the media?
4 How important do you think it is to have a musical education at school?

## English in Use 2 (Paper 3 Part 6)

### Lead-in

1 **Answer these questions.**
   1 Look at the film still. Do any girls you know play football? Why?/Why not?
   2 What do you think the film is about?

### Gapped text

▶ Task strategies pages 169 and 170

2 a **Read the text. What effect did the film have in India?**

   b **Do the task.**

   For questions **1–6**, read the text and then choose from the list **A–I** given below the best phrase to fill each of the spaces. Each correct phrase may only be used once. **Some of the suggested answers do not fit at all.**

---

## Inspired to play

*Bend it like Beckham* is a comedy film about a football-loving teenager from a traditional Punjabi family, who dreams of becoming a professional footballer. Although set in Britain, the film became a surprising hit in cinemas throughout India. **(1)**............. sang along with the songs, hundreds of schoolgirls sat marvelling at the heroine's football skills. They all had the same thought in their heads: that could be me. The months after the film opened saw an explosion of interest in the game among schoolgirls. **(2)**............. admired their footballing heroes on cable TV, but now they believe they can become heroes themselves. **(3)**............. has turned into the hottest new pastime, encouraging the Indian Youth Soccer Association to set up a girls-only league for the first time, with 25 matches being played over 18 weeks on Sunday

mornings. **(4)**............. are being coached daily for teams with names like *Daring Divas* and *Sensational Sizzlers*, and a big expansion in the sport is expected.

Interestingly, unlike the heroine's parents in the film, the majority of Indian families have no objections to their daughters playing and are supportive, even going along to cheer them at matches. Generally speaking, it is the boys who are the problem. **(5)**............. laugh at the girls and try to put them off. **(6)**............. the boys' outlook, it did a lot to assure parents that there was nothing strange about their daughters playing the sport. One thing the girls like about it, though, is not so much that they are challenging society's accepted views of society, but that they are doing something they really want to do.

---

**A** This success has been remarkable and

**B** What was once a tiny minority sport

**C** While the film may have not done much to change

**D** Even though many of them

**E** They are the ones who

**F** No matter how much these girls

**G** Girls from every part of Delhi

**H** Once they sat at home and

**I** While many in the audience laughed at the jokes and

### Discussion

3 **Discuss these questions.**
   1 What other sports have traditionally been seen as male only? Are attitudes changing?
   2 Have you ever been inspired by a film or a book to do something you've never done before?

# Language development 2

▶ Grammar reference page 186

## Nouns, adjectives, verbs + prepositions

**1 a** Match the sentence halves and mark the word + preposition combinations. Some of the sentences are from the text on page 162.

1 The film is about a teenager who dreams
2 Her parents objected
3 In India, there was an explosion of interest
4 More girls now discuss football
5 Many parents realise there's nothing strange
6 Football clubs no longer depend
7 The majority of families have no objections
8 Some parents still discourage their daughters

a in the game.
b with their friends.
c from playing football.
d of becoming a footballer.
e on boys for support.
f to their daughter's taking up the sport.
g to their daughters playing football.
h about their daughters playing the sport.

**b** Look at the patterns in Exercise 1a and complete these rules.

| |
|---|
| A Prepositions after verbs, nouns and adjectives always have an object. The object can be a ............... , pronoun or ............... . |
| B If the object of a preposition is a ............... , it must be in the *-ing* form. |
| C The *-ing* form can have its own subject. This may be put in the ............... form (formal English). |
| D Related verbs, nouns and adjectives often take ............... preposition. |

**2** Correct the mistakes in these sentences.

1 Someone presented to the singer with a big bouquet of flowers.
2 The critic aimed most of his comments to the writer.
3 First we had a discussion about the venue, then we discussed about the dates.
4 The success of the comedy saved from disaster the theatre.
5 The producer blamed on the press for the lack of ticket sales.
6 When his jokes failed, he resorted to shout insults at the audience.
7 The reason why I don't like music festivals is that I'm unaccustomed to sit in muddy fields all day.
8 What's the point to buy a ticket if you can't see anything?

**3** What are the missing prepositions?

1 The audience agreed ............... the critics ............... the singer's performance.
2 The theatre management apologised ............... the audience ............... the interruption.
3 Theatregoers complained ............... the sound quality ............... the manager.
4 I depend ............... my father ............... practical advice about running the company.
5 The director quarrelled ............... the producer ............... the ending.

## Preposition + -ing verb

**4** Rewrite the sentences using a preposition + *-ing* verb.
EXAMPLE: As a developing performer, he's always keen to learn new techniques.
*As a developing performer, he's always keen on learning new techniques.*

1 We were annoyed to find someone else sitting in our seats.
2 I'd like a new CD but I'm nervous to ask again.
3 My parents advised me not to go to drama school.
4 They insisted that everyone bought a ticket.
5 The doorman suspected that I had bought the tickets on the black market.
6 I'm sorry that I lost your CD.

## Confusing pairs

**5** Some verbs and adjectives can be used with different prepositions with a change of meaning. Complete the sentences with the correct word + preposition combination.

1 *hear of / hear about*
   a Have you ............... the new play?
   b I've ............... Hughes, but I've never seen any of his films.
2 *shout to / shout at*
   a He ............... something ............... me, but I couldn't hear with all the noise.
   b Please don't ............... me, it wasn't my fault.
3 *anxious for / anxious about*
   a Families of the survivors hadn't heard anything, so they were ............... news.
   b I'm ............... Tom – he doesn't look well.
4 *care for / care about*
   a The only thing he ............... is money.
   b I don't much ............... those friends of his.
5 *laugh at / laugh about*
   a We ............... it when we got home, but it wasn't funny at the time.
   b You shouldn't ............... your own jokes.

## Writing 2  Review (Paper 2 Part 2)

**Lead-in**

1 Discuss these questions.

   1 How often do you read reviews of TV programmes, films, new CDs, books, etc.?

   2 Does reading a review ever influence your decision to see a film, buy a CD, etc.? Why?/Why not?

**Understand the task**

▶ Writing reference page 199

2 Read and analyse the two tasks below. Then choose which question you would like to answer. What will make it a good answer?

Who is the patron saint of Spain?

**TASK ONE**

An international student magazine to which you subscribe has asked readers to review two TV programmes of a similar genre which are popular in your country. Your review should compare and contrast the programmes, and say which programme you prefer.

Write your **review** in approximately 250 words.

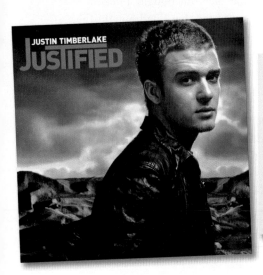

JUSTIN TIMBERLAKE
JUSTIFIED

**TASK TWO**

An international music magazine has asked readers to send in reviews of two very different audio CDs they have heard recently. Your review should comment on

• the musical style and intended audience
• the quality, e.g. of the lyrics, vocals, sound

and say which CD is more successful.

Write your **review** in approximately 250 words.

**Plan your review**

3 a Decide which two TV programmes or audio CDs you will review. Make some notes on the points in the task.

   b Look at the paragraph plans below, which show alternative ways to approach your review. Which will you choose and why?

**Plan A**
**Paragraph 1:** Introduction
**Paragraph 2:** Compare and contrast (e.g. content/style/ intended audience)
**Paragraph 3:** Compare and contrast (e.g. quality)
**Paragraph 4:** Summary and recommendation

**Plan B**
**Paragraph 1:** Introduction
**Paragraph 2:** Discuss first item
**Paragraph 3:** Discuss second item
**Paragraph 4:** Summary and recommendation

   c Select the best points from your notes and write them in your plan.

**Language and content**

**4 a** These are words and phrases which can be used to make evaluations in a review. Decide which are positive and which are negative and write them in the appropriate column below.

> *(particularly) memorable   (entirely) predictable   (truly) original*
> *(really) lively   (excruciatingly) boring   (totally) unconvincing*
> *over the top   (extremely) popular   riveting (viewing)   (almost) inaudible*
> *(incredibly) stylish   (vastly) overrated   entertaining   (profoundly) moving*
> *(quite) sophisticated   (absolutely) hilarious   (refreshingly) different*
> *(a bit) flat   (beautifully) recorded*

| Positive | Negative |
| --- | --- |
| | |

**b** Choose expressions from the list that you can use in your review.

| Comparing and contrasting | *X is a bit/considerably more original than …*<br>*X isn't quite as good as …*<br>*While/Whereas X is … , Y is …*<br>*Neither … /Both …* |
| --- | --- |
| Balancing an opinion | *I found (the lyrics incomprehensible at times/the host infuriating), but … / However, …*<br>*Although (the lead singer has a great voice/the show is a big hit with the public), …*<br>*Even so, (her performance will stay in the memory for a long time/the show makes great family viewing).*<br>*Despite this/In spite of this/And yet (I enjoyed nearly every track on it/it doesn't really spoil the programme).*<br>*On the other hand, (I wouldn't go out of my way to buy it/the concept doesn't really work).* |
| Expressing preferences | *If I had to choose one …*<br>*I'd rather … than …*<br>*I much prefer …*<br>*Give me … any day!* |
| Summarising | *So, (two different artists but) …*<br>*All in all, (if you're going to buy one disc/watch one programme this week) …*<br>*Quite simply, (this is the best …)* |

**Write your review**

**5** Now write your review, using some of the ideas and language above.

**Check your answer**

**6** Edit your work using the checklist on page 188.

▶ Writing reference page 188

▶SRB  p113

# Module 10: Review

**1** **Decide which word or phrase best fits each space.**

1 He built his reputation performing across the ........ of the country.
   **A** the full width   **B** length and breadth
   **C** great lengths   **D** height and width

2 During his mime act, he doesn't utter ........ .
   **A** a thing   **B** at all   **C** a word   **D** the least

3 In my view, Puccini's operas are ........ overrated.
   **A** vastly   **B** profoundly   **C** absolutely
   **D** excruciatingly

4 She was absolutely ........ that she wasn't going to pay any more for the tickets.
   **A** obdurate   **B** immovable   **C** adamant
   **D** steadfast

5 He turns his charm on and off like ........ .
   **A** a light   **B** a tap   **C** the TV   **D** the gas

6 No ........ singer would work without good musicians to back them.
   **A** self-respecting   **B** self-satisfied   **C** self-assured
   **D** self-important

7 I've got a really ........ headache this morning!
   **A** harsh   **B** brutal   **C** malicious   **D** vicious

8 The producers claimed they were not ........ manufacture a star.
   **A** meaning to   **B** taking aim to   **C** out to
   **D** arranging to

9 Many ........ young artists can learn a lot from the older comedians.
   **A** aspiring   **B** encouraging   **C** expectant
   **D** impending

10 At the risk ........ the obvious, you'll need to book your tickets early.
   **A** to state   **B** in stating   **C** of stating   **D** by stating

11 The special effects were ........ – there were just too many of them.
   **A** over my head   **B** to cap it all   **C** over and above
   **D** over the top

12 I'd like to set ........ a new charity for out-of-work actors.
   **A** in   **B** up   **C** off   **D** about

**2** **Rewrite the ideas in italics using the words in brackets. Add any other words necessary.**

1 As soon as he came on stage, I *started to laugh.* (*burst*)

...............................................................................

2 I *discovered* one of her old records in a second-hand shop yesterday. (*stumbled*)

...............................................................................

3 I *don't mind* you going to the show. (*objections*)

...............................................................................

4 It's a tradition *that's been around for a long time.* (*established*)

...............................................................................

5 Many amateur stage productions *underpinned* his later success in movies. (*basis*)

...............................................................................

6 *His only passion is* music. (*consuming*)

...............................................................................

7 Do you think *his performance will ever improve?* (*prospect*)

...............................................................................

8 He's *not working* tonight. (*duty*)

...............................................................................

**3** **Complete the sentences by putting one word in each gap.**

1 I agree ............. you ............. that production of *Carmen* at the Opera House – it was stunning!

2 ............. listened to their latest record, I think they've become very predictable.

3 I'm very nervous ............. going for an audition.

4 I saw that programme you like last night and, ............. put it bluntly, I think it's rubbish!

5 I've never heard ............. Justin Timberlake. Is he famous?

6 ............. by the noise, my son put his hands over his ears.

7 Not ............. it easy to get hold of her directly, I decided to phone her agent instead.

8 My sister advised me ............. ............. anything in the new shop – it's too expensive!

9 She's not afraid to laugh ............. herself – it's one of her most endearing qualities.

10 After ............. the film, we went to a restaurant and had a late-night meal.

**4** **Find and correct the ten mistakes with participle clauses and prepositions.**

To have had my car stolen the day before and still to feel completely devastated, I decided to dance the night away in my favourite club. Annoyed with finding it full when I got there, I had to resort to argue with one of the security guards to let me in. Even then, he insisted in me waiting until some people had left. For understanding my frustration, you need to realise that, been a regular there for many years, I love the place and don't much care about being treated as an ordinary clubber. Anyway, having complained at the manager about being left out in the cold, I was let in and, to lose myself in the music and the dance, I forgot my troubles in an instant.

# Reference material

# Exam reference

## Paper 1: Reading (1 hour 15 minutes)

There are four parts to this paper, with a total of around 3,500 words and 45–50 questions.

Parts 2 and 3 each consist of one continuous text, but Parts 1 and 4 may be divided into sections on a related theme. Part 4 is the longest, at up to 1,200 words. The texts come from a variety of sources, including newspaper and magazine articles, non-fiction and informational material. Questions carry one or two marks each. Notes can be made on the question paper, but your answers must be transferred to the answer sheet before the end of the exam.

**Task strategy (all tasks)**
- Read the title and any subheading and skim the text rapidly to get a general sense of what it's about and how it's organised.
- Read the instructions carefully before you begin.

## Part 1: multiple matching

This task requires you to match questions or statements to a text or texts. There are 12–18 questions, which carry one mark each.

The task tests your ability to locate relevant ideas and information in the text. Close reading is unnecessary and could waste time.

**Task strategy**
- Read the questions and mark key words.
- Read through the text section by section.
- Use parallel phrases and ideas in the questions and text to help you find the information you need.
- Read that section of text carefully to make sure it has exactly the same meaning as the question.
- If you are unsure, go on to the next question. It will be easier to answer when you have dealt with more questions.

## Part 2: gapped text

In this task, six or seven paragraphs have been removed from the base text and placed in jumbled order after the text. You have to decide where they fit. (There is one extra paragraph which does not fit anywhere.)

The task focus is on awareness of how the text is structured and the ability to predict the logical development of ideas, opinions and events. Careful reading is required.

**Task strategy**
- Read the main text carefully for meaning and to get a general idea of the text structure. How do the ideas develop? Are tenses important?
- Read the text around each gap carefully, and mark words that could refer to the missing paragraph. Try to predict what kind of information is missing.
- Read the extracted paragraphs and look for topic links, grammatical links (e.g. tenses, pronouns, articles, linkers, etc.) and lexical links (e.g. parallel phrases) with the main text.
- Read the whole text again in sequence. Does it make sense?

## Part 3: multiple choice

The text in this section is followed by between five and seven four-option multiple-choice questions. The questions are in the same order as the information in the text. Each question carries two marks.

This task tests detailed understanding of the text, including opinions and attitudes, and an ability to deduce meaning from context. Close reference to the text is required, in order to eliminate similar answers. The final question may depend on interpretation of the whole text.

**Task strategy**
- For each question, read the stem and locate the relevant part of the text.
- Try to complete the sentence or answer the question in your own words.
- Look at the four options and decide which one is closest to your own answer.
- If you are not sure of the answer, try to eliminate the ones that can't be correct.

## Part 4: multiple matching

This part of the paper is similar to Part 1, except that the text is longer, requiring you to deal with up to 1,200 words, and answer between 12 and 22 questions. As with Part 1, Part 4 tests your ability to locate specific information quickly. Remember, the text will contain information you do not need.

**Task strategy**
As for Part 1.

# Paper 2: Writing (2 hours)

For this paper, you have to produce two pieces of writing, each of around 250 words. The task types could include formal or informal letters, reports, proposals, articles, information leaflets, etc. The type of writing, the target reader and the purpose for writing are always specified in the instructions.

Each question carries equal marks. Task achievement is a key feature of assessment in *both* parts. An answer which does not include all the relevant information will not receive good marks, however good the language is.

▶ See the Writing checklist on page 188.

## Part 1

▶ See the Writing reference pages 189–191 for an example. Part 1 is compulsory and is based on input material of up to 400 words, in the form of letters, notes, adverts, etc. relevant to the context. These texts must be read very carefully, as they will form the basis of the text you produce. Appropriate selection and expansion of the key points is vital, avoiding irrelevance, repetition, deviation, etc.

## Part 2

▶ See the Writing reference pages 192–199 for examples. In Part 2, you have to choose one of four tasks. The last one is usually work-related and should not be attempted by students who have no relevant work experience. You should follow the instructions carefully and use appropriate layout, style and register according to the text type chosen.

# Paper 3: English in Use
## (1 hour 30 minutes)

There are six parts to this paper, each based on an input text. There are 80 questions, each worth one mark. You must write your answers on the answer sheet. Inaccurate spelling is penalised.

**Task strategy (all tasks)**

- Read the instructions carefully.
- Read the title and the whole text for general understanding before starting the task.
- When you've finished, read the whole text again to check your answers make sense and fit grammatically.
- Check your spelling is correct.

## Part 1: lexical cloze

This is a four-option multiple-choice task with 15 gaps, based on a text of around 250 words. The test focus is vocabulary, so although all the options might fit grammatically, only one option is appropriate to the context. Phrases, collocations, idioms, phrasal verbs and linkers may all be tested.

**Task strategy**

- Read the text carefully.
- Look at the sentence before and after the gap and think about what kind of word fits each space.
- Choose which answer, A–D, fits the grammar and the meaning.
- If you aren't sure, cross out the answers which you know are incorrect.

## Part 2: open cloze

You have to read a text of around 250 words and complete 15 gaps (one word for each gap). The test focus is on grammatical structure. The missing words will generally be grammatical and include articles, pronouns, prepositions, conjunctions, etc. Some will form part of phrasal verbs and fixed phrases.

**Task strategy**

- Read the text carefully, noting the answers you are confident of.
- For the others, look at the context and the words around each gap. What kind of word is needed to fit the meaning and grammar?
- Put only one word in each space. Don't use contractions.

## Part 3: error correction

There are two possible versions of this task, based on a 200-word text. In the first version, most lines contain an unnecessary word. Most of the errors are grammatical. Some might not fit in with the sense.

In the second version, most lines contain an incorrect spelling or inappropriate punctuation mark, for example missing capital letters, unclosed speech marks, wrong use of apostrophes.

Each line of text is either correct or contains one error. Out of 16 lines, no more than five lines will be correct.

**Task strategy**

- Read the text carefully, sentence by sentence (not line by line).
- For tasks involving unnecessary words, mark any words you think should not be there.
- For tasks involving spelling and punctuation errors:
  - mark any words you think may be incorrectly spelt (check there are no other errors on that line);
  - mark any punctuation marks you think may be wrong or missing.
- Read the whole sentence again to check.
- When you have finished, make sure you have marked no more than five lines as correct.
- When you check your answers to tasks involving spelling and punctuation, try reading from right to left to help you focus on each word.

## Part 4: word formation

This is a word-building task based on two short, unconnected texts of around 125 words each, with a total of 15 gaps. You are given the base form of 15 words and you have to put them into the correct form to fit the context. This task tests affixation, especially noun formation and the use of prefixes to modify meaning.

**Task strategy**
- Read and complete the first text before moving on to the second text.
- Read each sentence, not just the line with the gap.
- Decide what kind of word is needed in the space.
- Change the form of the word on the right to fit the grammar and meaning. Check if a negative or plural form is needed.

## Part 5: register transfer

There are two texts of around 150 words each, both containing the same information, but written in a contrasting register. For example, the first text may be a formal article, and the second an informal letter. You must complete 13 gaps in the second text with one or two words, using information from the first text. The words must be appropriate in style and tone to the new context. This section tests range of expression and the ability to use an appropriate register for the context.

**Task strategy**
- Read both texts quickly for general understanding.
- Look at the gaps in the second text, and mark which information in the first text you have to re-express.
- Think of synonyms and paraphrases, in the style of the second text, for the expressions you have marked. The words you need do not occur in the first text.
- Read the second text again to check that the information is the same, the grammar is correct, the sentences make sense and the style is appropriate.

## Part 6: gapped text

This part consists of a 250-word text from which six phrases or short sentences have been removed. You have to select the appropriate phrase to fit each gap. There are three phrases which do not fit at all. The task focuses on structure and coherence.

**Task strategy**
- Read the title and the whole text once for meaning.
- Look at the gaps, and read the options.
- To decide which of the extracted phrases fits each gap, ask yourself:
  - Does the meaning fit? Does the grammar fit?
  - Are there any grammatical links (e.g. pronouns, link words, punctuation)?
  - Are there any vocabulary links (e.g. repeated words)?

# Paper 4: Listening
## (approximately 45 minutes)

This paper has four parts, each based on a recorded text or texts. These are taken from a variety of authentic sources and then recorded in a studio to ensure clarity. Each part is heard twice, except for Part 2, which is heard only once.

There are two possible task types for each part. The instructions, which are recorded as well as printed on the page, are followed by a pause, giving you time to read through the task for that section. Notes can be made on the question sheet during the exam, but at the end you are given time to transfer your answers to the answer sheet provided.

**Task strategy (all tasks)**
- Read and listen to the instructions so you know what you are going to hear.
- In the time provided, read through the task to help you predict the content/missing information.
- Remember that the task summarises information in the recording, so you won't hear exactly the same sentences. Listen for similar ideas.
- For sentence or note-completion tasks, write no more than three words in each space. The words you need are all on the recording – don't change them. Don't repeat words and ideas on the page.
- While transferring your answers to the answer sheet, check that:
  - your answers make sense and fit grammatically
  - the key words are spelled correctly
  - your handwriting is legible.

## Part 1: sentence completion/note-taking

You will hear a monologue (e.g. an announcement, radio broadcast, telephone message, speech, talk, lecture) lasting about two minutes. It is played twice. You have to complete a set of gapped sentences or notes that summarise the main information in the text. There are between eight and ten questions, which follow the order of information in the text. You only need to write a word or short phrase in each gap – usually concrete nouns or noun phrases.

The task tests your ability to follow the structure of a text and extract specific information and stated opinions. In **sentence completion** tasks, answers must fit grammatically into the sentence. In **note-taking** tasks, you are usually required to complete gaps in a table or complete lists under headings. Answers must fit logically according to these prompts.

**Task strategy**
- Use the context to help you predict the missing information before you listen.
- Listen for discourse markers to help you follow the structure of the talk.
- Check and complete your answers during the second listening.

## Part 2: sentence/note completion

The text is an informational monologue as for Part 1. However, this time it is played only once and the key information needed for the task is recycled in some way. For example, some answers may be repeated and others will be reinforced in the text that follows.

**Task strategy**
- Listen for signals that help you predict when the information you need is coming up.
- Listen for explanations, examples and repeated information that confirm your answer.

## Part 3: sentence completion/multiple choice

This section is a conversation (an interview or discussion) between two or more speakers, lasting around four minutes. There are between six and ten questions of one mark each, and the main focus is on the attitudes and opinions of the speakers. The task will most often be four-option multiple-choice questions.

**Task strategy (multiple choice)**
- Read the questions or sentence stems and mark key words.
- Listen for the answers to the questions. Remember that you're listening for the opinion or attitude of the speaker – don't be influenced by your own opinions on the subject!
- Decide which of the options is nearest to your answer. Remember the words in the options that give you the answer will not be the same as in the recording.

## Part 4: multiple choice/multiple matching

In this section, you will hear five short monologues of around 30 seconds each on a related theme. There are ten questions in all, which focus on aspects of overall meaning. You have to identify and interpret information about the context, the speakers and their opinions, as well as recognising functions and attitude.
In the **multiple-choice** option, there are two questions for each of the five speakers, with three options to choose from.
In the **multiple-matching** option, there are two tasks (1 and 2). Each task requires you to select the five correct options from a list of eight possibilities.

**Task strategy (multiple matching)**
- Read the question for each task carefully, so you know what you have to listen for.
- Read the options A–H in both tasks and mark key words.
- The first time you listen, complete Task 1. The second time you listen, complete Task 2.
- Listen carefully for the main point each speaker makes, and expressions they use to indicate their attitudes and opinions.

# Paper 5: Speaking
## (approximately 15 minutes)

This paper is divided into four parts. The standard format is two candidates and two examiners: the interlocutor, who asks the questions and assesses, and the assessor, who listens and assesses, but does not take part. Each part is designed to prompt a range of spontaneous language based on prompts. It is important to speak as much as possible in order to demonstrate your ability to use a range of language, but it is equally important to include your partner where appropriate and encourage his/her contribution. Assessment is based on performance in the whole of the speaking test, based on the following criteria:
- accuracy and appropriacy of grammar and vocabulary
- fluency, coherence and range of language
- comprehensible pronunciation of individual sounds, stress and intonation
- ability to interact with others in order to complete a social, transactional or interactive task.

You are not assessed on your ideas, but examiners can only assess you on the language you produce, so if you do not contribute, you will not do well.

**Task strategy (all parts)**
- Listen to the examiner's instructions carefully so you know what you have to do.
- Don't be afraid to ask him/her to repeat the question if necessary.
- Use a wide range of structures and vocabulary. This is your chance to show your command of spoken English.
- Avoid repeating yourself.
- Speak clearly so the examiners can hear.
- Give yourself thinking time by using expressions such as *Let me think* or *I haven't given this much thought before, but I suppose …*
- Paraphrase if you can't think of a word.
- In Parts 1, 3 and 4, participate fully but don't dominate – encourage your partner to speak as well.

## Part 1: social interaction (three-way conversation) (3 minutes)

This part is a three-way conversation between the candidates and interlocutor in which you have to answer the examiner's questions about yourself, find out personal information about your partner based on prompts given by the interlocutor, and answer your partner's questions. The focus is on social interaction.

### Task strategy
When asking questions:
- Keep your tone friendly and sound interested!
- Encourage your partner to expand his/her answers.
- When asking questions from prompts, avoid repeating the same words.

When answering questions:
- React naturally – don't use prepared answers.
- Answer as fully as you can – don't be monosyllabic.
- Keep talking – don't pause too long.
- Invent opinions if necessary.

## Part 2: individual long turn (4 minutes)

In this task, you have to talk for about one minute without interruption, commenting on or reacting to a visual prompt, usually a set of pictures around a particular theme. Tasks involve the language of comparing and contrasting, describing, speculating or hypothesising. You and your partner may each have a completely different task. In this case, you are each asked to comment briefly after your partner has spoken (about 20 seconds). Alternatively, you may have a 'shared task', i.e. the same task as your partner (with a different set of pictures). At the end of the shared task, you and your partner look at both sets of pictures and answer a question together (up to a minute).

### Task strategy
- Make sure you don't simply describe the pictures – your response should include hypothesis or speculation from the start.
- Keep talking, but try to finish within the time limit.
- Organise your ideas and express yourself coherently.
- When your partner is speaking, listen but don't interrupt.

## Part 3: collaborative task (two-way interaction) (4 minutes)

In this section, you and a partner are given visual prompts, usually a set of pictures on a theme, and asked to collaborate on making a decision or solving a problem. There is no one correct answer, but you are expected to discuss the prompts (the first part of the task) and work towards a conclusion (the second part of the task). You don't have to agree. At the end, you are asked to report on and justify the outcome of your discussion.

This task requires a range of linguistic skills to keep the conversation going, such as paraphrasing, asking for clarification and using conversational 'fillers' rather than leaving long pauses. It also tests a range of communication strategies: an ability to invite the opinions of your partner, discuss, evaluate, collaborate, negotiate and reach some kind of agreement.

### Task strategy
- Make sure you discuss the first part of the task before you come to a conclusion.
- Give your opinions, but take care not to dominate.
- Invite your partner to give his/her opinion and develop what he/she says.

## Part 4: developing the discussion (three-way conversation) (4 minutes)

In this part, the examiner leads a discussion which develops the issues raised in Part 3 in a broader and more abstract way. You may be asked to respond to the same or different questions.

### Task strategy
- Participate in developing the discussion. Don't just give one-word answers.
- Respond to and develop the points made by your partner.
- Don't interrupt your partner or dominate the discussion.

# Grammar reference

## Module 1

### 1 Tense forms (page 13)

#### A Continuous forms

**1 Used to talk about temporary events**
*I'm working in the supermarket at the moment.*
(present continuous)
*I was backpacking around India this time last year.*
(past continuous)
*I'll be filming in Mexico this time next week (then I'm coming home).* (future continuous)

**2 Used to show an event is ongoing**
*I'm studying French this year.* (present continuous)
*He's been working here for two weeks (and he still is).*
(present perfect continuous)
*I was watching TV when the phone rang.*
(past continuous: event in progress)

**3 Used to focus on the action/situation**
*She's always leaving the door open.*
(present continuous: characteristic behaviour)
*I've been cooking all day. I'm exhausted.*
(present perfect continuous: leading to present result)

**Notes**
- Some verbs are not normally used in the continuous. These are:
  - verbs that describe states of being, e.g. *appear, be, deserve, doubt, exist, hate, own*
  - verbs of sense and perception, e.g. *smell, taste, think*
  - verbs used to perform an action, e.g. *agree, apologise, promise*

  When these verbs are used in the continuous, they become actions:
  *I'm thinking of going out (= I'm considering).*
- Some verbs which describe physical feelings, e.g. *feel, hurt*, can be used in the simple or continuous form with little or no difference in meaning: *How are you feeling / do you feel?*

#### B Perfect forms

We use perfect forms to talk about things which happen before or leading up to another time/event:
*I've been a travel writer for a long time.*
(present perfect: time up to the present)
*Listen, I've found out something very interesting about this university.*
(present perfect: past event/action with present relevance)
*I'd already met Jamie Oliver, so he knew who I was.*
(past perfect for a prior event in the past)
*William will already have left by the time we get there.*
(future perfect for something completed before a specific time in the future)

**Note**
*for* = a period of time, e.g. *for six weeks*
*since* = a point of time, e.g. *since last June*

#### C Tense forms often confused

**1 Present perfect and past simple**
- Present perfect (= thinking of past and present together)
  *Oh, no! I've left the tickets at home.*
  (a past action with present relevance)
  *I've been all over the world.* (general experience)
  *I've lived here for three years.* (an unfinished time period)
- Past simple (= thinking only of the past)
  *I met her yesterday.*
  (completed action at a specific time in the past)
  Compare:
  *The president has arrived.* (present perfect: recent past)
  *His plane landed at ten o'clock.*
  (past simple: completed action)

**2 Past continuous and past simple**
- Past continuous (= long temporary action/state not complete at a time in the past)
  *At six o'clock, I was driving home.*
- Past simple (= short completed action)
  *As I was driving home, I had an accident.*

**3 Present perfect simple and present perfect continuous**
- Present perfect simple (= completed actions when we are interested in the result)
  *No, thanks. I've already read that book three times.*
- Present perfect continuous (= interested in the action or to emphasise how long)
  *I've been learning English in a private school for three years.*

**4 Past perfect simple and past perfect continuous**
- Past perfect simple (= to stress that one event finished before the other began)
  *I'd finished my dinner before she got there.*
- Past perfect continuous (= for a longer/continuous period up to a specified time in the past)
  *Before I came to London, I had been working in Paris.*

**5 will and going to**
- *will*
  *Tom will fail his driving test.*
  (prediction based on personal opinion)
  *Wait. I'll help you.*
  (spontaneous decision, offer)
- *going to*
  *Look at those clouds. It's going to rain.*
  (prediction based on evidence)
  *I'm going to get a new job.*
  (plan: decision already made)

**6 Present simple and present continuous for future reference**

- Present simple
  The bus **leaves** at 7.35. (timetables and programmes)
- Present continuous
  We**'re leaving** the country very soon.
  (personal arrangement already made)

**7 *will* and future continuous**

- *will*
  I**'ll see** him tomorrow. (neutral prediction)
- Future continuous
  I**'ll be seeing** you next lesson. (inevitable event)
  Next week, we**'ll be sitting** on the beach.
  (temporary event in progress in the future)

**8 Present simple or present perfect for future time**
  We use present simple or present perfect, not *will*, for future time after time conjunctions, e.g. *after, as soon as, once, until*:
  I'll phone you **as soon as I check / I've checked in**.

**D Expressions with future meaning**

**1 For fixed/planned events**

- *be to* + infinitive to talk about official, formal arrangements, e.g. in a radio commentary
  The Prince **is to meet** everyone concerned with the charity.
- *be due to* + infinitive (*due* = expected to happen at a particular time)
  The ceremony **is due to** start at 9 a.m.

**2 For events that will happen very soon**

- *be about to* + infinitive
  She looks as if she**'s** (just) **about to burst** into tears.
- *be on the point/verge of* + *-ing*/noun
  The talks **were on the point/verge of collapsing/collapse**.

**3 To talk about probability**
  *be likely/unlikely to* + infinitive / *expect* (somebody/ something) *to* + infinitive
  The country**'s likely to get** poorer next year.
  We **expect** the country **to get** poorer.

**4 To talk about certainty**
  *be bound/sure to* + infinitive
  Don't lie to him. He**'s bound to/sure to find out**.

**E Future in the past**

**1** To talk about the future from a viewpoint of the past, we can use:
  *was/were going to* + infinitive
  I **was going to phone** you yesterday, but I forgot.
  (unfulfilled intention)

**2** We can transfer any verb/expression with future meaning to the past using:
  *was/were about to, was/were due to, would (have), was/were to have*
  I **was about to go out** when you called.
  We **were due to go out** at six.
  I thought you **would finish / would have finished** before now.
  The Queen **was to have come** down the Mall. I don't know what went wrong.

## 2 The passive (page 19)

**A Use**

**1** We use a passive construction when:

- the 'doer' (agent) of an action is not known:
  Our office **was broken into** last night.
- it is obvious who the agent is or it is not important at the time of speaking:
  I **was given** a new contract yesterday. (obviously by my employer)
- we don't want to say who the agent is:
  Some mistakes **were made** in the preparation of the report. (We don't want to say who made the mistakes – possibly to protect them or ourselves!)

**2** When we wish to focus on the agent, we use *by* + agent:
  My husband was badly injured **by a lorry**. (The new information (*a lorry*) is brought into focus by putting it at the end of the sentence.)

**3** The passive is more common in writing than speaking and can sound formal and impersonal. It is often used:

- in orders and rules:
  All money **must be paid** by the end of the week.
- to talk about events and achievements:
  The company **was founded** in 1912.
- to talk about processes:
  First, strips of wood **are put** through the machine.

It is often used in academic and scientific English.

**Note**
The passive cannot be used with:

- intransitive verbs (verbs with no direct object):
  It ~~was arrived~~.
- state verbs (e.g. *be, have, seem*): A bath ~~is being had by Jane~~.

**B Form**

**1 Active versus passive forms**

| | Active | Passive |
|---|---|---|
| modal verb (present) ➔ modal verb + *be* + past participle | All students **must take** an entrance exam. | An entrance exam **must be taken** by all students. |
| modal verb (past) ➔ modal verb + *have been* + past participle | They **should** not **have elected** him. | He **should** not **have been** elected. |
| *make, see, hear, help* ➔ *be* + past participle + *to*-infinitive | They **made** me **do** it. They **heard** him **shout**. | I **was made to do** it. He **was heard to shout**. |
| *let* ➔ no passive form | They **don't let** candidates use dictionaries. | Candidates **are not allowed/permitted** to use dictionaries. |

**2 Passive -*ing* forms and infinitives**

When verbs are followed by an -*ing* or infinitive form, these forms can be made passive:

- verb + passive infinitive
  *The film star **agreed to be photographed**.*
- verb + -*ing* form
  *I'm tired of **being lied to**.*

**3 *need* + -*ing* can have a passive meaning**

*The cups **need washing**. = The cups **need to be washed**.*

## C Impersonal passive structures

The following structures can be used with reporting verbs:

- subject + passive verb + *to*-infinitive
  *He **is claimed/said/thought to be** the greatest composer ever.*
  *They **are believed/reported/thought to have become** extinct.*
- *It* + passive verb + *that* clause
  *It **is thought/expected/said/understood that** the weather will get worse.*
- *There* + passive verb + *to be*
  *There **are thought/expected/said/known to be** huge food shortages.*

## D *have/get* + object + past participle

We can use this structure:

1 to talk about something which someone else does for us because we asked them to (*get* is more informal than *have*):
  *Have you **had** your hair **cut**?*
  *I want to **get** the house **redecorated**.*

2 like a passive, for things that happened by accident or unexpectedly, usually something unpleasant; it is fairly informal:
  *How **did** your car **get damaged**? I've **had** my bike **stolen**.*

# Module 2

## 1 Relative clauses (page 29)

### A Relative pronouns and adverbs

1 A relative pronoun can be the subject of a relative clause:
  *I talked to the woman **who/that** believes in ghosts.* (I talked to the woman. **She** believes in ghosts.)
  *Gavin, **who** is very superstitious, always wears a good-luck charm.* (Gavin always wears a good-luck charm. **He** is very superstitious.)
  *Judy's the woman **whose** parents have just retired.* (Judy's a woman. **Her** parents have just retired.)

**Note**

We cannot:
- use a subject pronoun after a subject relative pronoun:
  *I talked to the woman **who** ~~she~~ believes in ghosts.*
- omit a subject relative pronoun:
  *I talked to a woman believes in ghosts.* ✗

2 A relative pronoun can be the object of a relative clause:
  *Steve Cohen, **who** I saw in London, is absolutely incredible.*
  *Steve Cohen, **whom** I saw in London …* (formal)
  (Steve Cohen is absolutely incredible. I saw **him** in London.)

*The tricks **which/that** he performed made everyone gasp.* (He performed tricks. **They** made everyone gasp.)

**Note**

We cannot use an object pronoun and an object relative pronoun in the same relative clause:
*The tricks **which** he did ~~them~~ made everyone gasp.*

3 Relative adverbs include *where* (places), *when* (times) and *why* (reasons). They can be the subject or object of a relative clause. Alternatives to *when* and *why*:
  *1895 is the year **when / in which** he was born.*
  *I know the reason **why / that** they came here.*

4 The relative pronoun *which* can be used to refer to a whole sentence, not just the subject/object:
  *He was very quiet, **which** is unusual for him.*
  *He arrived at nine, **which** was when he was expected.*

  We can also say …, *which was how/why/what/where* …:
  *The train was delayed, **which was why** he was late for work.*

## B Defining relative clauses

These identify or classify a noun/pronoun. They are necessary for the sense of a sentence. We do not use commas:
*He is someone **who** is generally very lucky.*

**Note**

We can omit the defining relative pronoun if it is an object:
*He's the man **(who/that)** I met when we were volunteers together.*

## C Non-defining relative clauses

These add extra information and are not necessary to the sense of a sentence. The extra information is separated off by commas. Non-defining relative clauses are more common in written than spoken English:
*The phone, **which had been quiet all evening**, suddenly rang.*

**Notes**
- We cannot omit the relative pronoun.
- We cannot use *that* instead of *which*.

## D Words used with relative pronouns

**1 Prepositions and prepositional phrases**

- A preposition can go at the end of a relative clause or before the relative pronoun:
  *It's a mystery **which** there is no explanation **for**.*
  (less formal)
  *It's a mystery **for which** there is no explanation.*
  (more formal)

**Note**

After a preposition, we use the pronoun *which* (not *that*) for things and *whom* (not *who*) for people.
*Is this the place **which/that** we used to eat **in**?* (informal)
*Is this the place **in which** we used to eat?* (formal)

- Prepositional phrases are often used in non-defining relative clauses:
  *It might rain, **in which case** we'll have to go home.*
  *I waited for him until seven, **at which point** I gave up.*
  *Pharaoh Tutankhamun's tomb was opened in 1922, **since when** many strange things have happened.*

2 Words such as *all, both/neither, some, many of* are often used before the relative pronoun in non-defining clauses:
*The builders of the Pyramids were skilled craftsmen, **many of whom** died during the construction.*

3 The following words may be used before a relative pronoun in defining relative clauses with *who* (not *whom*) and *that* (not *which*): *someone/something, anyone/anything, everything, some, all, many, little, much, those*:
***Anyone who** sees the Sphinx is impressed.*
*I disagreed with **much that** was said.*

## E Nominal relative clauses

In these clauses, the whole relative clause functions as a noun. Nominal relative pronouns include: *what, whatever, whoever, whichever, when, where, who, how, why*:
*Tell me **what** you did yesterday.* (= the things that you did)
***Whatever** he did must have been terrible.* (= whatever things)
*You can invite **whoever** you want.* (= any person who)
*This is **where** I was born.* (= the place where)
*That's **why** I like it.* (= the reason why)
*You're not **who** I thought you were.* (= the person who)

## F Replacing relative clauses

1 We can often reduce a relative clause by omitting the relative pronoun and the auxiliary verb:
*The man ~~who was~~ living next door …* (active meaning)
*The wall, ~~which was~~ built during Roman times, still stands.* (passive meaning)

2 We can sometimes replace a relative clause containing a modal with a *to*-infinitive:
*There's no one here **to speak to**.* (= who I can speak to)
*Sue is the best person **to ask**.* (= that you can ask)

## 2 Nouns (page 35)

### A Uncountable nouns

1 These refer to things we think of as a 'mass', rather than individual, countable things. They usually have no plural form and are used with a singular verb:
*accommodation, advice, clothing, equipment, food, flu, luggage, patience, weather*, etc.
*Progress **is** very slow.*

2 We do not normally use the indefinite article (*a/an*) with uncountable nouns. Instead, determiners like *some, any*, etc. may be used:
*Here is ~~an~~ some advice.*
*There isn't ~~an~~ any evidence.*

3 We can use the definite article with uncountable nouns when we are talking about a specific example of something:
*Can you give me back **the** money I gave you?*

However, we do not use the definite article to talk about things generally:
***Money** is the root of all evil.*

4 To make uncountable nouns countable, we use phrases like these:
***a bit of** help, **a piece of** evidence/information, **a pile of** rubbish/books, **a slice of** bread/cake, **a spoonful/two spoonfuls of** (sugar)*

## B Countable or uncountable nouns?

1 Many nouns can be countable or uncountable depending on the context:

| Uncountable | Countable |
| --- | --- |
| ***Life** here is very good.* | *Many **lives** were saved.* |
| ***Time** is short.* | ***Times** were hard.* |
| *Don't stay out in the **cold**.* | ***Colds** are common in winter.* |
| ***Science** is not a popular subject.* | *The **sciences** are squeezed of funds.* |

2 Some uncountable nouns can be used with the indefinite article. They are usually qualified by an adjective or phrase:

| Uncountable | Countable + adjectival phrase |
| --- | --- |
| ***Knowledge** is power.* | *He has **a good knowledge** of the area.* |
| *I've got no **time**.* | *Have **a good time**.* |
| ***Tolerance** is a virtue.* | *He showed **a great deal of tolerance**.* |

## C Subject–verb agreement

1 Uncountable nouns ending in *-s* are followed by a singular verb:
*aerobics, athletics, genetics, maths, news, physics, politics*, etc.
*No news **is** good news.*

2 These nouns are always followed by a plural verb:
* Nouns ending in *-s*, usually clothes and tools:
*pyjamas, shorts, trousers; glasses* (= spectacles), *pliers, scissors*
To make these singular, we usually use *a pair of*:
*a pair of trousers*
* Nouns made up of many 'parts':
*the authorities, belongings, cattle, contents, goods, (the) people, (the) police, remains*

3 The noun *whereabouts* can be followed by a singular or plural verb:
*His **whereabouts is/are** unknown.*

4 Collective nouns (nouns referring to groups)
* These may be used with a singular verb if we think of them as a **single unit**, or with a plural verb if we are referring to **members of the group**. We use *the* with these nouns:
***The staff is** excellent.* (= thinking of an impersonal unit)
***The staff are** excellent.* (= thinking of the people who work there)
*The media **is/are** very powerful.*
Other examples include: *army, audience, choir, committee, headquarters, orchestra, press, public, team*
* We generally use a singular verb after *a/an* + collective noun:
***An** army of volunteers **is** on its way.*

- We generally use a plural verb after the following expressions when they are followed by *of* + plural noun: *the majority/minority (of), a number (of), a couple (of)*
  *Only a minority of people **support** the new law.*
  *A number of people still **cling** on to the old beliefs.*
  Compare:
  *A small minority **disagree/disagrees** with the ruling.*

5 If a plural subject describes a single unit, e.g. an amount or quantity, we usually use a singular verb:
  ***Thirty kilometres is** a long way.*
  ***Five euros is** not much.*
  ***Six per cent is** a big increase.*

## D Determiners, pronouns and quantifiers

### 1 Before nouns

- **With a countable or uncountable noun:**
  *some/any, (not) enough, half/all (of), a lot of/lots of, more/most, no, plenty of*

- **With a countable noun:**
  *a few (= some), few (= almost no), (not) many, one/both (of), each (of), every, either/neither (of), several*

- **With an uncountable noun:**
  *a little (= at least some), little (= almost none), (not) much, less, the whole*

### 2 Determiner or pronoun?

Most of the words in the above section can be used as determiners (before a noun) or pronouns (on their own).
***Most people** enjoy sport.* (determiner)
***Some of your ideas** are crazy.* (pronoun)
*'Which one do you want?' '**Either** is OK.'* (pronoun)

**Notes**

- *no* and *every* are determiners, never pronouns.
- *none* is a pronoun, never a determiner.

### 3 each, every

- We use *each* to talk about two or more things or people, considered separately:
  *She held a bag in **each** hand.*

- We use *every* to refer to all the people or things in a particular group (more than two):
  ***Every** road in the centre was blocked.* (= all roads)

- In some contexts, we can use *each* or *every* interchangeably:
  ***Each/Every** person in the group joined in.*

- We can use *each* (not *every*) as a pronoun:
  *We **each** have our own skills.*
  ***Each** of us went our own way.*

- We can use *each/every* + *one of*:
  *We played several games and lost **each/every one of** them.*

- *Each* and *every* are followed by a singular verb:
  ***Each** of us **has** a job to do.*

### 4 all, both

- We use *both* to talk about two people, things, etc. together, and emphasise that each is included:
  ***Both** films were boring.* (determiner)
  *'Which one shall I buy?' 'Why not get **both**?'* (pronoun)

- We use *all* to refer to the whole of an amount, thing, or type of thing, or every one of a number. We don't usually use *all* as a pronoun on its own:
  *I haven't seen him **all** week.* (determiner)
  *'Which one do you like?' 'I like **all** of them.'* (pronoun)

5 **the whole** (adjective, noun)
  We use *(the) whole* to refer to all of something, often instead of *all of*:
  *We wasted **the whole day** looking for it.*
  *Climate change affects **the whole (of the) planet**.*

6 **either, neither**
  We use *either* and *neither* to refer to one or the other of two things or people. Strictly speaking, they are followed by a singular verb, but a plural verb is common in spoken English.
  *'You can have **either** tea or coffee.' '**Neither**, thank you.'*
  *I wouldn't want to do **either** of these jobs. **Neither** of them is very interesting.*

7 **no, none**
  *No* is a determiner, *none* is a pronoun. In formal English, they are followed by a singular verb, but a plural verb is more common:
  *'For those who believe, no explanation is necessary. For those who do not, **none** (= no explanation) will suffice.'*
  ***None** of us is/are perfect.* (= not one of us, for a group of three countable nouns or more)

# Module 3

## Modals and semi-modals (page 50)

### A Obligation and necessity: *must/have (got) to, need to*

1 **must/mustn't**
- Used to express strong obligation when we impose this on ourselves:
  *I **must** go to the doctor's.*
  *I **mustn't** forget to take out insurance.*
- Used to express a strong opinion:
  *We **must** all do our bit for the environment.*
- Used to give instructions, usually in writing:
  *This appliance **must** be earthed.*

2 **have to or need to for an obligation imposed by someone else**
  *This report **has to/needs to** be finished by Monday.*

3 **must, have to and need to express general necessity**
  *Everyone **needs to** take a holiday at least once a year.*

4 **Other ways of expressing obligation and necessity**
- *be required to* + infinitive:
  *You **are required** by law **to wear** a seat belt.*
- *be to* + infinitive:
  *We **are** all **to report** to the Principal's office.*
- *had better* + infinitive:
  *We **had better leave** before it gets dark.*
- *feel/be obliged* + *to*-infinitive:
  *Many parents **feel obliged to support** their children.*
  *You **are obliged to report** to the police once a week.*

### B Lack of necessity

1 **not have to, need not, not need to**
  *You **don't have to/needn't/don't need to** get up early today.* (It's not necessary.)

**Note**

*Need* has two past forms with different meanings:

*She **didn't need** to take a coat. It wasn't cold.* (We don't know if she took a coat or not.)

*She **needn't have** taken a coat.* (She took one, but it wasn't necessary.)

**2   Other expressions**

*be under no obligation to*

*You **are under no obligation to** buy anything.*

## C   Prohibition and criticism: *mustn't, shouldn't, can't, couldn't, may not, should(n't) have*

**1   *mustn't* or *shouldn't***
   - Used for prohibition imposed by the speaker:

*You **mustn't** start a fight!* (strong prohibition)

*You **shouldn't** be so thoughtless!* (weaker prohibition)

**2   *can't* or *may not***
   - Used for prohibition imposed by someone else:

*You **can't** drive a car yet, you're too young.*

*Candidates **may not** leave the room during the exam.* (formal)

**3   *couldn't***
   - Used for prohibition in the past:

*As children, we **couldn't** stay up later than 10 p.m.* (= were not allowed to)

**4   *should(n't) have* + past participle**
   - Used to express regret or criticism of a past action:

*I **should have become** a doctor, but I didn't. I wish I had.* (regret)

*You **shouldn't have done** that.* (criticism)

**5   Other ways of expressing prohibition**

*Smoking is **forbidden/not permitted** here.*

## D   Advice, recommendation: *must, should, ought to, had better*

**1**   *must* for strong advice and recommendations:

*You **must** visit the castle.*

**2**   *should/ought to* when the advice is less strong:

*You **should/ought to** protest.*

*You **shouldn't** go on strike.*

**Note**

We rarely use *ought to* in questions and negative statements.

**3**   *had better (not)*

*I'd better go and get ready.*

*You **had better not** tell your mother.* (= It is not a good idea.)

## E   Permission: *can, could, may, might*

*'**Can** I use your car?' 'Yes, you **can**.' / 'No, you **can't!**'*

***Could** I ask you to do me a favour?* (tentative, polite)

*'**May** I leave the office early today?'* (more formal)

*'Yes, you **may**.' / 'No, you **may not**.'*

*I wonder if I **might** have a word with you?* (formal, polite)

## F   Ability: *can, can't, could, might, be able to*

**1**   *can/can't* for general ability in the present and future:

*I **can** sing. I **can't** come tomorrow.*

**2**   *could* for general ability in the past:

*I **could** play the piano when I was six.*

**3**   *was able to* for ability in a specific situation in the past:

*I **was** finally **able to** pass my driving test last week.*

**4**   *wasn't able to* or *couldn't* for negative general and specific ability in the past:

*They **couldn't/weren't able to** make the wedding on time.*

**5**   *could/might* + *have* + past participle for a past ability or opportunity not used:

*He **could have gone** to college, but decided against it.*

**6**   Other ways of expressing ability:

*I **managed to** (was able to) raise some money for charity last week.* (suggests success in the face of difficulty)

*Scientists have not yet **succeeded in** finding a cure for cancer.*

## G   Possibility, probability: *can, could, may, might, should*

**1**   *can, could, may* for things that are theoretically possible and happen sometimes:

*Temperatures **can** reach −20° at night in the desert.*

*These chemicals **could/may** cause cancer.*

**2**   *could, may, might* for possibility in the present or future:

*It **could** be weeks before he returns.*

*There **may** well be a strike next week.*

*I **might** be late for the meeting.*

**3**   *could* for theoretical possibility in the past:

*My father **could** be really strict with me when I was young.*

**4**   *can, could, may, might* + *have* + past participle for specific past possibilities:

*She **may/might/could have been** held up in the traffic.* (It's possible she was.)

**5**   *could/might* (+ *have* + past participle) to express criticism/annoyance:

*You **might** at least say 'thank you'!*

*They **could/might have let** us know they weren't coming!*

**6**   *may, might (well)* to acknowledge something is true, before introducing a contrast:

*He **might (well)** be a good actor, but he can't sing.*

**7**   *should/shouldn't* for probability:

*It **should** be a nice day tomorrow.*

*Peter **should** be arriving any moment now.*

*It **shouldn't** be too difficult to find the way.*

## H   Deduction: *must, can't, couldn't*

**1**   *must* for something we are sure about because of evidence:

*He **must** be a vegetarian. He doesn't eat meat.*

**2**   *must* + *have* + past participle to express a deduction about the past:

*There are a lot of broken windows. There **must have been** a riot.*

**3** *can't/couldn't*, not *mustn't*, in negative sentences:
*He **can't/couldn't** be her father. He looks too young.*
*He **can't/couldn't** have phoned. I've been in all evening.*

## I Uses of *will, won't, would*

### 1 Intentions, predictions, certainty

- Intentions:
*I **will** pass that exam!*
- Predictions about the future:
*Sue and Anna **won't arrive** until this evening. They **will be** tired.*
- Predictions made in the past:
*He said he **would/wouldn't** be late.*
- Certainty about the present based on knowledge or expectations:
*'I heard a knock at the door.' 'That **will be** the postman.'*
*As you **will have realised**, we are behind schedule.*
*They only left two hours ago, so they **won't be** home yet.*
- Certainty or deductions about the past:
*I became an apprentice when I left school. I **would have been** 14.*

### 2 Frequency, habits, characteristics

- Habits and typical behaviour in the present:
*Accidents **will happen**.*
*As soon as the illusion fades, the public **will turn** on their idols.*
*This car **will do** 0 to 60 in ten seconds.*
- Past habits:
*He **would sit** for hours watching the birds.*
- To express annoyance:
*She **will play** music at full volume.*

### 3 Willingness and refusal

*The doctor **will** see you now.*
*He **won't** talk to me!*
*They **wouldn't** let us into the country. (past)*

## J Offers, promises, suggestions, requests, orders: *can, could, may, might, will, shall, would*

### 1 Offers and promises

*Can/May I **help** you?*
*I'll **come** with you if you like.*
*Shall I **carry** that for you?*
*Would you **like** a cup of tea?*

### 2 Suggestions

*You **could join** a club.*
*You **might think** of taking a gift.*
*We **can/could get** a takeaway.*

### 3 Requests

*Can/Could you **help** me?*
*What **shall** I **bring**? (asking for advice)*
*You **wouldn't lend** me £10, would you?*

### 4 Orders

*All payments **shall** be **made** in cash.*
*Passengers **will** please **proceed** to the gate.*

**Note**

In question tags, *shall* is preferred to *will* in first person singular tags:
*I'll do that, **shall** I?*

# Module 4

## Noun clauses (page 67)

Noun clauses are groups of words that function like a noun in a sentence and can be referred to by *it* or *that*. Like nouns, they can act as the subject, object or complement of the sentence. They normally refer to abstractions (e.g. ideas, processes, facts) rather than people or things. Noun clauses use the following structures.

### A *that*-clauses

**1** Following nouns, e.g. *danger, evidence, fact, idea, likelihood, opinion, possibility*:
*There is **evidence that** more people are becoming aware of Multiple Intelligence Theory.*

**2** Following adjectives, e.g. *clear, interesting, likely, possible, sad, sure, true*:
*It is **encouraging that** more teachers are adopting its ideas.*

**Note**

With this structure, we usually start the sentence with *It*. We don't omit *that* except following *It's a shame/pity (that)* …

**3** Following thinking and reporting verbs (as object), e.g. *believe, explain, know, say, suggest, understand*:
*Multiple Intelligence Theory **suggests that** people learn differently.*

**Note**

We often omit *that* after a verb.

**4** *that*-clause as subject
*That*-clauses can be used as subject in formal English:
***That his theories were revolutionary** is clear.*

### B Clauses beginning with a question word

**1** As subject of the sentence
***What is good for one learner** might not be good for another.*
***Whoever wrote this music** is a genius.*

**2** As object of the sentence
*Do you know **when he is coming**? (NOT ~~when is he coming?~~)*
*I'm always forgetting **where I've left things**.*

**3** Following *be*
*The question is **how far intelligence is genetically determined**.*

**4** Following a preposition
*It depends **on who you know** not **what you know**.*
*Have you read **about how you can improve your memory**?*

**5** With *to*-infinitive clauses
*He showed me **how to solve the problem**.*
*I don't know **what to say**.*

**6** *if/whether (or not)*
- We use *if* or *whether* in indirect *Yes/No* questions:
*John asked **if/whether** I wanted to go to the cinema.*
- We use *whether* rather than *if* when talking about a choice:
*I didn't know **whether** to go (or not).*
***Whether (or not)** the theory is true is arguable.*

- We usually use *if* when the noun clause is object of a verb:
  *I've often wondered **if he was genuine**.*

## C  *-ing* and *to*-infinitive clauses

### 1  As subject
***Taking extra classes** might benefit some learners.*
***To achieve the best results for everyone** must be the aim
of all schools.* (formal)

**Note**
An introductory *It* structure is more common than a *to*-
infinitive as subject of a sentence in neutral or spoken English:
***It** must be the aim of all schools to achieve the best results for
everyone.*

### 2  As object
*I enjoy **being looked after**.*
*I want **everyone to be happy**.*

### 3  Following *be*
*My ambition is **to become a neurologist**.*
*My main worry is **not being good enough to pass**.*

### 4  Following a noun or adjective
*We had some difficulty **finding the place**.*
*My plan **to leave the country** failed.*
*It is important **to adopt a variety of approaches**.*

### 5  Adding a subject to a *to*-infinitive clause
When there is a subject in a *to*-infinitive clause, we
usually add *for*:
*It's impossible **for me** to go with you.*

### 6  Verb + object + *-ing* clause
When the main verb is followed by an object + *-ing*
clause, we use an object, or, in formal language, a
possessive form:
*I don't mind **him/Peter (his/Peter's) getting** a pay rise.*

# Module 5

<h2 style="background:black;color:white">1  Gradable and ungradable adjectives<br>(page 77)</h2>

## A  Modifying gradable adjectives

Most adjectives are 'gradable' because they describe qualities
we can think of in terms of a scale, and therefore can be
weaker or stronger.

1  Gradable adjectives, e.g. *important, slow, valuable,
   vigorous,* can be made stronger using *extremely,
   incredibly, most* (formal), *pretty* (informal), *rather,
   really, terribly, very:*
   *It's **pretty obvious** that he's not interested.*
   *The talk was **most interesting**.* (formal)
   *I thought he was **rather nice**.*

**Notes**
- We cannot use *absolutely* with gradable adjectives.
- The modifier *dead* may be used only in informal English:
  *The concert was **dead good**!*

2  Gradable adjectives can be made weaker using *a
   (little) bit, fairly, quite* (= *fairly*), *relatively, slightly,
   somewhat* (formal):
   *He's **quite rich**, but not a millionaire.*
   *We were **somewhat disappointed** with the service.*
   *The hotel was **relatively/fairly cheap**.*

## B  Modifying ungradable adjectives

'Ungradable' adjectives, e.g. *brilliant, correct, disastrous,
exhausted, furious, identical, perfect, unique,* indicate extreme
or absolute qualities.

1  The extreme/absolute quality can be stressed using
   *absolutely, completely, quite* (= *completely*), *really,
   totally, utterly:*
   *They were **absolutely furious**.*
   *This vase is **quite unique**.*

**Note**
*Absolutely* cannot be used with all ungradable adjectives. In
some cases, *completely, totally* or *utterly* are preferred (see
Section D below).

2  We can say that something is very nearly in an
   absolute state using *almost, nearly, practically, virtually:*
   *The tank is **almost empty**.*
   *The two vases are **virtually identical**.*

## C  Gradable and ungradable

Some adjectives can be gradable or ungradable, depending
on the context:
*The beach was **fairly empty**.*
(gradable = There were not many people.)
*The beach was **absolutely empty**.*
(ungradable = There were no people.)

## D  Adverb + adjective collocations

Some adverbs tend to collocate with certain adjectives:
***bitterly*** *cold, disappointed, opposed*
***completely*** *different, incomprehensible, new, sure*
***deeply*** *ashamed, attached, divided, unhappy*
***entirely*** *beneficial, different, satisfactory, unexpected*
***heavily*** *armed, dependent, polluted*
***highly*** *contagious, critical, intelligent, likely, sensitive*
***painfully*** *aware, obvious, sensitive, slow*
***perfectly*** *balanced, normal, safe, serious*
***seriously*** *damaged, hurt, rich, wealthy*
***totally*** *harmless, inadequate, unbelievable*
***utterly*** *different, disastrous, impossible, useless*
***widely*** *available, held, publicised, used*

<h2 style="background:black;color:white">2  Conditionals (page 83)</h2>

## A  Overview

### 1  Zero conditional: real events/situations, things which are always true
*If* means the same as *when*.
- present + present
  *If/When I **work** late, I always **get** home tired.*
- past + past
  *If/When the weather **was** bad, we **used** to stay indoors.*

**2  First conditional: possible or likely events/situations (future)**

*If* + present + modal verb / present continuous (with future meaning) / *going to* / imperative
*If it **snows** tomorrow, the match **will/may/could** be cancelled / I'm **staying** at home.*

**3  Second conditional: unlikely or unreal situations (present or future)**

*If* + past + *would/could/might* + infinitive
*If you **met** your favourite actor on the street* (unlikely), *what **would** you do?*
*If I **became** President* (but I won't), *I'**d build** more hospitals.* (in the future)
*If I **were** you* (but I'm not), *I'**d take** warm clothes.* (= advice)

**4  Third conditional: unreal/impossible past situations**

*If* + past perfect + *would/could/might* + *have* + past participle
*If we **had known** about the blizzard, we **wouldn't have set out**.* (but we didn't know)
*If you **had listened** more carefully* (but you didn't), *you **would have understood**.* (= criticism)

## B  Mixed conditionals

Mixed conditional structures combine the verb forms from two different conditional patterns. The most common combinations are:

- unreal past + unreal present
  *If we **hadn't got lost**, we'**d be** there by now.*
- unreal present + unreal past
  *If I **were** a more ambitious person* (but I'm not), *I'**d have become** a politician.*

## C  Alternatives to *if*

Other conjunctions can be used to introduce conditions:

- *unless* (= *if ... not* or *only if*)
  ***Unless** the weather improves, we will have to cancel the game.* (If the weather doesn't improve ...)
  *She won't go to sleep **unless** you tell her a story.* (She will only go to sleep if you ...)
- *providing/provided (that)*, *on condition that*, *as/so long as* (= *only if*)

**Note**

These conjunctions are not used with the third conditional.

*I'll lend you the money **providing (that)** you pay it back.*
*I'd lend you the money **as long as** you paid it back.*

- *but for* (= *if it had not been for*, *if ... not*)
  ***But for** your warning, we wouldn't have realised the danger.* (If it had not been for your warning, / If you had not warned us, ...)
- *whether ... or not* (= *it doesn't matter which of these situations*)
  ***Whether** governments like it **or not**, they have to give more aid to the developing world.*
- *suppose/supposing*, *what if* (used to talk about imaginary situations)
  – The present tense suggests the condition may be fulfilled:
  ***What if** your plan fails, what then?*

– The past tense suggests the condition is unlikely:
  ***Suppose** you won the Lottery, what would you do?*
- *assuming that* (= *in the possible situation that*)
  ***Assuming (that)** you're right, we should turn left here.*
- *in case* (as a way of being safe from something that might happen)
  *Take your umbrella **in case** it rains.*
- *otherwise* (= *if not*)
  *Let's hope the weather improves. **Otherwise** (= If it doesn't), we'll have to cancel the picnic.*

## D  Omission of *if*

*If* can be omitted and the auxiliary verb moved in front of the subject (inversion). This structure is formal.

- *should* suggests that the condition is unlikely:
  ***Should** you ever find yourself in Oxford, we would be glad to see you.* (If you should ever ...)
- *were* suggests that the condition is unlikely:
  ***Were** the company to collapse, many people would lose their savings.* (If the company collapsed ...)
- *had*
  ***Had** I known earlier that you wanted to join the team, I'd have put your name on the list.* (If I had known ...)
  *My horse would have won **had** he not fallen at the final fence.* (... if he had not fallen ...)

# Module 6

## 1  Emphasis: cleft sentences (page 93)

Cleft, or 'divided', constructions can be used to emphasise particular items of information in a sentence by putting them in a separate clause. They are common in spoken English, and can also be used to signal emphasis in writing, where it cannot be indicated by intonation.

### A  Emphasis with *What, The thing that, The place where, The reason why*, etc.

1  **wh- clause (with a verb) + a form of *be* + emphasised information**

This structure can be used:
- to put emphasis on the subject, object or complement of a sentence:
  ***Regular exercise*** (subject) *keeps you healthy.*
  → *What keeps you healthy is **regular exercise**.* (focus on the subject)
  *I enjoy **taking regular exercise**.* (object)
  → *What I enjoy is **taking regular exercise**.* (focus on the object)
  The clauses can be reversed.
  ***Regular exercise*** *is what keeps you healthy.*
  ***Taking regular exercise*** *is what I enjoy.*
- to put emphasis on the action in a sentence. The wh- clause must contain a verb. We use a form of the auxiliary *do*. The emphasised part usually contains an infinitive:
  *I decided I needed to keep fit, so I joined a health club.*
  → *I decided I needed to keep fit, so **what I did was to join** a health club.*

2 This structure can also be used to focus on a thing, person, place, time or reason, but usually with the addition of an introductory phrase, e.g. *the thing that, the person who,* etc. The *wh-* clause acts like a relative clause:

**The (one) thing that** (really) keeps you healthy is regular exercise.
**The people who** live next door are very friendly.
**The place where** I go for a workout has got some great classes.
**The reason (why)** the gym is popular is that it's got good equipment.
**All I'd (ever) wanted to be** was reasonably healthy.
**All I know is (that)** vitamins are very expensive.

## B Emphasis with *It + be*

This structure can put emphasis on most parts of a sentence except the verb. It often implies a contrast with the previous statement:

*Sarah wanted a job as a physiotherapist in the capital.*
→ *It was **Sarah** who wanted a job as a physiotherapist.* (emphasising the subject)
→ *It was **a job as a physiotherapist** that Sarah wanted.* (emphasising the object)
→ *It was **in the capital** that/where Sarah wanted a job as a physiotherapist.* (emphasising the prepositional phrase)

## 2 *-ing* or infinitive after verbs (page 99)

▶ See also *Patterns after reporting verbs,* page 185.

## A Verbs followed by *-ing*

### 1 Verb + *-ing*

The verbs marked * can also be followed by an object + *-ing*:
*adore\*, advise, allow, appreciate\*, avoid\*, can't bear\*, can't help\*, consider, contemplate, deny, detest\*, dislike\*, enjoy\* fancy\*, finish, forbid, imagine\*, involve\*, keep, mention\*, miss\*, permit, practise, recommend, resent, resist\*, suggest, understand\**
*Have you **considered taking** up yoga?*
*They **forbid/allow/permit** smoking here.*

### 2 Verb + object + *-ing*

Further verbs followed by object + *-ing* include:
*catch, discover, feel, find, hear, leave, notice, observe, see, spot, want, watch*
*She **caught** him **cheating** in the exam.*
*I don't **want** you **going** home alone.*
▶ See also Section D on page 183.

**Notes**
- In more formal style, we can use a possessive form for the object:
  *I can't understand **him/John/his/John's** making such a fuss.*
- The verbs *advise, allow, forbid, permit, recommend* are followed by a *to*-infinitive, not an *-ing* form, when they have an object:
  *I **advise taking out** insurance for the trip.*
  *I **advise you to take out** insurance for the trip.*
  *I don't recommend **staying** here.*
  *I don't recommend **you to stay** here.*

## B Verbs followed by infinitive

### 1 Verb + *to*-infinitive

The verbs marked * can also be followed by an object + *to*-infinitive.
*afford, agree, appear, arrange, attempt, choose\*, dare\*, deserve, expect\*, force, guarantee, help\*, hope, intend\*, manage, need\*, neglect, prepare, pretend, refuse, volunteer, want\*, wish\*, yearn*
*He **appeared to be** discovering the truth.*

### 2 Verb + object + *to*-infinitive

Further verbs followed by object + *to*-infinitive include:
*advise, allow, cause, command, compel, encourage, forbid, force, get, instruct, invite, leave, oblige, order, permit, persuade, recommend, remind, request, tell, urge, warn*

**Note**
*for* is used before object + infinitive with these verbs:
*arrange, long, plan, wait, yearn*
*I **long for them** to return.*

### 3 Verb (+ object) + infinitive without *to*

The following verbs take an infinitive without *to*:
*had better, let, make, would rather*
*You**'d better** go.*
*Please **let me come** with you.*
*He **made me finish** my report.*

**Notes**
- *hear, make, see* are followed by infinitive with *to* in the passive:
  *We **were made to walk** home.*
- *let* is replaced by *be allowed to* in the passive.
- *dare, help, need* can be followed by infinitive with or without *to*:
  *Can you **help me (to) carry** this case?*

## C Verbs + *-ing* or *to*-infinitive

### 1 With little difference in meaning

*attempt, begin, can't bear, can't stand, continue, hate, like (= enjoy), love, prefer, start*
*I **started watching/to watch** the programme.*

With verbs of liking/preference, the *-ing* form tends to refer to general activities, and the *to*-infinitive to a specific activity:
*I **like swimming**.* (in general)
*I **like to swim** every weekend.* (I think it's a good idea.)

**Note**
We use the *to*-infinitive after *would like/love/prefer*:
*'Would you **like to go** out?' 'I'd **prefer to stay** at home this evening.'*

### 2 With a change in meaning

- *forget/remember*
  *I **remember/forget bringing** the key.* (looking back)
  *Please **remember**/Don't **forget to bring** the key.* (looking forward)
- *go on*
  *Please **go on telling** us about it.* (continue)
  *He **went on to become** president.* (do something next)

- *mean*
  Managing well **means communicating** well. (involves)
  We **meant to get** up early. (intended)
- *regret*
  I **regret leaving** school so early. (feel sorry)
  I **regret to inform** you that your contract will not be renewed. (formal: used in official letters or statements)
- *stop*
  She **stopped working** for the gallery ages ago. (no longer do something)
  She **stopped to buy** a programme. (stop and change activity)
- *try*
  **Try going** for a run. (to see what happens)
  **Try to get** more exercise. (make an effort)

### D  Sense verbs: *feel, hear, notice, see, smell, taste, watch*

Sense verbs, or verbs of perception, can be followed by:

1  object + *-ing* form when we are describing an action in progress or a repeated action:
   I **heard him singing** a great song.

2  object + infinitive when we are describing a single or completed action:
   I **heard him sing** a great song.

# Module 7

## Past tenses for hypothetical meanings
### (page 115)

We use past tenses after the following expressions to describe situations in the present, past or future which are imagined or unreal:
*wish / if only, It's (high) time, would rather/sooner, would prefer, as if/though, suppose/supposing, what if*

### A  *wish / if only*

1  We use *wish / if only* + past when we want a present situation to be different:
   I **wish / If only we had** more money. (but we haven't)
   I **wish I was** (formal: **were**) a bit taller. (but I'm not)

2  *wish + would* is used to express a wish for something to change in the present or future.
- We often use it to criticise or complain about someone or something:
  I **wish** Peter **would** wear smarter clothes.
  I **wish** the weather **would** improve.
- *I wish + would* cannot be used to refer to oneself:
  I **wish I could** (not ~~would~~) stop smoking. (but I can't)
- We cannot use *would* for an impossible change:
  If only the earth ~~would be~~ was (formal: **were**) square.

**Note**
Notice the difference between *wish* and *hope*. If we hope something will happen, we believe it is possible and likely:
I **hope** they **will** come. (= I want them to and I think it's likely.)
I **wish** they **would** come. (= I don't believe it's likely.)

3  We use *wish / if only* + past perfect to express regret about a past situation:
   I **wish we'd had** something to eat earlier. (but we didn't)
   **If only** I **hadn't missed** my appointment. (but I did)

4  Differences between *wish* and *if only*:
- *if only* is usually more emphatic than *I wish*.
- We can put a subject between *if* and *only* for emphasis:
  **If only you / If you only** knew what I've been going through.

### B  *It's time*

We use this expression to say that something is not happening and it should be:
**It's (high) time you gave up** playing computer games. (You should give them up!)

### C  *would rather/sooner, would prefer*

**I'd rather / I'd sooner** you didn't ask me for any more money. (Please don't!)
**I'd prefer it if** you didn't ask me for any more money.

**Notes**
- If the speaker and the preference are the same, we use an infinitive, not the past tense:
  **I'd rather/sooner watch** TV. (not ~~to watch~~)
  **I'd prefer to watch** TV. (not ~~watch~~)
- We can also say *I'd prefer you not to go.*

### D  *as if / as though*

- We use the past after *as if / as though* to indicate that the situation is unlikely:
  He acts **as if/though he was** (formal: **were**) a teenager. (In fact, he's in his thirties.)
- We use a present tense to indicate that something is likely:
  He **looks as if/though he is** a teenager. (And he probably is.)

### E  *suppose/supposing, imagine, what if*

We use these expressions to ask about an imaginary situation in the present or future, and its possible consequences:
**(Just) suppose/supposing/imagine** you won the lottery, how would you spend the money?
**What if** you had hurt yourself – what would have happened then?

# Module 8

## 1  Emphasis (page 125)

### A  Emphasis using negative introductory expressions

The following expressions can be placed first in a sentence for emphasis. The subject and verb are then inverted. We use *do/does/did* if there is no auxiliary.
- *little, never, rarely, scarcely*:
  **Never** have I seen so many people.
  **Little** did we know that he had followed us.
- *no sooner … than, barely/hardly … when*:
  **No sooner had** he got the job **than** he asked for a pay rise.
  **Hardly** had I got through the door **when** the phone rang.

- *at no time, under no circumstances, on no account, no way* (informal):
  **Under no circumstances** should you let anyone in.
- *not since, not for, not a (person/thing), not only … (but also)*:
  **Not since** the 90s has he written such a superb novel.
  **Not a soul** did we see on our journey.
  **Not only** do they want a pay increase, they (**also**) want reduced hours.
- *only* + time expression or prepositional phrase:
  **Only now / after all these years** has the crime been solved.
  **Only when I got to the airport** did I realise I had forgotten my passport.

## B Emphasis through 'fronting' parts of the sentence

'Fronting' involves moving elements of a sentence to the front in order to:
- start with the most important information;
- provide an emphatic contrast with the previous sentence;
- provide a link with what came before by putting known information at the front of the sentence.

**Note**
In order to avoid ending a clause or sentence with *be* as a result of fronting, we normally invert the subject and verb.

1 Fronting the object or complement
  *I don't know **what we're going to do**. → **What we're going to do** I don't know.*
  *It took me **ages** to finish that assignment! → **Ages** it took me to finish that assignment!*
  *I don't believe **that**. → **That** I don't believe!*

2 Fronting adverbials and verbs of place or movement (+ inversion)
  *And now we are in the market place. **Here** stood the old Corn Exchange building. **Opposite** is the church.*
  *We arrived at our camp. **Then** began the slow process of acclimatisation.*
  ***Into the room** swaggered the Count.*

**Note**
We don't invert the subject and verb:
- if the subject is a pronoun:
  *Here stands his statue. Here it stands. ~~Here stands it.~~*
- with time phrases
  *~~At eight o'clock went off the alarm clock.~~*

3 Fronting comparative or superlative phrases, *so, such* (when not followed by a noun), *also* (+ inversion)
  *She has made five films to date. Her latest film is **particularly good**. → **Particularly good** is her latest film.*
  *The storm was **so terrible** that the ship sank. → **So terrible** was the storm that the ship sank.*
  *His financial position was **such** that his friends started to worry. → **Such was his financial position** that his friends started to worry.*
  *The house loomed out of the darkness. **Also visible were** several dogs guarding the door.*

4 Fronting *as* and *though*
  *Try **as** they might, they could not win the race.*
  *Exhausted **though** he was, he stumbled on.*

5 Fronting noun clauses
▶ See *Noun clauses* (Section A4), page 179.

# 2 Comparisons (page 132)

## A Review of comparison

### 1 Comparative structures
- to a higher degree:
  *Boston is small**er**/saf**er** than New York.*
  *Living in the centre is **more** fashionable these days.*
- to the same degree:
  *Congestion in London is (just) **as** bad **as** it is in Paris.*
  *He's **as** good **a** policeman **as** his father was.*
  *Both cities are **equally** beautiful.*
- to a lower degree:
  *The city is **not as/so** safe **as** it used to be.*
  *It's not **such a** safe city **as** it used to be.*
  *That's **not such a** good idea.* (implied: *as you might think*)

### 2 Superlative structures
*Mexico City is one of **the** larg**est** cities in the world.*
*Prison is **the most/least** effective way of dealing with such crimes.*

## B Modifying comparisons

1 To express a big difference, we can use:
- *a great deal, (quite) a lot, considerably, far, (very) much* + comparative
  *It's **much easier** to get around today.*
- *by far (and away), easily* + superlative
  *This is **easily the best** book I've ever read.*
- *nothing like, not nearly, nowhere near as … as*
  *Graffiti is **nowhere near as serious** a crime **as** murder.*
- *just about* + superlative
  *He's **just about the nicest** person I know.* (= extremely nice)

2 To express a small difference, we can use:
- *barely, a bit, hardly any, a little, scarcely (any), slightly, somewhat* + comparative
  *The house is **scarcely bigger** than a rabbit hutch.*
- *nearly, not quite as … as, much the same as …*
  *The city is **much the same as** it was 50 years ago.*

## C so/such; too/enough (result)

- *so* + adjective + *that*-clause
  *The demonstration was **so peaceful that** most of the police left.*
- *such a* + adjective + noun + *that*-clause
  *It was **such a peaceful demonstration that** most of the police left.*
- *too* + adjective (+ *for*) + *to*-infinitive
  *It was **too dangerous** (**for** us) **to** go out at night.*
- *(not)* adjective + *enough* (+ *for*) + *to*-infinitive
  *It was**n't** safe **enough** (**for** us) **to** go out at night.*

## D Other types of comparison

1 Repetition of the same comparative form to emphasise increase or decrease:
*I'm getting **colder and colder / more and more anxious**.*

2 *the … the* to say how a change in one thing affects another:
**The more** *I see you,* **the more** *I like you.*
**The less** *you know,* **the better**.
**The longer** *we stand here in the rain,* **the worse** *I feel.*

3 To contrast two similar qualities:
*His behaviour was **more** strange **than** suspicious.* (His behaviour was strange rather than suspicious.)
*I'm **not so much** angry **as** relieved.*

## E *as* versus *like*

1 *like* + noun = *similar to*
*He looks **like a criminal**.* (but he's not)

2 *as* + name of job, etc. = role, function
*He works **as an 'extra'** in films.* (That's his job.)

## F Ways of expressing preferences

We sometimes use comparative forms when expressing preferences:
*I'd **want/prefer to** pay an on-the-spot fine **rather than** go to court.*
*I'd **(far) sooner/rather** live in Chicago **than** New York.*

# Module 9

## Reported speech, reporting verbs (page 141)

### A Review of reported speech

#### 1 Tense changes
To report something said in the past using a past tense reporting verb, we usually use a tense one step further back in the past. This is sometimes called 'backshift'.
*'We're getting married.'* (present)
→ *He **said** they **were** getting married.* (past)
*'I met Peter recently.'* (past)
→ *He **said** he **had met** Peter recently.* (past perfect)

We do not backshift:
- when the reporting verb is in the present tense:
  *He **says** (that) they**'re getting** married.*
- when the reporter sees the past events from the same point of view as the speaker:
  *He said he **was pleased** (that) my exam results **were good**.*
- when we report modals *would, should, might, could, ought to*:
  *You **should** learn to swim.* → *He said (that) she **should** learn to swim.*
- with the past perfect:
  *'They**'d already left**.'* → *He told me they**'d already left**.*

We can choose to backshift or not when present and future events are still true:
*'Come after lunch.'* → *He suggested (that) I **came/come** after lunch.* (It is not lunchtime yet.)

#### Note
*shall* changes to *would* when it refers to the future and *should* when it is a suggestion:
*'We **shan't** see you tomorrow.'* → *They said (that) they **wouldn't** see us the next day.*
*'**Shall** we open the window?'* → *They suggested (that) they **should** open the window.*

#### 2 Changes of pronouns and adverbs
If the person, place or time of reporting is significantly different from the words in direct speech, we change pronouns and adverbs.
*'I'll see you here tomorrow.'*
→ *He said he would see **me there the next day**.* (spoken three days later in a different place)
→ *He said he'll/would see **me here tomorrow**.* (spoken today in the same place)

#### 3 Word order in reported questions
- To report questions, we use the same order as in statements:
  *'When are you going?'* → *He asked me **when I was going**.*
  *'Have you seen my wallet?'* → *She asked him **if he had seen her wallet**.*
- With *what/who/which* questions + *be* + complement, *be* can go before the complement:
  *'Which is our bus?'* → *She wanted to know **which was our bus/which our bus was**.*

### B Patterns after reporting verbs

▶ See *Verbs followed by infinitive*, page 182.

#### 1 Verb + *that*-clause
Some of these verbs can also be followed by a *to*-infinitive or an *-ing* form (see below):
*add, admit, agree, announce, answer, argue, claim, complain, confess, decide, deny, expect, explain, hope, promise, repeat, suggest, swear, threaten, warn*

#### 2 Verb + *that*-clause (+ *should*)
*advise, beg, demand, insist, prefer, propose, recommend, request, suggest*
*She **advised** (that) the house **should** be sold immediately.*
*I **recommended** (that) he **should** see a lawyer.*

#### Note
- In more formal contexts, we can omit *should*:
  *She advised (that) the house **be** sold immediately.*
  *I recommended (that) he **see** a lawyer.*
- In less formal contexts, we use an ordinary tense:
  *I recommended (that) he **saw** a lawyer.*

#### 3 Verb + *to*-infinitive
*agree, ask, claim, decide, demand, expect, hope, intend, offer, promise, refuse, swear, threaten*
*She **asked to see** the manager.*

#### 4 Verb + object + *to*-infinitive
*advise, ask, beg, command, encourage, expect, forbid, intend, invite, order, persuade, recommend, remind, tell, urge, warn*
*They **told/warned him** not **to be late**.*
*You **are forbidden to smoke** in the building.*
*I **invited them to stay**.*

**5 Verb + *-ing* form**

*admit, deny, mention, propose, recommend, regret, report, suggest*

They **regretted leaving/having left** so soon.

**6 Verb (+ object) + preposition (+ object/genitive) + *-ing***

*accuse sb of, apologise (to sb) about, apologise for, blame sb for, complain (to sb) about, comment on, confess to, insist on, object to*

They **accused me of telling** a lie.

He **confessed to stealing** the money.

They **insisted on me/my going** with them.

**Note**

Some reporting verbs may be followed by a *wh-* clause:

He **commented on how** tall she'd grown.

▶ See also *Noun clauses*, page 179.

## C Impersonal report structures

The following impersonal structures can be used after verbs of mental processes, e.g. *accept, agree, argue, announce, believe, claim, hint, know, hope, say, feel, report, repute, suggest, think*, to avoid mentioning the agent and/or to focus attention on the last part of the sentence. This structure is generally used in written English, often in newspapers.

**1 It + passive + *that*-clause**

**It is said (that)** he is extremely rich.

**It is believed (that)** the city was established in Roman times.

**2 Subject + passive + *to*-infinitive / perfect infinitive**

**He is said to be** extremely rich.

**The city is believed to have been** established in Roman times.

# Module 10

## 1 Participle and *to*-infinitive clauses
### (page 156)

▶ See also *Replacing relative clauses* (section F), page 176

Participle clauses allow us to express ourselves economically, both in speech and writing.

## A *-ing* participle clauses

We can use *-ing* participle clauses:

**1** to show that two actions occurred at the same time, or one happened immediately after another:

I sat there **twiddling my thumbs**. (= As I sat there, I twiddled my thumbs.)

**Turning to the crowd**, he smiled and waved. (= He turned to the crowd and smiled.)

He finally resigned, thus **ending days of speculation**. (= When he resigned, he ended days of speculation.)

**Note**

A perfect participle can be used to emphasise that one thing happened before another:

**Having taken off** his shoes, he walked upstairs.

**2** to suggest a cause, reason or result, especially with stative verbs such as *be, believe, feel, have, know, want*:

**Feeling ill**, I decided to stay at home. (= I felt ill, so I decided …)

**Wanting to become more independent**, he left home. (= Because he wanted …)

He felt at home in the village, **having lived there for many years**. (= … because he had lived …)

**3** to replace adverbial clauses of time or contrast. The participle clause is introduced by a conjunction:

**On seeing** her brother, she gave him a big hug. (= When she saw …)

**Before leaving** the room, he turned off the light. (= Before he left …)

**While/Although admitting** he'd been very stupid, he refused to apologise. (= While/Although he admitted …)

## B *-ed* participle clauses

These participle clauses have a passive meaning and are more frequent in written English. They can be used to suggest cause, reason and condition:

I applied for the job, **convinced** I could do it. (= … because I was convinced …)

**Told well**, my jokes are as funny as anyone's. (= If they are told well, …)

The job **successfully completed**, they left. (= The job was successfully completed, so they left.)

**Notes**

- If the subject of a participle clause is not stated, it must be the same as the subject of the main clause.
- If the subject of a participle clause is stated, it can be different from the subject of the main clause:

  It being high season, **all the hotels** were fully booked. (= As it was high season, all the hotels …)

## C *to*-infinitive clauses

*To*-infinitive clauses may be used to express purpose and sometimes consequence, condition or result:

He went back into the house **to get** the tickets. (purpose = *in order to get*)

I got to the theatre **only to find** the show had started. (unexpected consequence = *and found*)

I've been there often enough **to know** my way around. (result = *and therefore know*)

**To see** him, you'd never think he was 60 years old. (condition = *If you saw*)

▶ See also *Attitude clauses and phrases* (Section 2), page 203.

## 2 Nouns, adjectives, verbs + prepositions (page 163)

## A General rules

**1** When verbs, nouns and adjectives are followed by a preposition, the preposition is always followed by an object. This can be a noun, pronoun or the *-ing* form of a verb:

I'm not interested **in the opera / in going** to the opera.

**2** When we use a subject with the -*ing* form, it can be put in the possessive form in more formal English:
*We depend on **his/him** giving us the money.*

**3** Related verbs, nouns and adjectives often take the same preposition:
*We don't **object to** the proposal.*
*We have no **objection to** the proposal.*

**Note**
Some verbs, nouns and adjectives can be followed by different prepositions with a change in meaning. Compare:
*The other children laughed **at** him.* (negative = *made unkind remarks*)
*We laughed **about** the incident later.*

## B Verb + preposition patterns

A preposition is required after some verbs to link the verb to the object. The combination may give a new meaning.

**1 Verb + preposition + noun/-*ing***
*agree on sth/with sb, aim for, believe in, care about/for, count on, dream of, hear about/of, laugh about/at, object to, pay for, quarrel with, resort to, shout at/to*
*My boyfriend and I don't **agree on** everything.*
*Do you **agree with** increasing taxes?*
*We're **aiming for** a big increase in sales.*
*The rebels **resorted to** violence / committing violent acts.*

**2 Verb + direct object + preposition + indirect object**
*aim sth at sb/sth, blame sb for sth, blame sth on sb, discuss sth with sb, explain sth to sb, save sb from sth*
*This programme is **aimed at** teenagers.*

**Notes**
- The direct object must come before the preposition and indirect object:
*I explained ~~to him the problem.~~* → *I explained the problem to him.*
- If the order of the objects is changed, different prepositions are used:
*I **blame him for** the poor results.*
*I **blame** the poor results **on him**.*
*They **presented the actress with** the award.*
*They **presented** the award **to the actress**.*

**3 Verb + direct object + preposition + -*ing* form**
*accuse sb of -ing, advise sb against -ing, discourage sb from -ing, prevent sb from -ing, suspect sb of -ing*
*The Foreign Office **advises** tourists **against travelling** to certain countries.*

**4 Verb + preposition + object + preposition + object**
Verbs used in this pattern are usually reporting verbs.
*agree with sb about sth, apologise to sb for sth, complain to sb about sth, depend on sb for sth, disagree with sb about/over sth, quarrel with sb about/over sth, rely on sb for sth*
*I **agreed with** the others **about** the need for speed.*
*She **apologised** to him **for** having to leave early.*

**5 Verb + preposition + subject + -*ing***
*depend on, insist on, rely on sb/sth -ing*
*Success **depends on** us/our **getting** the product out on time.*
*Her parents **insisted on** Mary/Mary's **coming** home by 11 p.m.*

## C Noun + preposition patterns

*amazement at, anger about/at, apology for, belief in, delay in, effect of, increase in, insistence on, point in/of, prospect of, success in, taste for*
*What's the **point of going** there now?*
*There's no **point in worrying**.*

**Notes**
- Related verbs and nouns often take the same preposition:
*insist on, insistence on*
- Some nouns are followed by a preposition although the related verbs are not:
*discuss sth, have a discussion about sth; fear sth, have a fear of sth*

## D Adjective + preposition patterns

Many adjectives describing feelings and opinions are followed by a preposition.
*afraid of, annoyed about sth, annoyed at/with sb, disappointed about/at/with, disappointed in sb, excited about/at/by, interested in, keen on, nervous about/of, proud of, scared of, sorry about sth/for -ing*
*She's very **excited about** her forthcoming trip.*
*I was very **excited at/by the prospect of seeing** her again.*
*He was **nervous about** his exams.*
*They were **nervous of** their teacher at first.*

**Note**
Related adjectives, verbs and nouns often take the same preposition:
*be interested in, take an interest in*
*depend on, be dependent on*

# Writing reference

## Contents

## Assessment

Acceptable performance at CAE is represented by Band 3. Each piece of writing is given an 'impression mark' based on the general impression mark scheme below.

### Band 5

Minimal errors; resourceful, controlled and natural use of language, showing good range of vocabulary and structure; task fully completed, with good use of cohesive devices; consistently appropriate register; no relevant omissions; not necessarily a flawless performance. Very positive effect on target reader.

### Band 4

Sufficiently natural; errors only when more complex language is attempted; some evidence of range of vocabulary and structure; good realisation of task; only minor omissions; attention paid to organisation and cohesion; register usually appropriate. Positive effect on target reader achieved.

### Band 3

Either (a) task reasonably achieved; accuracy of language satisfactory and adequate range of vocabulary and range of structures; or (b) an ambitious attempt at the task, causing a number of non-impeding errors, but a good range of vocabulary and structure demonstrated; minor omissions, but content clearly organised. Would achieve the required effect on target reader.

The general impression mark scheme is used in conjunction with a task-specific mark scheme, which focuses on criteria specific to each particular task. This summarises the key areas indicated in the task, which need to be included to achieve Band 3 or above:

- Content
- Organisation and cohesion
- Range of structures and vocabulary
- Register and format
- Target reader

## Writing checklist

- Have you included information about all the points in the task? Check back to the parts you marked.
- For Part 1 tasks, have you used your own words and avoided copying from the input?
- Have you used the appropriate organisation and layout for the piece of writing you have been asked to produce? For example:
  - Letter: have you included appropriate opening and closing formulae?
  - Article: have you written clearly organised paragraphs with a topic sentence and relevant examples?
  - Leaflet, guidebook entry, report, proposal: have you considered using headings to present the information clearly?
- Have you included appropriate language related to the task and used a good range of vocabulary? For example:
  - Character reference: language of recommendation and vocabulary related to work and personality
  - Leaflet: language of description and persuasion
  - Guidebook entry: language of description, facts related to the place being described
  - Report, proposal: language of description, evaluation and recommendation
- Is your sentence structure sufficiently complex to show a good command of English?
- Have you used the appropriate register consistently (formal, neutral or informal)?
- Would your target reader be informed?
- Have you written about 250 words?
- Are your grammar, spelling and punctuation accurate? Are there any errors that might cause comprehension difficulties?

# Part 2: Character reference

▶ See pages 20–21 for work on character references.

## Task

A colleague at work has applied for a job as Chief Administrator of an international school and you have been asked to write a character reference for the applicant. You should indicate how long and in what capacity you have known the applicant, comment on his or her administrative skills and mention any information about the person's character (e.g. ability to form relationships with colleagues, manner with the public) that you think might be relevant to the job.

Write your **character reference** in approximately 250 words.

## Model answer

Start by explaining your relationship or your working experience with the person.

Use a more formal impersonal style, without contractions.

To whom it may concern

MILENA KAIRBEKOVA

Milena Kairbekova and I have worked together in the Worldwide Travel Agency for the last four years. When she started with the company, she worked in my department as a sales assistant, selling holidays directly to customers. Last year, when one of the sales managers left, she was asked to take over his role.

In the time that Milena worked as a sales assistant, she proved herself to be very competent and very careful in all administrative matters. She was also reliable and punctual, and rarely absent from work. Milena was popular with customers, who liked her relaxed, friendly manner and the care she took over their travel arrangements.

Talk about the person's strong points.

Use a new paragraph for a different point.

As a colleague, I have always found Milena to be thoughtful and considerate. She has built up good relationships at work and is liked and respected by everyone. She is also enthusiastic in everything she does and is very hard-working.

When Milena was promoted to sales manager, she had some difficulty getting used to the new role. At first, she was less relaxed, and some of my colleagues found her a bit bossy. However, Milena is an intelligent person and soon realised that her manner was wrong and, without losing any authority, she changed and became friendly and supportive.

In a confidential reference, include any weaknesses, but if you are recommending the candidate, leave the reader with a positive impression.

Say why the candidate would be suitable for the job.

Milena informed me recently that she is looking for a greater challenge, and it is clear from the job description that the post you are seeking to fill would suit her enormously. She would undoubtedly do an excellent job, and I have no hesitation in supporting her application.

Give your final recommendation.

## Further practice

Your friend would like to apply for the scholarship advertised below and has asked you to write a character reference for him/her.

> The Wisbech Trust offers a one-year scholarship for a suitable person to study in a university in an English-speaking country. The grant covers all study costs, travel to and from the country and adequate living expenses. The chosen candidate should be academically able, interested in the chosen country, and be prepared to work as part of a team on an area of research decided by the university.

Write your **character reference** in approximately 250 words, explaining why your friend would be suitable.

# Part 2: Leaflet/Information sheet

▶ See pages 36–37 for work on leaflets.

## Task

You are a member of a student committee in a college which admits a number of international students each year. The committee has decided to give more support to these students, and you have been asked to produce a leaflet in English, giving information and advice in a number of key areas, such as accommodation, study facilities and the social programme.

Write the **leaflet** in approximately 250 words.

## Model answer

Give your leaflet a title. Remember who you are and who you are addressing.

Break your leaflet into short sections and give a heading to each section.

## WELCOME TO THE COLLEGE

New students are sometimes confused by life in a busy college, so here are a few handy tips to get you going.

Say what the aim of the leaflet is. Adopt a relaxed, friendly tone.

### Finding somewhere to live

You have probably already fixed up your accommodation, but if not, don't forget the Accommodation Office can find accommodation
- on campus
- with a private family
- in self-catering accommodation.

If you are unhappy where you're living, just go and see the Accommodation Officer. Providing you give a week's notice, she can move you somewhere else.

Make each section short and light. Have an introductory sentence followed by bullet points or numbered points if there is a list.

### Making your study rewarding

There are a number of extra facilities to help you with your classroom learning. We have
- a reading room for quiet study
- an extensive library with a range of reference materials, newspapers and journals
- a computer centre with easy Internet access.

Make sure you build each of these into your programme at least once a week. You'll be amazed what you'll find there!

### Enjoying yourself in your spare time

Because it is important to relax and make friends in the college, we have a wide variety of social activities. These include
- excursions to places of interest
- societies and clubs where you can meet people with similar interests (from architecture to jazz to politics!)
- parties and dance evenings
- sports activities.

Whatever your interest, make sure that in your first few days you come and talk to one of our team of social organisers who will help you decide what is right for you.

**Remember:** we are here to make sure your stay is truly unforgettable.

Finish on a friendly note.

## Further practice

The tourist office in your town has asked your help in producing a leaflet to persuade people to come to the area out of the main tourist season. Write a leaflet, addressed to travel agents, highlighting the main visitor attractions and give any practical information they need to know.

Write the **leaflet** in approximately 250 words.

# Part 2: Report

▶ See pages 52–53, 126 and 133 for work on reports.

## Task

You are on the <u>Leisure Committee in your college</u>. This is an extract from a letter you receive from the Town Council.

> Could you carry out a survey and write a <u>report on the leisure facilities for young people</u> in the town, addressing the following questions:
> - What <u>facilities</u> do young people use?
> - Are the facilities <u>adequate or inadequate</u> and <u>why</u>?
> - In what <u>other ways</u> could the town <u>help young people</u>?

Write your **report** in approximately 250 words.

## Model answer

**List the aims of the report and say where you got your information.**

**Use clear headings linked to the question.**

**Use numbers or bullet points for a list.**

**Save your recommendations for the end.**

### REPORT ON LEISURE FACILITIES FOR THE YOUNG

**Introduction**

The aims of this report are to:
1 give an overview of the town's leisure facilities used by young people
2 comment on whether the facilities meet their needs
3 recommend extra support that the town could give.

As preparation for this report, I interviewed a cross-section of students in my college and other young people in the town.

**Current Facilities**

At present, the town has only a few facilities used by young people: a cinema, a sports hall, a night club and a couple of restaurants.

**Strengths and Limitations**

While the people I interviewed liked the town, and in particular loved the beautiful park near the centre, the general feeling was that the young people in the town are badly served for the following reasons:
- the cinema has only one screen and is too small
- the sports hall has no outside facilities and no swimming pool
- there are no cheap coffee bars where young people can sit and talk
- there are no cultural facilities, like an art gallery or a good library.

Most young people I spoke to felt the town's facilities were mainly aimed at middle-aged people and the old.

**Recommendations**

In my view, an action group should be set up, consisting of local business people and young people to draw up a plan for future developments in the town. They should look at:
- how businesses can be encouraged to set up extra leisure facilities for the young
- what extra facilities the town can reasonably provide out of local taxes.

**Don't use the same words as the input.**

**Use an impersonal formal style.**

**Make your points clearly and succinctly.**

## Further practice

You are a student in the Information Technology Department of an international college. You have been asked to write a report for an international survey about how the students in your college use the Internet. You should cover the following points:
- current use (e.g. how much it's used, where it's used and what for)
- benefits and disadvantages (if any)
- future use in the college (e.g. in the classroom).

Write your **report** in approximately 250 words.

# Part 2: Article

▶ See pages 68–69 and 84–85 for work on articles.

**Task**

You see this announcement in an international student magazine.

### THE GLOBAL VILLAGE

We are preparing a special edition of our magazine dedicated to the effects of 'globalisation' on young people in different countries. Write an article about the most important aspects of this issue as it affects young people in your country – for example, technology, shopping or tourism.

Write your **article** in approximately 250 words.

**Model answer**

*Think of a title that will make the reader want to read the article.*

*Make sure you focus on young people in your country, as the question says.*

*Start with a strong opening sentence that introduces the topic.*

### Going global – the solution or the problem?

For better or worse, the world is becoming a smaller place. National markets have grown closer together, and national borders have become less important. Companies now operate all over the world and aim their products particularly at young people. In my country, many young people have access to the Internet, they watch foreign films on satellite TV and they listen to foreign music. In the evenings, they eat in restaurants owned by foreign companies and speak to their friends abroad on their mobile phones.

Most young people in my country say that 'globalisation' is a good thing. There is more choice in the shops, goods are more stylish than they were before, living standards have gone up, and we can travel anywhere in the world. They also believe we have greater freedom of information and a better understanding of foreign cultures.

However, some young people in my country see the situation very differently. They feel that our traditional way of life and our local identity are under threat. They say that mass tourism is ruining our natural heritage, and that the spread of English is destroying our national language. They resent the fact that large international companies, who care mainly about profits, are becoming so important that they have more influence than our own democratically elected government. Some of them take to the streets in protest.

Clearly there are arguments on both sides, but one thing we can be certain of is that globalisation will not go away.

*Remember who you are writing for and keep the style fairly neutral for this topic. You are not being asked for your opinion.*

*Finish the article with a strong sentence.*

**Further practice**

You see the following announcement in a college magazine.

### HOW TO PASS EXAMS

We would like our readers to share their ideas and experiences. Write an article suggesting the best ways of preparing for exams, saying what you should or should not do on the day of the exam.

Write your **article** in approximately 250 words.

# Part 2: Formal letter

▶ See pages 78 and 116–117 for work on formal letters.

## Task

You have received this letter from a hotel after a recent visit.

> Thank you very much for filling out our feedback questionnaire. We are sorry to see that you were not satisfied with your arrival arrangements. Would you be so kind as to provide us with detailed comments and make suggestions for improvement? We trust the rest of your stay was satisfactory and will happily give you one night's free accommodation the next time you visit us.

Write your **letter of complaint** to the hotel in approximately 250 words.

## Model answer

*Use formal language.*

*Write 'Dear Mr Stephens'/'Dear Ms Jenkins' if you know the name of the person.*

*Say why you are writing.*

*Explain what the problem was. Give details about what happened. Try to remain factual but polite.*

*Give further details.*

*Don't make your language too forceful or you will have a negative effect on the reader.*

*Don't forget to answer all parts of the question.*

*Try to end on a positive note.*

*Use a formal ending.*

Dear Sir/Madam

I am writing in response to your letter asking for detailed comments about our stay at your hotel.

When my husband and I first arrived to check into the hotel, we were surprised that there was no one at the reception desk. We rang the bell, but no one took any notice. After a very frustrating wait, a young receptionist appeared. We explained we had been waiting for ten minutes and were surprised by his rather gruff reply.

Eventually, after an incredibly slow check-in, we were given a key and went to our room, only to find that it had not been cleaned. The bed was unmade, and there were dirty towels on the floor. We went back down to reception to complain, and were given a rather weak apology, and told to wait until the cleaners could be found. We asked to be moved into a different room, but this was refused without explanation. All in all, it was another hour before our room was cleaned and we could settle in.

Clearly, the two problems were staffing and training. There need to be more staff working in reception at the time of day when most guests arrive, and they need to be better trained in dealing with guests. There also need to be more cleaners.

Fortunately, things got better after we had settled in, and the rest of the stay was satisfactory. We appreciate the offer of a free night's accommodation and will gratefully accept the next time we are in the area.

Yours faithfully

## Further practice

You are looking for a job where you will have an opportunity to use your English, and have seen this advertisement in an international magazine.

### International Summer Camp – Helpers required.

We are looking for helpers to work in our summer camp for two weeks in July for children aged 11–16. The job is residential, and applicants should have a good command of English.

*Do you have*
- relevant experience?
- good communication skills with young people?
- something unique you could bring to the job?

Write your **letter of application** in approximately 250 words.

# Part 2: Brochure/Guidebook

▶ See pages 100–101 for work on guidebooks.

**Task**

You have been asked to write a section of a guidebook for visitors to your country about a local amenity, such as a public park, a theme park or a wildlife park.
You should say

- why the place is worth visiting
- what there is to see and do there.

Write your **guidebook entry** in approximately 250 words.

**Model answer**

### Mexico City

When Mexico City starts to feel too busy, the best solution is to make your way to Chapultapec Park, the weekend playground for those who live in the capital. It's the city's largest green space, and people come here to unwind – to have a picnic or go for a walk. There's also a wide range of cultural and sporting facilities on offer if you're feeling energetic.

Chapultapec Park is located at the end of the Paseo de la Reforma, the city's main boulevard. It is divided into three sections and covers about 1,600 acres (about 2.5 square miles), which makes it one of the biggest city parks anywhere in the world.

There are seven museums in the park, including the wonderful Papalote Children's Museum. There is also the splendid National History Museum in Chapultapec Castle. This is filled with period furniture, as well as hundreds of paintings, which depict the history of Mexico from the Aztecs to today. The emphasis is on the colonial era, when the Spanish ruled Mexico, and later military history.

However, the one museum that you really must not miss is the National Anthropology Museum, which houses displays of priceless artefacts of Mexican culture, including the Aztec calendar stone.

If you are travelling with children, the world-class zoo is another place you should definitely visit. The zoo's star attraction are the giant pandas. It was here in 1980 that the first baby panda was born outside China.

Other attractions include a large amusement park, and children will also enjoy taking a paddle boat on one of the lakes or a tram ride.

*Side annotations:*

- Try to create a visual picture. Remember, you are writing a description.
- Include some specific examples to bring the description to life.
- Use a fairly neutral style and keep it consistent.
- Use some adjectives like this, but sparingly.
- Give lots of facts that will interest the potential tourist.
- If you are describing a single place, there is no need for an introduction or conclusion.

**Further practice**

You have been asked to write a section of a guidebook for visitors to your country. The following publicity information describes the aim.

> The Best Buy section is for tourists who like to buy typical local products, such as clothes, rugs and souvenirs, at a good price, whether in a market or a shop.

You should write about **one or two** places in your area, covering

- where the place is
- what it's like
- what makes it a good place to shop.

Write your **guidebook entry** in approximately 250 words.

# Part 1: Letter and note

▶ See pages 116–117 for work on letters and notes.

## Task

You are on the <u>committee of an animal rights group</u> in your college, and the secretary has emailed you to explain why you should <u>write a letter to your local paper</u> concerning a <u>new medical research centre, sponsored by a drug company</u>, that is planned for your area. He has also sent you a number of extracts from questionnaires received in a recent survey to get <u>students' views on the new centre</u>.

Read the email and the comments and then, using the information carefully, write <u>a letter to the newspaper</u>, as well as <u>a covering note to the editor</u>, Laura Kovaks.

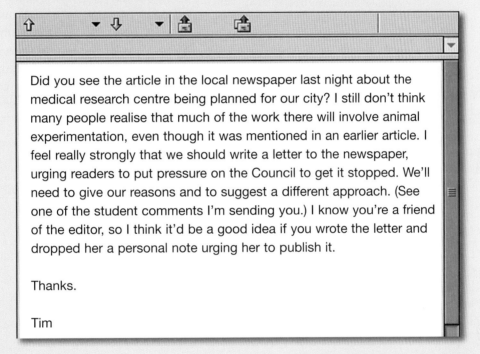

Did you see the article in the local newspaper last night about the medical research centre being planned for our city? I still don't think many people realise that much of the work there will involve animal experimentation, even though it was mentioned in an earlier article. I feel really strongly that we should write a letter to the newspaper, urging readers to put pressure on the Council to get it stopped. We'll need to give our reasons and to suggest a different approach. (See one of the student comments I'm sending you.) I know you're a friend of the editor, so I think it'd be a good idea if you wrote the letter and dropped her a personal note urging her to publish it.

Thanks.

Tim

OK, so drug companies don't just want to make profits. They want to save lives as well. But don't those guys realise how much suffering they cause animals in the name of scientific research? What right have they to treat animals in this way?
TOMÁS LEE

The research centre calls itself 'highly reputable', which means nice and respectable on the outside, but inside what they do to animals is terrible.
GINO CRESTANI

Drug companies argue that if they are going to make progress in curing diseases like cancer, they have no choice but to experiment on animals. But have they really looked for other types of solutions? There are numerous safe alternative remedies, such as homeopathy, which could be more rigorously tested through scientific means, but which the medical profession simply pooh-pooh.
NADIA ROTOVA

According to one paper I read, drugs tried out on animals don't necessarily work on humans. In fact, some have caused serious illness.
MICHÈLE RICCI

Now write a **letter** to the newspaper for the animal rights group, explaining why you think the plans for the research centre should be stopped (approximately 200 words) and a covering **note** to the editor (approximately 50 words). You should use your own words as far as possible.

## Model answer (Part 1: Letter and note)

### Letter

Use a formal register.

No need to include addresses.

To the Editor

I am writing concerning the new so-called 'highly reputable' medical research centre that a drug company wants to set up in our area, and wonder whether your readers realise that live animals are to be used in experiments there. While we accept that the company doesn't simply want to make profits, but also wants to cure illness and save lives, the experiments the centre will carry out will cause unnecessary suffering to animals.

Make sure you have processed carefully ALL the information provided in the input and combined it. Don't miss any out or you will lose marks. Only add extra information if you have covered all the essential points.

Rephrase the wording of the input.

We do not agree that the companies have no option but to use animals in their research. Many patients get very effective treatment for their illnesses through alternative therapies, like homeopathy, which doctors and scientists like to dismiss as not worth thinking about. Why don't the drug companies conduct research in these areas? The medicines are at least safe.

There have also been recent newspaper reports that show that although a drug may be successful in curing an animal, it does not necessarily mean it will help a human. There have even been cases where the drug itself has done the patient serious harm.

Conclude by restating in a forceful way the reason you are writing.

We believe the local community needs to wake up to the truth about the new centre and pressurise the Council into rejecting the plans.

### Note

Friendly tone.

Hi Laura!

I wonder if you could do me a favour. I read about the new medical research centre last night and want to remind your readers it will involve nasty experiments on animals. I've written a letter on behalf of our animal rights group. Any chance of you publishing it?

Informal register.

Don't forget what you have been asked to do! And keep the note concise.

All the best

Jamie

# Further practice (Part 1: Letter and note)

You recently went to Australia for three months on an <u>overseas work-experience placement programme</u> organised by your college. When you returned, a friend of yours who also took part in the programme sent you <u>an article from the local newspaper</u> with her comments. Read the letter from your friend, the newspaper article and her comments. Then write a <u>letter to the editor</u> saying <u>why the article is inaccurate</u>, and <u>a note to your friend</u> explaining <u>what you've done</u>.

Just read this absurd article! I think one of us needs to write to the newspaper and put them right. Maybe get them to apologise. Bad publicity like this will get back to Australia and mean the scheme won't run next year.

Love,

Tania

This year's work placement scheme in Australia was not the success the college was hoping for. For a start, only six of the promised 16 took part and they were all male. This was despite the fact that the companies offering the placements had said they preferred a balance of male and female volunteers. Then apparently, according to one company employee we spoke to, our students made a poor impression, which reflects badly on our town. They were frequently late for work because they were staying out most nights with their friends on the programme. When the company complained to the placement organiser about their behaviour, our students said the work was boring and they were given no leisure time. Clearly, the future of such placement programmes is in doubt.

*Oh yes it was!* (to "not the success")

*Well, I went and I'm hardly male!* (to "they were all male")

*True.* (to "volunteers")

*How ridiculous! I hardly ever met up with the others in the evenings.* (to "staying out most nights with their friends")

*Mine even organised sightseeing tours for us!* (to "boring and they were given no leisure time")

*It was very interesting.* (to "the work was boring")

Then, using the information, write a **letter** to the editor of the paper (in approximately 200 words) and a **note** to your friend (approximately 50 words).

# Part 2: Proposal

▶ See pages 148–149 for work on proposals.

## Task

> You study at an international college, and your student committee is concerned that the college pays too little concern to environmental issues, such as
> - energy efficiency
> - use of environmentally friendly products
> - waste.
>
> The committee has asked you to write a proposal to your principal giving reasons why a consultant who can advise on these matters should be brought in.
>
> Write your **proposal** in approximately 250 words.

## Model answer

Break up the proposal into sections and include sub-headings.

Make it clear where the proposal is coming from and why.

Use the passive voice to 'distance' the criticisms.

Conclude with your suggestion.

Have a suitable neutral title.

Be clear, concise and direct.

Use a detached tone.

Use formal language.

The aim of the proposal is to persuade the reader about your suggestion, so you need to show conviction without being offensive.

### PROPOSAL TO IMPROVE COLLEGE ENVIRONMENTAL POLICY

**Introduction**

In the view of the student committee, the college at present does too little to conserve natural resources, reduce pollution in all its activities and influence and encourage others to be more aware of environmental issues.

**Efficient use of energy**

From our own observations, there is considerable waste in terms of energy, including lighting, water heating and refrigeration. However, at present, staff and students appear unaware of the need for conservation and to reduce consumption.

**Environmentally friendly products**

The companies that supply detergents and pesticides are at present not encouraged to provide the college with environmentally friendly products, endangering the college environment and the health of the people who work there.

**Waste**

Little attention is given to ways of reducing waste and making it easier to reuse and recycle paper, glass, aluminium, plastics and other college waste, using the most environmentally friendly means. This indicates a lack of responsibility in such matters and compares unfavourably with other colleges we know.

**Committee recommendation**

We propose that a group of environmental consultants is brought into the college to examine what we do and suggest ways in which we can make college members aware of environmental issues and encourage them to get involved. Some of us have had personal experience of the consultants Johnson and Co., and we believe they would be a suitable choice. We urge the college to take this matter forward as a matter of urgency.

## Further practice

> You work for an international tour company which, in the summer, recruits large numbers of untrained students to work on its campsites in a number of roles: dealing with arrivals and departures, organising children's activities and solving general problems. Your company director has asked you to write a proposal for a training programme indicating
> - the sort of training that will be required
> - how long the training will take
> - how the company will benefit.
>
> Write the **proposal** in approximately 250 words.

# Part 2: Review

▶ See pages 164–165 for work on reviews.

## Task

The editor of an international student magazine has asked you to write a <u>review</u> of <u>two action films</u> you have seen recently. <u>Compare</u> the two films from the point of view of

- <u>the story</u>
- <u>the acting</u>.

Write your **review** in approximately 250 words.

## Model answer

Catch your readers' attention in the opening sentence.

Make the plot summary very brief: your aim is evaluation.

Write an equal amount on each film.

Include evaluative adjectives as you go along.

Give your personal recommendation.

Include negative points as well as positive points.

If you are reviewing two films, use the language of comparison and contrast.

### TWO ACTION FILMS

Never mind the plot, just watch the action and the special effects. That seems to be the message of *Die Another Day*, the 20th in the James Bond series, and *Matrix Reloaded*, the follow-up to the incredibly successful *Matrix*.

*Die Another Day*, about a wealthy lunatic who's threatening the safety of the world, moves very quickly, really too quickly at times, and the plot is so confused that the characters never get the chance to develop properly. Having said that, the action sequences are fantastic and the visual effects are stunning. Pierce Brosnan makes a believable Bond, the best since Sean Connery, and Halle Berry as his ruthless ally is amazing, playing a character just as uncomplicated as Bond himself.

The action in *Matrix Reloaded*, a science-fiction movie about a group of humans struggling for freedom against a machine army, is much slower to get started and, unlike Bond, there is a lot of phoney philosophical talk mixed in with the comic-book story-telling. Fortunately, once the action starts, there are lots of fights and chases, done of course with all the incredible special effects that we expect in a Hollywood movie. The actors who play the heroes are all impressively physical in their numerous fight scenes, but unfortunately elsewhere their performances are rather wooden. Only Harold Perrineau as the navigator brings some life to the film with his shouts of 'Yes!' from the control room when something goes right. He at least seems not to take his part too seriously.

So, all in all, if it's action, excitement and escapism you want, these two films are for you.

## Further practice

Your college magazine has asked you to write a review of two magazines or newspapers (they can be online publications) that appeal to different kinds of readers. Say in what ways they are different and what makes them popular with their readers, giving your personal views about the publications.

Write your **review** in approximately 250 words.

# Linking devices

In a coherent piece of writing, all the ideas are relevant to the main point and are presented in a logical sequence. A cohesive piece of writing uses linking devices to signal the relationship between the ideas clearly and to avoid unnecessary repetition.

## Logical links

1  **Expressions which link ideas within a sentence (conjunctions)**
   - Addition: *and, as well as*
   - Time: *after, as, as soon as, before, once, since, until, when, while*
   - Contrast/change of direction: *although, but, despite, even if, even though, in spite of, while, whereas*
   - Reason/result: *as, because, since, so*
   - Purpose: *(in order) to, so that*

   Note: *and, but, so* usually only go in the middle of the sentence. All the other conjunctions can go either in the middle or at the beginning of the sentence.

2  **Expressions which link ideas across sentences (adverbials)**
   - Addition: *also, as well, besides, furthermore, in addition, moreover, too, what's more*
   - Time: *afterwards, beforehand, eventually, finally, first, in the end, lastly, later, meanwhile, next, secondly*
   - Example/Illustration: *for example, for instance*
   - Contrast/Change of direction: *even so, however, nevertheless, nonetheless, on the other hand, still, yet*
   - Reason/Result: *as a result, because of this, consequently, that's why, therefore*
   - Conclusion: *in conclusion, in summary, last of all, to conclude*

   Notes
   1  *As well, too* go at the end of a sentence.
   2  *Finally, later, eventually, also, therefore, consequently* usually go at the beginning of the sentence.
   3  All the other adverbs normally go at the beginning of the sentence.

## Grammatical reference links

1  **Reference words**
   - Personal pronouns (*he, they, her, their, its,* etc.)
     *I met your father.* **He's** *very young.*
   - Articles (*the, a, an*)
     *He's got two children.* **The** *son is a doctor and* **the** *daughter is a teacher.*
   - Determiners (*this, that, these, those*)
     **That** *idea was very original.*
   - Relative pronouns (*who, which*)
     *I met your father,* **who** *is very young.*

2  **Other substitutions**
   - *there, then*
     *The Ritz is a good hotel. We stayed* **there** *last July. It was very busy* **then**.
   - *one, ones*
     *We missed the bus so we got a later* **one**. *They will be the* **ones** (= the people) *who will benefit.*
   - auxiliary verbs (*do/does/did, have/had, can/could,* etc.)
     *Tom likes fish and so* **do** *I* (= I like fish too).
     '*I couldn't go to the show.*' '*Neither* **could** *I.*'
     (= I couldn't go to the show either.)
   - *so, such*
     *She was very lively as a child and remained* **so** *throughout her life.*
     *He was very rude.* **Such** *behaviour* (= behaviour like this) *is not acceptable.*
   - *if so / if not*
     *Do you eat meat?* **If so** (= if you eat meat), *I'll cook chicken.* **If not** (= if you don't eat meat), *I'll do a vegetable stew.*
   - Relative clauses
     *I sat out in the sun without wearing sunscreen,* **which** *was very stupid of me.* (*which* refers to the whole of the previous clause)

3  **Omission**
   Sometimes, we can omit words altogether.
   *We could stay in, but I'd prefer not to ~~stay in~~.*
   *He never offers to clean or ~~he never offers to~~ wash the dishes.*
   *Sally likes tea but not* (= she doesn't like) *coffee.*

## Lexical reference links

1  **Parallel expressions**
   *Science fiction is full of descriptions about how humans might look in the future. It may seem rather far-fetched to think we will have electronic arms and legs, laser vision or be able to fly, as* **the genre** (= science fiction) *would have us believe.* (Reading, Module 6, page 88)

2  **Repeated key words**
   For example, in an article on the topic of stress, the word *stress* may be repeated several times to remind the reader of the topic.

# Punctuation

## 1 Capital letters
- To begin a sentence: *We saw him yesterday.*
- For the pronoun *I*, names, titles, countries, nationalities, streets, cities, days of the week and months (not seasons) of the year:
  *Mr Jones, the Welshman, Oxford Street, last Friday, last spring, in May*

## 2 Full stops
- To mark the end of a sentence: *I'm very homesick.*
- For abbreviations: *Prof. (= Professor), a.m. (= in the morning)*
- With decimals, prices and time: *At 4.30 the price rose 3.3% to £4.99.*

Notes
1 Full stops are not used with abbreviations where the last letter of the abbreviation is also the last letter of the word: *Mr* for *Mister*, *Dr* for *Doctor*.
2 With some abbreviations, full stops are a matter of style and are sometimes omitted: *6 am, the UK*

## 3 Apostrophes
- To indicate possession: *my brother's house* (= one brother); *my brothers' house* (= more than one brother); *my parents' house*

Notes
1 When a word ends in *-s*, a second *-s* is not necessary: *Mr Hughes' dog*
2 The possessive pronoun *its* has no apostrophe: *The hotel has **its** own pool.*
  *It's* is a contraction of *it is* or *it has*: *It's mine. Jack's got a new car.*
3 Be careful not to use an apostrophe with numbers and abbreviations when the *s* is used to indicate a plural, not possession:
  *the 1900s, CDs*

## 4 Commas
- To separate items in a list: *I bought apples, pears(,) and bananas.*
- To separate off an introductory word, phrase or clause:
  *Happily, the weather was fine in the end.*
  *In my view, smoking should be banned.*
  *When it rains, I take an umbrella.*
  *If you're thirsty, have a drink of water!*
  *Being a nice person, he offered to help.*
- Around inserted phrases and clauses:
  *John, as we all know, is lazy.*
  *He is, however, very intelligent.*
  *Sue, who works in a bank, is a friend of mine.*
  *The woman, hungry after a long journey, started to eat.*
- To separate some final elements such as question tags and participle clauses:
  *You're tired, aren't you?*
  *I didn't go, not being interested in such things.*
- In direct speech: *'It's late,' he said. He said, 'It's late.'*
- Optional before *and, or, but*: *Tom tries hard(,) but Sue doesn't.*

Note: the use of the comma before *and* in a list is much more common in American English than in British English.

## 5 Speech marks
- To separate direct speech from the rest of a sentence.

Notes
1 A comma is used to set off a direct quotation from the rest of the sentence, and a capital letter to start the quotation: *John shouted, 'Come out of the water now!'*
2 If a quoted sentence is split up, the second part does not begin with a capital: *'That,' he said, 'is my house.'*
3 Commas or full stops at the end of a quoted speech are inside the speech marks.

## 6 Other punctuation
- Colon (:)
  - to introduce a list: *The hotel has everything: a gym, a sauna, …*
  - before a phrase that gives more information or an example: *He got poor marks: not surprising when you consider how little work he did.*
  - to introduce a quotation. *As Shakespeare said: 'All the world's a stage.'*
- Semi-colon (;)
  - to separate two main clauses that are closely linked in meaning, so that a full stop would be too strong a break between them: *He was once poor at English; now he's a Professor of English.*
- Dash (–)
  - in informal writing, to separate a part of a sentence which adds extra information:
    *The second man – Tom Jones – was well known to the police.*
    *I've been to Paris – in fact, I went there last year.*

# Spelling

## Spelling changes

**1 Words ending in -ch, -sh, -s, -ss, -x, -z, -zz**
- Add -es instead of -s: bun**ches**, wa**shes**, addres**ses**, coa**xes**, bu**zzes**

**2 Words ending in consonant + -y**
- Nouns/verbs change -y to -ie when a suffix is added: enquir**y** ▶ enquir**ies**, fl**y** ▶ fl**ies**, tid**y** ▶ tid**ier**
- But -y doesn't change before -ing: carr**y** ▶ carr**ied** ▶ carr**ying**
- Change -y to -i for other suffixes: myster**y** ▶ myster**ious**; pit**y** ▶ pit**iful**, bus**y** ▶ bus**ily**, heav**y** ▶ heav**iness**

**3 Words ending in vowel + -y**
- Add -s: journ**eys**, p**ays**
- But for past participles, change -y to -i and add -d: l**ay** ▶ l**aid**
- Note these adverbs: d**ay** ▶ d**aily**, g**ay** ▶ g**aily**

**4 Words ending in -f/-fe**
- Add -s: gul**fs**, chie**fs**
- But note: thie**f** ▶ thie**ves**. Also: self, shelf, loaf, leaf, knife, wife, life, half.

**5 Words ending in vowel + -o**
- Add -s: rad**ios**, shamp**oos**

**6 Words ending in consonant + -o**
- Add -es: potat**oes**, tomat**oes**, her**oes**

**7 Words ending in -e**
- Drop silent -e after a consonant and before a vowel: strid**e** ▶ strid**ing**, invit**e** ▶ invit**ation**
- But keep -e in words like lik**e** ▶ lik**eable**, dy**e** ▶ dy**eing** and -ee words: s**eeing**, agr**eeable**

**8 Words ending in -ie**
- For -i suffixes, e.g. -ing, change -ie to -y: d**ie** ▶ d**ying**, l**ie** ▶ l**ying**
- For -e suffixes, drop one -e: d**ied**, l**ied**

**9 Words ending in -c**
- To keep the /k/ sound, add -k: pani**c** ▶ pani**cking**
- Add -al to -ic words for -ly words: franti**c** ▶ franti**cally**

**10 Words ending in a consonant**
- For words ending in a vowel + a consonant, with the last syllable stressed, double the only or final consonant: fi**t** ▶ fi**tter**, prefe**r** ▶ prefe**rring**, occu**r** ▶ occu**rred**
- In British English, words ending in -l or -p are normally doubled even if the stress is on other syllables (<u>travelling</u>, <u>handicapped</u>)

- -s is sometimes doubled: <u>focused</u> or <u>focussed</u>
- Don't double the final consonant of
  - words with two vowels before the final consonant: pl**ai**n > pl**ai**n**er**
  - words with two final consonants: fa**st** > fa**ster**

**Some useful rules**
- -ise (verb) / -ice (noun): advi**se**/advi**ce**
  Note the American English for some verbs: real**ize**, computer**ize**
- -ie when the sound is /iː/ except after -c: ach**ie**ve, n**ie**ce (but rec**ei**ve)
  Exceptions: s**ei**ze, prot**ei**n
- -ei for other sounds: n**ei**ghbour, l**ei**sure, th**ei**r, w**ei**ght, for**ei**gn
  Exception: fr**ie**nd

## Hyphens

Hyphens are used to join words to form compound nouns or adjectives and to add affixes. They are important in
- numerical expressions: a five-star hotel, a thirty-minute wait
- compound adjectives which come before the noun: blue-eyed, up-and-coming
- affixes to help pronunciation (co-operate) or to avoid confusion: resent/re-sent.

## Endings often misspelt

- Adjectives
  -ible/-able: vis**ible**, irresist**ible**, respons**ible**, lov**able**, valu**able**, advis**able**
  -ful: cheer**ful**, hand**ful**, success**ful**
  -ent/-ant: perman**ent**, confid**ent**, ignor**ant**, observ**ant**
  -ous/-eous/-ious: marvell**ous**, courag**eous**, anx**ious**
- Nouns
  -ence/-ance: influ**ence**, differ**ence**, correspond**ence**, assist**ance**, attend**ance**, appear**ance**
  -al/-le/-el: propos**al**, circ**le**, quarr**el**
  -er/-or/-ar: offic**er**, solicit**or**, fact**or**, burgl**ar**
  -ary/-ery/-ory/-ry: libr**ary**, robb**ery**, direct**ory**, fact**ory**, poet**ry**
  -tion/-sion/-ssion: rela**tion**, occa**sion**, posse**ssion**
- Verbs
  -cede/-ceed: pre**cede**, re**cede**, ex**ceed**, pro**ceed**

## Commonly misspelt words

accommodation, approximate, biscuit, building, business, campaign, compare, desert/dessert, development, different, disappoint, disguise, embarrass, exhaustion, familiar, follow, frequent, guarantee, guilty, immediately, immigrant, individual, interest, leisure, medicine, mountaineer, necessary, occupation, pastime, pleasant, professional, pronunciation, receipt, separate, scissors, similar, surface, technical, through

# Attitude clauses and phrases

Attitude, or comment, phrases are not an integral part of the sentence, but indicate the speaker's/writer's attitude to the action or event, or a comment on its truth.

## 1 Finite attitude clauses

**As far as I know**, she's coming next week.
**As I said**, we will need to leave very early.
John is leaving, **as you know**.
**As we shall see**, this decision was to cost him his life.
I can't help you, **I'm afraid**.
**Believe it or not**, he passed all his exams.
**As it turns out**, she didn't need to come.
**You know**, it might be a good idea to go by train.
I can't be the driver. **You see**, I don't know how to drive.
**The truth is**, nothing has changed since the election.

## 2 Non-finite attitude clauses

These include participle and *to*-infinitive phrases:
**All things considered**, we've done very well.
**Considering** (the problems we've had), we've done very well.
We've done very well, **considering** (the problems we've had).
**Taking everything into consideration**, I think we've earned a break.
**Generally (speaking)**, women earn less than men.
**To be honest**, I didn't really like the book.
**Judging by** his recent performance, he should win the cup.
**Speaking from memory**, I'd say it's about ten miles from here.
**Strictly speaking**, we shouldn't be here.
**To tell the truth**, I'd forgotten all about it.
It's fairly risky. **Or to put it another way**, don't try this on your own.

## 3 Sentence adverbs

A Giving your opinion about/reaction to some event
*annoyingly, funnily (enough), hopefully, luckily, naturally, oddly (enough), rightly, strangely, (not) surprisingly, understandably, worryingly*
**Hopefully**, the government will change its mind.
**Oddly enough**, someone asked me the same question only yesterday.
There's a lot of talk, **quite rightly**, about the dangers of smoking.

B Commenting on the truth or likelihood of some event
*actually, arguably, certainly, clearly, definitely, doubtless, evidently, obviously, presumably, really, surely, as a matter of fact, in fact, of course*
**Actually**, what happened was that …
**Doubtless** he will be promoted before long.
**Of course**, his father is the managing director.
**Surely** you don't mean that?

C Emphasising what you have said
*indeed, as a matter of fact, in fact*
I don't mind at all. **Indeed**, I'm pleased to be asked.

D Admitting something is true
*admittedly, granted*
Her technique needs improving, **granted**, but she puts great feeling into her performance.

E Explaining how you are speaking
*frankly, honestly, personally, seriously*
**Personally**, I think it's a terrible idea.
I don't like him, **quite frankly**.

F Generalising
*as a rule, by and large, in the main, on the whole*
**As a rule**, I don't have breakfast at weekends.
**By and large**, the conference went very well.
**In the main**, the climate is very mild.
**On the whole**, things turned out for the best.

# Sentence structure

## 1 The main sentence patterns of English

**A Main clause: subject + verb (+ complement/object)**
A sentence in English must have at least a subject + a verb.
*The shop is closing.* (S+V)
*Coffee bars are a favourite with customers.* (S+V+C)
*Some stores employ a number of entertainment techniques.* (S+V+O)
The subject always comes before the verb, except in questions and some special cases for style or emphasis.

   ▶ Grammar reference pages 181 (omission of *if*, cleft sentences), 183–184 (fronting and inversion)

**B Main clause + coordinating conjunction (*and, or, but, so*) + main clause**
*Shopping is something we all have to do(,)* **but many people go shopping just for fun.**

Note: A comma is optional before a conjunction in British English.

**C 1 Main clause + subordinate clause**
   *I love going to parties* **as I'm a very sociable person.**

   **2 Subordinate clause, + main clause**
   **Although I enjoy lying on the beach doing nothing,** *I couldn't do it for very long.*

Note: A comma is used when the subordinate clause comes first.

**D Main clause + inserted information**
**Unfortunately,** *there is not a lot to do in the evenings.*
**To tell the truth,** *most evenings I prefer to stay at home and read a book.*
*Going to work,* **believe it or not,** *is some people's idea of a good time.*
**Not finding it easy to relax when I come home from work,** *I usually watch TV.*
*My father enjoys life to the full,* **which is amazing for someone his age.**

**E Main clause. Linking expression + main clause**
*I only enjoy myself when I'm with people I like.*
**That's why** *I only go out with friends.*
*Taking part in online auctions can be fun.* **What's more,** *you can find some real bargains.*

The basic sentence patterns can be combined into complex sentences containing more than one clause.
*Strolling through a town centre on a Saturday, the country's busiest shopping day, you might come across such things as drama workshops, a fairground ride or even a brass band raising money for charity, all of which are part of a campaign to encourage people into town.*

## 2 Fragments

A group of words that does not contain a subject and verb and does not express a complete idea is a **fragment**.
*She decided to study French. Because she loved the language so much.* ✗
We can attach the fragment to the previous sentence:
*She decided to study French because she loved the language so much.* ✓
*John promised to pay me back the money. Which he didn't do.* ✗
*John promised to pay me back the money, which he didn't do.* ✓
We can add a subject to the second sentence:
*John promised to pay me back the money. He didn't do so.* ✓

## 3 Run ons

When two complete, independent clauses are run together with no adequate punctuation to mark the break between them, this is a **run-on** sentence.
*My job is very time-consuming, I have no time for a social life.* ✗ A comma alone is not enough to join two independent clauses.
*My job is very time-consuming. I have no time for a social life.* ✓ Split the ideas into two separate sentences with a full stop.
*My job is very time-consuming and as a result, I have no time for a social life.* ✓ Add a suitable linking expression.

# Speaking material/Keys

## Unit 2B: Speaking (p.33)
### Exercise 4a

INTERLOCUTOR

First of all, we'd like to know a little about you.
- Where do you both live?
- What do you enjoy about living there?

Now I'd like you to ask each other something about:
- entertainment and leisure facilities in this area
- an ambition you would like to fulfil
- a change you would like to make to your life in the future.

Thank you. *(Ask further questions as necessary.)*
- What have you liked most about studying English?
- What interesting things have happened in your life recently?
- If you could go anywhere you wanted on holiday, where would it be?

## Unit 3A: Listening 1 (p.43)
### Exercise 3c

CHARLIE: Well, I've been collecting something or other ever since I can remember. First, it was plastic dinosaurs, then a bit later my friends were all into model aeroplanes, so I started collecting them, too. Then when I was 11, for some reason my dad gave me a signed photograph of the film star Cary Grant. I wasn't a particular fan of his, but I realised that just the fact that I had this one signature made people – even grown-ups like my parents' friends – look up to me somehow. So I started building up a collection.

## Unit 4B: Speaking (p.65)
### Exercise 5a

E

F

# Unit 5A: English in Use 1 (p.76)

## Exercise 4

1   Do tour operators have a responsibility for preserving the local environment and culture?
2   Would you be willing to pay more to companies that benefit local communities and conservation?
3   Would your holidays be more enjoyable if you could learn a little of the language and visit local wildlife conservation and social projects?

# Unit 6A: Listening 1 (p.91)

## Exercise 3e

> As a doctor, I'm very aware that our way of life today is very different from that of a generation ago. We spend our days sitting in front of computer screens, and our evenings watching television. I don't think we're any more greedy than previous generations, but we're certainly less active, so there's a rising problem of obesity. At the same time, many of us are increasingly stressed compared with past generations. There's one simple way of solving both these problems and that is exercise. This will burn off the extra weight, and it's also one of the best treatments for stress.

# Unit 6B: Speaking (p.97)

## Exercise 5b

Look at your pictures, which show aspects of the past. Compare and contrast these pictures, saying what they tell us about how people used to live, and how you think the people might be feeling. You have about a minute for this.

# Unit 8A: English in Use 1 (p.124)

## Exercise 1a

A  The National Lottery in the UK
B  A breakfast cereal
C  The Yellow Pages (a business telephone directory)

# Unit 8B: Speaking (p.128)

## Exercise 1d

- Increasing police numbers and resources (94%)
- Increasing penalties for offenders (93%)
- Greater cooperation between the police and the public (94%)
- Reporting information to help the police detect crime and catch criminals (97%)

# Unit 9B: Speaking (p.144)

## Part 1

INTERLOCUTOR
First of all, we'd like to know a little about you.
- Where do you both/all live?
- How long have you been studying English?
- Have you been studying English together?
- What countries have you visited/would you like to visit?
- What country would you most like to visit?

Now I'd like you to ask each other something about:
- your reasons for studying English
- any other languages you have studied
- something you would like to do in the future.

Thank you. (Ask further questions as necessary.)
- What have you enjoyed most about studying English?
- What have you disliked most about studying English?
- What important events have happened in your life recently?
- What has been the most memorable event in your life?
- How would you feel about going to live abroad permanently?
- If you could meet somebody famous, who would it be?

(Stop the discussion after three minutes.)

Thank you.

## Part 2

INTERLOCUTOR
In this part of the test, I'm going to give each of you the chance to talk for about a minute and to comment briefly after you have both spoken. You will each have a pair of photos showing different rooms. Candidate A, it's your turn first. Here are your photos. Please let Candidate B see them. I'd like you to compare and contrast photos A and B, saying what the rooms tell you about the kind of people who live there. Don't forget, you have about one minute for this. Would you start now, please?

(Stop the candidate after one minute.)

Thank you. Now, Candidate B, compare and contrast photos C and D. Don't forget to say what the rooms tell you about the owners, and what kind of people live there. You have a minute for this. Would you start now, please?

(Stop the candidate after one minute.)

Thank you. Now, would you like to look at all the photos again and talk together about which room you think is the most attractive? You only have a short time for this, so don't worry if I interrupt you.

(Stop the candidates after one minute.)

Thank you.

## Part 3

INTERLOCUTOR
Now I'd like you to discuss something between yourselves, but please speak so we can hear you. Here are some photos which show different ways of keeping up to date with international events. Talk to each other about how useful each of these are as ways of keeping up to date, and then decide which two are likely to give you the most reliable information. You have about four minutes for this.

(Stop the candidates after four minutes.)

Thank you. So, which two do you think are likely to give you the most reliable information?

## Part 4

INTERLOCUTOR
(Select any of the following questions as appropriate. Stop the discussion after four minutes.)

- To what extent do you believe what you read in newspapers?
- Do you think television news coverage can always give both sides of every story?
- To what extent might journalists actually influence the events they report on?
- Have 24-hour news broadcasts made the world a better place?
- Some people say that 'no news is good news' – do you agree?
- Is free access to information always a good thing?

Thank you. That is the end of the test.

---

Unit 5A: English in Use 1, Exercise 4

Results of polls of UK tourists:
1  90% said yes.
2  Almost 50% said yes.
3  Over 75% said yes.

**Pearson Education Limited**
Edinburgh Gate
Harlow
Essex CM20 2JE
England
and Associated Companies throughout the world.

www.longman.com

© Pearson Education Limited 2005

The right of Jan Bell and Roger Gower to be identified as authors of this Work has been asserted by them in accordance with the Copyright, Designs and Patents Act 1988.

First published 2005
Third impression 2007

ISBN 978-0-582-82391-4

Set in 10.5/13.5 Minion

Printed in China GCC/03

## Authors' Acknowledgements

With grateful thanks to Heather Jones, Bernie Hayden, Catriona Watson-Brown and all the team at Longman.

## Publishers' Acknowledgements

The publishers and authors would like to thank the following people and institutions for their feedback and comments during the development of the material:

Anne Alexander (Spain), Katerina Anastasaki (Greece), David Corkill, Rolf Donald (UK), Marek Doskocz, Piotr Gralewski (Poland), Drew Hyde, Nick Kenny, Jacky Newbrook (UK), Nick Shaw (Spain), Arek Tkacz (Poland).

We are grateful to the following for permission to reproduce copyright material:

Bloomsbury Publishing Plc for an extract adapted from *They F\*\*\* you up: How to Survive Family Life* by Oliver James published by Bloomsbury; Classic FM Magazine for an extract adapted from 'Henry meets Evelyn Glennie' by Henry Kelly published in *Classic FM Magazine* April 2003 © www.classicfm.com; Crimestoppers for an extract from 'Crimestoppers' Success Story' published on www.crimestoppers-uk.org; Paul Daniel at English National Opera and Jane Gilchrist for the text of an interview about *Operatunity*; Amanda Holloway at BBC Worldwide for an extract adapted from 'Operatunity' published in *BBC Music Magazine*; Carl Honoré and Orion Publishing Group Limited for an extract adapted from *In Praise of Slow* by Carl Honoré published by The Orion Publishing Group; The Independent for extracts adapted from 'People don't want to know how it's done' by Cole Morton published in *The Independent on Sunday* 6th October 2002 and 'Is this the body of the future?' by Elizabeth Heathcote published in *The Independent* 13th November 2002 © The Independent; Adrian Levy and Cathy Scott-Clark for an extract adapted from 'How television corrupted the Himalayan Kingdom of Shangri-La' by Adrian Levy and Cathy Scott-Clark originally published in *The Guardian Weekend* June 2003; Telegraph Group Ltd for extracts adapted from 'Now, they ask for my autograph' by Elizabeth Grice published in *The Daily Telegraph* 10th October 2002, 'Life in the slow lane' by Richard Robinson published on www.Telegraph.co.uk 13th October 2002, 'Fame who needs it?' by David Gritten published in *The Daily Telegraph* 9th November 2002 © Telegraph Group Limited 2002 and 'Be lucky – it's an easy skill to learn' by Richard Wiseman published in *The Daily Telegraph* 8th January 2003 © Telegraph Group Limited 2003; Origin Publishing for an extract adapted from 'Meeting the real Doctor Doolittle' by Graham Southorn published in *Focus Magazine* August 2002 www.focusmag.co.uk; John Pawsey, agent for Anne Mustoe for an extract from *A Bike Ride* published by Virgin Books Ltd 1991 and information published on www.annemustoe.co.uk; Pearson Education Limited for an extract adapted from *Brilliant Interview: What Employers Want to Hear and How to Say It* by Ros Jay; Solo Syndication for extracts adapted from 'Calls of the Wild' by Andrew Wilson published in *The Daily Mail Weekend* 22nd June 2002 © The Daily Mail and 'Is little Jack really on the road to a life of crime?' by David Cohen published in *The Evening Standard* 11th December 2002 © The Evening Standard; Times Newspapers Limited for extracts from the articles 'Two's company' by Candida Crewe published in *Times Magazine* 23rd February 2002, 'We love T-Shirts' by Sheryl Garratt published in *The Times* 22nd June 2002 © The Times 2002, 'Demons that drive us to row it alone' by Jonathan Gornall published in *The Times* 29th January 2003, 'The Cash Lady Sings' by Richard Morrison and 'Indian girls discover a bent for Beckham' by Catherine Philp published in *The Times* 26th February 2003 and 'Dark days under the curse of the sacrab ring' by Miranda Seymour published in *The Sunday Times* November 2003 © The Times 2003; Wikipedia for an extract from 'Victor of Aveyron' published on www.wikimedia.org; and Sarah Woodward and Peter Richards for extracts from 'Roaming the past' by Sarah Woodward published in CAM, the University of Cambridge Alumni Magazine 2002.

## Photo Acknowledgements

We are grateful to the following for permission to reproduce copyright photographs:

A1 Pix/Superbild/Bernd Ducke for page 17 (right); Advertising Archive/Nike for page 75; Art Directors & Trip for pages 87 (bottom right), 116, /Spencer Grant for page 17 (bottom left), /Judy Austin for page 76, /Australian Picture Library for page 78, /W. Jacobs for page 79, /Helene Rogers for pages 128 (bottom left), 157, /C. Webb for page 145 (top left), /Ron Bambridge for page 145 (bottom right); Bridgeman Art Library/The Stapleton Collection for page 87 (left), /Bibliothèque des Arts Decoratifs, Paris for page 114 (top); Bubbles for pages 95 (right), 135 (top right), (left); Cadogan Guides for page 100 (bottom); Cancer Research UK for page 52; Cartoonstock.com/Adey Bryant for page 139, /Elmer Parolini for page 141, /Carroll Zahn for page 155 (left), /Clive Francis for page 155 (right); Collections/John & Eliza Forder for page 17 (top left), /Gary Smith for page 110, /John Vere Brown for page 145 (centre right); Copeland Interactive Services Inc, (owner@collectr.com) for page 43, Corbis/Bettmann for pages 23 (left), 132, 206 (top right and bottom right), /Paul Hardy for page 28, /Rob Lewine for page 33 (bottom left), /Walter Hodges for page 33 (right), /Alan Schein for page 34, /Louise Gubb for page 46, /Chuck Savage for pages 55 (right), 127, /Dex Images Inc. for page 64, /David Raymer for page 65 (top right), /Reuters/Toby Melville for page 71 (top right), /Reuters for page 81 (top left), /Ecoscene/Peter Hulme for page 80 (left), /Chuck Keeler for page 82, /NewSport/Larry Kasperek for page 103 (left), /ZUMA/Branimir Kvartuc for page 103 (top right), /Bazuki Muhammod for page 103 (bottom right), /Didrik Johnck for page 106, /Archivo Iconografico, SA for page 114 (bottom), /Barry Lewis for page 119 (centre), /Chuck Savage for page 127, /Rune Hellestad for page 128 (right), /Arnold Cedric for page 128 (top left), /Tom Stewart for page 133, /Frank Lane Picture Agency/ Tom Hamblin for page 135 (bottom right), /Yang Liu for page 145 (centre left), /Patrick Ward for page 146 (bottom left), /Lawrence Manning for page 161 (centre left), /Royalty Free for page 161 (top left), /Will & Deni McIntyre for page 205 (top), /Sygma/Colin McPherson for page 129 (left), /Kent News and Pictures for page 129 (bottom right), /John van Hasselt for page 160; Dewynters/Alastair Muir, Hugo Glendinning, John Rogers, Tristram Kenton and Simon Turtle for page 156; Digital Vision/James Lauritz for page 146 (centre left and centre right); Getty Images/Hulton for page 206 (left), /Image Bank/Chip Porter for page 9, /Stephen Derr for page 16 (right), /Stone/Betsie Van der Meer for page 55 (left), /Robert Frerck for page 161 (top right), /Taxi/Eric O'Connell for page 65 (bottom right), /Justin Pumfrey for page 97 (right); Go Ape (www.goape.co.uk) for page 149 (right); John Birdsall Photo Library for pages 107 (top right), 151 (left); Impact Photos/Piers Cavendish for page 71 (left), /Mark Henley for page 119 (top), /Simon Shepheard for page 151 (top right); Image State/Agefoto/Joseph De Sciose for page 95 (left); /A. Farnsworth for page 96 (top), /Jeff Greenberg for page 96 (bottom), /Gonzalo Azumendi for page 120, /Jean-Marc Charles for page 146 (top left); *The Independent*/David Sandison for page 15, /Mark Chivers for page 24; John Frost Newspapers for page 39 (both); Kobal Collection for page 147; Life File Photo Library/Angela Maynard for page 65 (left); Magnum Photos/David Hurn for page 89; Jeff Moore (jeff@jmal.co.uk) for page 205 (bottom); National Portrait Gallery, London/Jillian Edelstein for pages 56 (top), 57, /Dudley Reed for page 56 (bottom); NHPA/Norbert Wu for page 35, /Iain Green for page 137 (top centre), /Andy Rouse for page 137 (centre bottom), /Peter Pickford for page 137 (top right), /Daniel Zupanc for page 137 (bottom right); The Outward Bound Trust (www.outwardbound-uk.org) for page 148; PA News Photos for pages 45, 104, 112 (left); Penguin Books/Robert Harding Picture Library for page 100; Photos 12.com for page 162; Photos For Books for pages 146 (top right), 161 (centre right); Popperfoto for page 151 (bottom right); Powergrid (www.powergridfitness.com) for page 91; Powerstock/Agefotostock/Terry Way for page 7 (top right), /Frank Siteman for page 11, /Peter Holmes for page 61, /Carlo for page 68, /Stefano Cellai for page 72, /Zoran Milich for page 113 (left), /Bartomeu Amengual for page 123; Punchstock/Stockbyte for page 7 (bottom right); Rex Features for pages 12, 164 (top), /C. Columbia/Everett for page 40, /Ray Tang for page 51, /Canio Romaniello for page 56 (centre), /James D. Morgan for page 161 (bottom); Robert Harding Picture Library for pages 7 (bottom left), 112 (right), /Penguin Books for page 100 (top); Ronald Grant Archive for pages 30, 140; Samsung for page 119 (bottom right); Still Pictures/UNEP/J. Juntawonsup for page 71 (bottom right), /A. Doto for page 80 (right), /Ron Giling for page 81 (bottom left); Topham for page 152, /Image Works for page 113 (top right), /Alan Carey for page 16 (left), /Fortean for page 23 (top right and bottom right), /ProSport for pages 32–33 (top left), /PA News Photos for pages 47, 58, 81 (right), 87 (top right), 107 (top left), 113 (bottom right), 129 (top right), 159, /Cruickshanks for page 84, /Karl Prouse for page 96 (left), /The Arena PAL Picture Library for page 107, /Empics for page 109, /Picturepoint for pages 119 (bottom left), 124, 131, 135 (top centre); *The Week* Limited (www.theweek.co.uk) for page 146 (bottom right); Zomba Recording Corporation/photograph by Steven Klein for page 164 (bottom).

Every effort has been made to trace the copyright holders and we apologise in advance for any unintentional omissions. We would be pleased to insert the appropriate acknowledgement in any subsequent edition of this publication.

Picture research by Liz Moore (liz@lizm.co.uk)
Illustrated by Francis Blake and Kveta Jelinek (both from *Three in a Box*)
Cover design by Raven Design
Designed by Roarr Design
Edited and project managed by Catriona Watson-Brown